CPIM PRODUCTION® & INVENTORY MANAGEMENT

Master Planning of Resources Reprints

Articles selected by the Master Planning of Resources Committee of the APICS Curricula and Certification Council

Preface

As an organization dedicated to furthering manufacturing and operations excellence, APICS strives to shed light on important issues and provide a forum for developing a better understanding of these issues. This volume is a modest attempt to answer the continual demand for updated definitions as well as additions to the body of knowledge. The assumption is that the reader is knowledgeable about the basics and is looking for additional insights.

The articles in this publication were selected by the Master Planning of Resources Committee based on relevancy of belonging to one of the three main topic areas, and on content which confirms and perhaps challenges our existing body of knowledge. The reprints give the committee the opportunity to quickly cover topics that spotlight state-of-the-art practices and processes.

The objectives of this compilation are as follows:

1. Provide supplementary material to the primary texts and references listed in the *Exam Content Manual* with relevant articles to help the candidate prepare for the Master Planning of Resources certification exam. Subjects adequately covered by the primary references are not included in these readings.

2. Furnish material that will provide practical information to the practitioners of production and inventory management, and reflect the latest knowledge on the subject. APICS members and other professionals should use these readings as a way to enhance their knowledge and to stay abreast of current and practical approaches to Master Planning of Resources .

3. Incrementally expand the body of knowledge associated with Master Planning of Resources. This allows the inclusion of material that has not yet had sufficient breadth of application or time to be considered part of the current body of knowledge. Therefore, the material in these readings may go beyond the current boundaries of the certification exam.

We encourage candidates to be familiar with this material, and to use it to augment their studies in the area of Master Planning of Resources. We recognize that there are many fine articles that could have been selected, and welcome recommendations for future inclusions.

It is our sincere wish that this volume inform the inquirer, support the test candidate, fortify the project manager, and sharpen the practitioner's skill.

The Master Planning of Resources Committee:

Carol Davis, CPIM, (Chair)
Karen T. Lykins, CPIM, CIRM
Ronald C. Parker, CFPIM
Bill Montgomery, CFPIM, CIRM
Philip Pitkin, CFPIM, CIRM

Contents

Reprinted from the 1998 APICS Conference Proceedings.

Listen to Us: Learn to Lead Your Company to Better Results with Sales and Operations Planning

Arne Brander, CPIM, and Tom Fischer, CPIM

In manufacturing resource planning (MRP II), sales and operations planning (S&OP) is often referred to as production planning and is the process which balances supply and demand. In this process, the company develops family forecasts which are translated into loads and compared with available capacity through the resource planning system. Inventory strategies such as chase and level are often the focal point and these are developed with the help of production-sales-inventory (PSI) charts with the result that performance measurements are often production and delivery oriented. An essential part of S&OP is balancing supply and demand, but one should not stop there.

S&OP can also be the process in which business decisions are taken and which aligns the three critical processes of Innovation, Supply Chain and Marketing & Sales to meet important strategic and tactical goals. It can even replace bureaucracy in your company. In order to achieve this you must select a cross-functional team which manages all important business issues with the customer as the focal point. This requires an S&OP agenda which makes business sense.

In enterprise resource planning (ERP), S&OP must be a customer-driven business process with a horizon of up to several years. It is the link between the strategic plan and the daily management of the operations as shown in **Figure 1** and should be a top management tool for managing the business. The S&OP links the strategic plan with operations and could be described as the "heart" of the operations.

Why S&OP at Ciba, Business Segment Whiteners?

Company and market background: The Business Segment Whiteners (BSW) is the major part of the Ciba Consumer Care division. The segment, present worldwide, is operating in four regions: Europe, North and Latin America, and Asia Pacific. The products, optical brighteners, are used in three industries: Detergents, Paper, and Textiles. The segment has several factories around the world which are integrated into the S&OP concept as shown in **Figure 2**. In

Europe, there are three S&OP processes, one for each industry, due to the fact that Europe has the worldwide R&D and three major factories. The European operations also coordinate the other regions.

The market trend is toward a stronger internationalization and many customers view their suppliers in a global context. Worldwide supply agreements are becoming increasingly common. In addition, international customers want to achieve synergies in issues such as technology, sourcing, and systems. This is particularly the case for the detergents industry. As a consequence of this trend it is important to manage a global optimum of activities such as the supply chain. The idea behind a global supply chain optimum is to:
- Take investment decisions which minimize total capital outlay and resulting costs.
- Create flows of supply which best utilize existing resources.
- Balance supply and demand in a way which gives the best customer service levels at the lowest costs even if this would lead to a suboptimization of the resources at the local level, i.e., optimization of the global business rather than regional optimization leading to global suboptimization.

In addition, the whiteners market is highly competitive. Important order winners are price, technical service, and innovation as well as supply chain excellence. Supply chain excellence not only encompasses on-time delivery to the customer, but also the capability of managing customer inventories. Managing these resources can only be done with an integrated global approach.

When we started to work with S&OP in the spring of 1996, the Ciba, Business Segment Whitener Head, Mark Garrett, gave us the following objectives:
- Create a customer-driven S&OP process which manages all value chain activities.
- Establish a transparent management information framework which makes an on-going process measurement possible at different levels and enables deploying corrective actions.

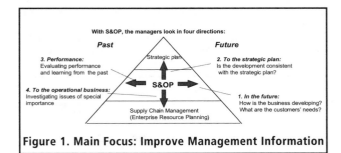

Figure 1. Main Focus: Improve Management Information

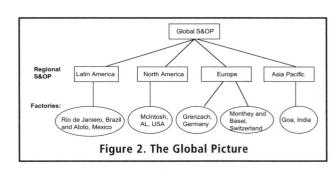

Figure 2. The Global Picture

- Secure cross-functional cooperation and operational excellence (OPEX).

The Start-Up: Create a Clear Focus of the Process

What is the company's value discipline? Or in other words, how do you achieve competitive advantage? Treacy and Wiersema mention in their book, *The Discipline of Market Leaders*, three different disciplines to achieve competitive advantage:

- *Operational excellence*: These companies deliver a combination of quality, price, and ease of purchase that no one in the market can match. They execute extraordinarily well, and the customer benefit is guaranteed low price and hassle free service.
- *Product Leadership*: Consistently strives to provide its market with leading-edge products or services.
- *Customer Intimacy*: Builds bonds with the customers and delivers what a specific customer wants.

The value discipline you choose will affect your business heavily. It was clear to BSW that the main emphasis must be operational excellence. This did not mean that the other areas were not important—in fact BSW also leads the industry's innovation. It means a balanced approach must be adopted as shown in **Figure 3**. The emphasis is not only on one issue but can vary from customer industry to customer industry. To achieve operational excellence requires streamlining the operations in order to offer value pricing and excellent service. One key element is to elongate the supply chain to include customers and suppliers. This requires:

- Getting direct information from the customer such as forecasts
- Managing the customer inventories and securing 100% availability of the goods
- Developing specific supply projects with the customer in order to reduce supply chain waste.

This can only be done with highly skilled personnel who have training and education such as CPIM.

Outlining the Way and Getting the S&OP Basics in Order

Integrating all departments to take joint decisions in a S&OP process is a challenge. The BSW S&OP framework, as shown in Figure 2, consists of 6 regional S&OP processes which are managed by one global S&OP process. The regional S&OP

was decided to be a monthly process and the global S&OP a quarterly process. S&OP is best implemented as learning by doing and thus a stepwise improvement process was selected. Each S&OP process was to reach excellence by evolving through four major phases, each marked by milestones, of which the last one, continuous improvement, never ends. See **Figure 4**.

How to Implement S&OP

The first step in getting the basics in order is to set up a common S&OP framework. The basic S&OP monitoring includes the definition of product families to which the SKU sales and forecasts are aggregated for overall load and capacity monitoring as well as performance measurements such as customer service levels. Further important groundwork includes:

Issues	Main Objective/Solutions
1. Define clear company objectives with S&OP.	Secure high plant utilization.
2. Define appropriate S&OP horizons and time buckets.	3 years with monthly buckets
3. Select the participants.	Marketing, Key account management, Supply chain management, R&D, Technical services
4. Establish meeting frequency.	Monthly
5. Set the agenda.	An example follows.

An Abbreviated Agenda for Managing the Business with S&OP

Business Issues

1. Minutes of the last meeting
2. Business Review—Sales and forecast development, profit analysis
3. Marketing Issues—Potential business, won and lost business analysis, competition, pricing, new introductions and phase-outs
4. Supply Performance Analysis—Factory reports including load and capacity development, supplier relations, supply related issues, customer service levels
5. Project update

Technical Issues

1. Research and development
2. Technical service
3. Production issues
4. Project updates

If you know what you want from the S&OP process, the battle is half won. A good way is to define milestones for the implementation which every process has to achieve. The first one (see **Figure 5**) is a pilot which demonstrates to the organization that S&OP works. The second milestone is the role-out which includes all other S&OP processes. Like many other processes, it is difficult to have a clear picture of the outcome in the very beginning. During the process one risks having a "moving" end target. This

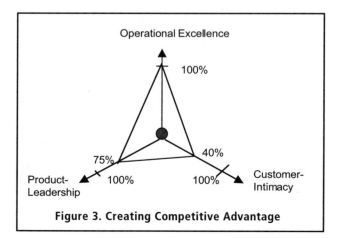

Figure 3. Creating Competitive Advantage

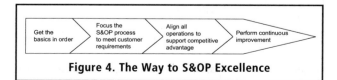

Figure 4. The Way to S&OP Excellence

is a part of the process and at a certain point it is necessary to close the implementation.

The Implementation Program

Are we committed?

Management support and commitment is a critical success factor. This includes not only top management, but also each regional S&OP head and everybody in the team. The S&OP vision must be shared by all managers and thus the concept must be "sold in." Verbal commitment is not enough. A successful S&OP implementation requires a cultural change and in order to achieve this, we must change what people do: S&OP must be performed by all managers. Creating enthusiasm is important and this will influence what people think and believe which is a prerequisite to achieve cultural change. One way is to constantly monitor the rate of success and communicate results. Good results will stimulate your teams.

The critical points initiating the process are:
- Some planning is necessary to initiate the process, but do not over plan.
- Exercise discipline. Do not accept any excuse for not finishing issues on time or completing actions.
- The process owner must regularly monitor the progress and be willing to correct poor performance.
- Accept your company's initial starting point and improve in each meeting.

Milestone 1—Run a Pilot and Demonstrate That it Works

We started the implementation with a business process in Europe which had already started performing S&OP. The standard agenda was used and, after a period of about five months, we had reached a level which we defined as stable excellence. The forecasting on SKU and family level was significantly improved and the link to the supply management was established. Marketing information was well integrated in the process. The success we had doing this demonstrated that S&OP worked. Significant achievements in managing the business can be done also during a relatively short time.

When you implement S&OP, during the first meetings you will probably find yourself putting it all together. Sales, forecasts, capacities and customer service levels are in focus. It is necessary to allow enough time for the first meetings. Some companies reserve a whole day in the beginning. If this is necessary, do it. After a while, a streamlining of the process will occur where the time usage is optimized.

With a cross-functional team you will probably have to spend half a day even after having streamlined the process— and half a day per month is worth getting your business under control.

Milestone 2—Role Out: The Worldwide Implementation

The next step was the worldwide implementation which included the two remaining European business operations and three continents: North America, Latin America, and Asia Pacific.

In the autumn of 1996 we established an educational framework with the objective to give the participants a clear picture of what S&OP is. The training had the standard agenda as a basis but now with a worldwide focus.

The training concept included the following major issues:
- Goals, procedures, methods, and tools
- Forecasting with the emphasis of implementing a standard concept
- Defining the families
- How to balance supply and demand which shows future utilization
- How to develop competitive advantage and integrate it in S&OP
- Identifying relevant performance measurements.

Critical Issue Number 1: How to Establish Future Demand

When improving management information for decision making, forecasting is of special importance. The main issue in any forecasting/budgeting system is to secure that the best possible forecasts are derived and maintained over the whole horizon. Best forecasting practices include clear responsibilities as well as the use of best methods for deriving and monitoring the forecast. In order to establish these best methods and procedures one must know the true behavior of the customer demand. Demand estimation can be done by using many different procedures or philosophies. The most common method uses time series of historical demand which are elongated to forecasts. This is also the only method which is widely supported by EDP forecasting systems.

As can be seen from **Figure 6**, the three different business operations have very different requirements. Forecasting excellence therefore must be achieved differently in the three industries.

Changing the Forecasting Game

The main objective is to integrate the company with the customers' planning process to avoid unnecessary forecasting . The forecasting philosophy at BSW is: If possible get requirements from the customers to feed your supply chain and pass this information on to the suppliers. This is something the customers appreciate because it secures 100% availability of stocks even in a changing market. Of course it is not possible to receive a forecast from all customers in a segment such as textiles with several thousand customers. But even here best practices are achieved in some countries by asking the biggest customers to provide forecasts. The "80/20 rule" can be used and the rest must be estimated.

In short forecasting excellence is secured by:
- Customer information
- Simple forecasting methods such as trend elongation

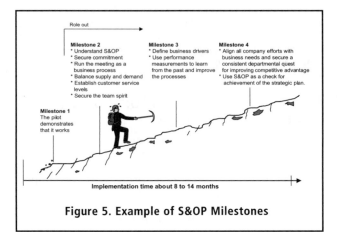

Role out

Milestone 2
* Understand S&OP
* Secure commitment
* Run the meeting as a business process
* Balance supply and demand
* Establish customer service levels
* Secure the team spirit

Milestone 3
* Define business drivers
* Use performance measurements to learn from the past and improve the processes

Milestone 4
* Align all company efforts with business needs and secure a consistent departmental quest for improving competitive advantage
* Use S&OP as a check for achievement of the strategic plan.

Milestone 1
The pilot demonstrates that it works

Implementation time about 8 to 14 months

Figure 5. Example of S&OP Milestones

		Important Forecasting Design Characteristics			
Business Operations:	Number of customers	1. Use of intrinsic methods in a bottom-up approach	2. Use of extrinsic indicators	3. Use of top-down approach	4. Use of customer information
Detergents	A few key accounts	No	No	Yes for budgeting purposes	Yes
Paper	Medium <200	No	No	Yes for budgeting purposes	Yes to some extent
Textiles	Many > 5000	Yes	No	Yes for budgeting purposes	No
Covered by commercial forecasting software		Yes	No	Sometimes	No

Figure 6. Different BSW Business and Forecasting System Design

- Extensive use of the best forecasting performance measurements such as the tracking signal, mean absolute deviation, and cumulative percent deviation.

Family Forecasting

This forecasting on the SKU level is performed by supply chain management and marketing. This level is too detailed for S&OP; forecasting for S&OP should be performed on the family level in order to reduce the complexity. The family is the highest level to which information can be summarized in a way that provides informational value for both the demand and the supply side. Out of about 300 SKUs, it was possible to establish 14 families which are monitored worldwide. The load factor for each family is established and thus the loads and capacities can be managed in all factories.

Critical Issue Number 2: Balance Worldwide Supply and Demand

The overall objective of integrating all factories into one management was to run the factories with optimal utilization worldwide. In order to do so we developed capacity monitoring on the family level with the help of a normal production-sales-inventory (PSI) chart. In addition this chart specifies the existing and planned plant utilization and import or export needs. This "capacity map" shows all regional demand and supplies over a three- year horizon. In this way, over and under capacity situations are highlighted and this information is used by the global management to balance worldwide capacities and thereby secure all supplies.

Milestone 3—The Customers' Needs Must Drive the Process

A customer-driven S&OP is a process in which customer long-term buying dimensions are identified and translated into a language which makes it possible to deploy strategies and actions which secure that all departments are actively supporting the company's competitive advantage. How the company wins orders is crucial and we spent a lot of time establishing these in all segments. We used the following definition of the business drivers.[1]

(1) Order Winners (OW)—Those competitive characteristics that cause a firm's customers to choose that firm's products and services over those of its competitors.

(2) Qualifiers (Q)—Those competitive characteristics that a firm must exhibit to be a viable competitor in the marketplace.

(3) Order Losing Sensitive Qualifiers (OSLQ)—Qualifiers which if not treated correctly can make a customer not choose a firm's products.

The result of this process is a list of the business drivers which is established for the different industries and regions:

- Technical service   OW
- Price   OW
- Innovation (products)   Q
- Product quality (conformance to specification)   OSLQ
- Delivery reliability (quantity and timing)   Q
- Delivery speed (lead time)   Q

These order winners and qualifiers form the basis for aligning all company strategies such as marketing, supply chain, production, and technical service. Do not underestimate the work of identifying and communicating the company's order winners and do not be surprised if, in the initial phase, the participants have a completely different opinion of what is important in the order winning process. When the business drivers are identified, all departments should secure that their operations support achieving competitive advantage. This was done through the deployment of functional strategies, policies and actions. It is very important to be sure about the order winners before the alignment is performed. In order to secure this we performed the following sequence:

1. Discuss competitive advantage and the business drivers in each S&OP team.
2. Define and weigh them and check the results with the sales force.
3. Monitor won and lost business with regard to how they are won and lost–ask the customer.
4. Review, when necessary, but at least once per year.

The order winners are the most important part of the performance measurement system and are measured on an on-going basis.

Milestone 4—Aligning All Operations

Corporate goals and customer potential are the driver for developing functional strategies. This input is used to define marketing strategy which defines issues such as products and services, markets, and customer targets (see **Figure 7**). Order winners assign the importance to an issue and must be monitored because they are the most important performance measurement.

How can the order winners be deployed? For example, if price were an order winner, the company wins orders by providing competitive pricing. Historical and especially future price monitoring is a key to success. Which price is the lowest possible will also be defined by the costs and, thus, constant cost reduction becomes a major goal. A very useful tool is to combine the forecasted price and cost development to a forecasted net margin which is used to highlight how the S&OP team views the future development. Monitoring this development and taking corrective actions when actual performance deviates from planned is an essential element.

How to Integrate Many S&OP Processes into One Global S&OP Process

The strategic plan (see Figure 1) outlines the company's direction. This plan should be used as a tool and updated as needed. In order to achieve a living strategic plan it must be integrated in the S&OP monitoring. This is an important task of the global S&OP.

When several S&OP processes are monitored by a global S&OP process, the main challenge is to establish the

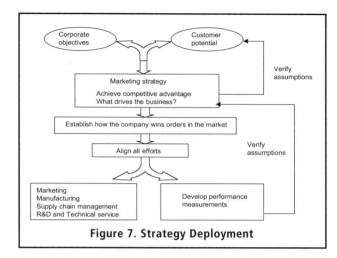

Figure 7. Strategy Deployment

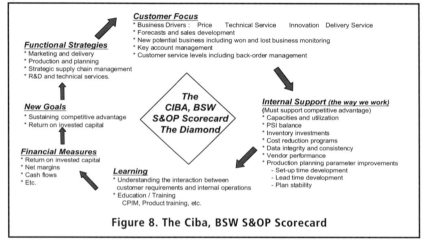

Figure 8. The Ciba, BSW S&OP Scorecard

framework for the information transfer between the levels. We recommend to:

- Let the country or regional S&OP processes be the "body" of information.
- Identify the major issues which are particularly important to monitor on an overall level, such as price development, worldwide capacity/load situation and general market development, in order to understand the customer needs better and align all the business operations.
- Let the global S&OP monitoring be action oriented, meaning that the agenda might consist of a business review and actions derived from the countries' S&OP processes.
- Compare the results with the assumptions in the strategic plan and develop actions.

Performance Measurements

You manage what you measure!

Implementing a set of pragmatic measurements was a primary goal and the measurements served two purposes:
- To secure the implementation process. We therefore used scorecards which showed the goal achievement such as a percent of final completion. All issues in the different milestones were monitored in this way.
- To install an on-going performance measurement system for managing the business. Business goals and

strategies were the starting point. The measurements (**Figure 8**) were divided into two categories, external and internal, the first of which focused on the customer and the second measured the company's process performance. A major step in order to improve is to learn from the measurement. This is done in order to identify optimal levels.

Continuous Improvement

The S&OP journey to excellence is unending. If improvements are not on an on-going basis, the value of the process will decline. Improvements should be done during the whole process but if you link several S&OP processes together it is important to secure that they do not drift apart from each other. A good way is to use the freeze/unfreeze procedure. This freeze and unfreeze procedure can be used with a three-month interval and during the freeze periods in between no major changes should be allowed.

Included in the process is streamlining which has simplification as the main focus. If your meetings take too long or there are too many issues in the meeting, the solution is often to downgrade issues which are under control and could be handled by S&OP supporting processes.

Remember

- This type of S&OP requires a substantial cultural change in most companies. Allow enough time.
- Give the people enough time and resources to investigate alternative ways to work in order to reach the optimum. But solidify one way of working which must be the best way. Show managerial commitment to discipline.
- Review and improve the processes according to defined milestones.
- Even if the logic behind S&OP is clear and understandable, many companies experience a resistance to change which comes from giving up individual "freedom." S&OP means a joint management responsibility where much of this individual "freedom" has to be relinquished to achieve common results. This is a challenge which will be handsomely rewarded if it is handled properly.
- The lack of good S&OP EDP tools often makes it necessary to self-program.
- Congratulate the participants when achieving good results and push on in the eternal quest for excellence.

Major S&OP Results

S&OP is an on-going improvement process which never ends. However, we have reached some very important results:
- S&OP has contributed significantly to the improvement of BSW financial results such as return on assets.
- The implemented S&OP processes are customer driven and customer needs are the focal point. Everybody understands what is most important to the customer and the efforts are coordinated correspondingly.
- The forecasting process is significantly improved which provides better management information and lower supply chain costs.

- A unique cross-functional team approach is used in the S&OP meetings which secures a business focus from different perspectives.
- The capacity reporting is markedly improved which helps determine optimal sourcing, reduce costs, and improve our competitiveness.
- During 1997 inventories were reduced by 30% without reducing the customer service levels.

Notes

1. See *Manufacturing Strategy* by Terry Hill or CPIM Participants Workbook System and Technologies.

About the Authors

Arne Brander, CPIM, studied in the United States where he received his Master of Science in operations management from the University of Wisconsin—Madison, as well as in Europe where he completed a Master of General Business at the Norwegian School of Management. Mr. Brander is partner with Bernd Remmers Consultants AG, Zug, Switzerland. One of his primary tasks is consulting in supply chain management with an emphasis on demand management and sales and operations planning. He consults with companies in Europe, North and South America, and Asia. His previous work includes many years of marketing management from Oslo, Norway. He has published the book *Forecasting and Customer Service Management*.

Tom Fischer, CPIM, studied in Germany where he received a Master of Science in mechanical engineering and business administration from Fridericiana University of Karlsruhe, Germany. Mr. Fischer is head of Warehousing and Distribution, BSW within the Strategic Supply Chain Group. During the S&OP implementation, he helped several S&OP teams achieve an excellent level through his profound knowledge of supply chain management and systems. His previous experience includes head of Supply Chain Management Business Operations Detergents and Business Operations Paper as well as project leader for several important supply chain projects such as MRP II, class A.

Reprinted from APICS—The Performance Advantage, *October 1991.*

The Master Schedule

John J. Bruggeman and Susan M. Haythornthwaite

The term master schedule refers to a time-phased planning chart used in master scheduling. Articles and books within our professional literature contain a great number of format variations on the master schedule. Each format is valid to the extent that it provides the user with a clear presentation of relevant data for master scheduling. Each of these formats has been developed to address a specialized application of the master schedule in a particular production environment, and to the extent that a unique master schedule format serves its environment, it is a perfectly good master schedule.

However, it is important to the professional to understand the basic attributes of the master schedule. This allows for interpretation of varied formats and provides a common ground for developing new formats for specialized applications.

Table 1 is the master schedule format developed for the APICS Master Planning certification exam. None of the terminology or layout should be foreign to a student or practitioner of master scheduling, but each piece of data has been given a specific definition to minimize misunderstanding. Specialized master schedules also have precise definitions of terms, but definitions may not be consistent among various specialized schedules. For this reason, we will review the APICS Master Planning exam master format in detail.

The Master Schedule Format

The master schedule format provides the following information:
- report identification
- scheduling guidelines
- time-phased variables

It is important to note here that the term master schedule refers to the entire form, whereas the term master production schedule refers to a single line on the chart, the schedule of production.

Report Identification

Each master schedule is for a unique item which is controlled by the master scheduler. This item is most commonly a "make" item, but in some instances a master schedule item may be subcontracted or purchased complete. The item number and a short item description appear in the header of the master schedule. The header also contains two important dates: the **run date**, which is the date on which the master schedule was run on the computer, and the **data date**, which is the date on which the master schedule data were last updated. For the purpose of the Master Planning exam, it is assumed that all records extracted from other files are synchronized as of the data date. The first period presented in the master schedule begins on the first working day following the run date.

Scheduling Guidelines

The header of the master schedule also contains scheduling guidelines, which include the current on-hand quantity of the item, the lot size and safety stock level, the item's lead time and the demand and planning time fences. Quantities are given in the item's standard unit of measure which, for the purpose of the exam, is a single unit (each). Times are given as periods which may be days, weeks or months. For calculation purposes, the length of the period is not important, but the number of periods specified is.

The item's **lead time** is stated as the number of periods from the order release to the completion of the order into available inventory. It is assumed that production begins upon order release; thus the lead time is the amount of time required to manufacture or purchase lower level components of the item.

Most master scheduled items have a lot size, which is a specific quantity calculated to be optimal for manufacturing the item. Often a master schedule will have an indication of the rule used for determining the lot size, such as an EOQ calculation or a lot-for-lot policy, but in the

Table 1. *Sample Master Schedule*

Item: 65650
Description: Sample MPS Part

Run Date: 01-01-92
Data Date: 12-31-91

Lead Time: 2
On-Hand: 40

Lot Size: 50
Safety Stock: 0

Demand Time Fence: 4
Planning Time Fence: 10

Period	1	2	3	4	5	6	7	8	9	10	11
Forecast	18	21	17	17	12	14	23	28	30	25	20
Customer Orders	19	20	15	20	6	20	4	6	12	0	0
Projected Available Balance	21	1	36	16	54	34	61	33	53	28	8
Available to Promise	1		15		24		40		38		
Master Production Schedule			50		50		50		50		

case of the simple standard master schedule format, this lot size can be accepted simply as the standard production quantity to be used by the computer in proposing orders for the master production schedule. This quantity is retained by the master scheduler when releasing orders to production.

The safety stock is additional inventory which is planned in advance as protection against unexpected fluctuations in demand or supply. The safety stock level determines the "zero" level used by the computer when it calculates and proposes master production schedule orders; the computer will attempt to keep the projected available balance above the safety stock level.

The on-hand quantity printed in the header of the master schedule indicates the quantity of the item which physically exists in inventory on the data date.

The two time fences associated with the master schedule provide stability and control. The **demand time fence** is the number of periods (beginning with period one) during which no changes can be made to the master production schedule without special authorization from management. If the demand time fence is four periods, then the master production schedule is frozen through the end of period four.

The **planning time fence** is the number of periods (beginning with period one) during which the component will not reschedule master production schedule orders. If the planning time fence is ten periods, then the master scheduler is responsible for maintaining the master production schedule through the end of period ten. Beyond this time fence, the computer will propose orders as required to meet the greater value of forecast or customer orders.

In the master schedule table, the demand and planning time fences are highlighted with heavy lines. In the exam itself, heavy lines are not used to highlight these time fences. It is assumed that the student has learned to interpret time fence information from the header of the master schedule.

Time-Phased Variables

The body of the master schedule is a time-phased planning chart with period numbers at the top of each column. As stated previously, the actual length of these periods is irrelevant to the process of master scheduling (days, weeks, and months are dealt with identically.

The first line appearing on the master schedule chart is the forecast. The forecast is the period-by-period projected demand for the master schedule item, and it represents the total of all projected demands, including such demand as service parts. In professional literature and specialized applications of the master schedule, this line is often broken down into two or more lines (indicating separate sources of demand) which are summed in calculating the total demand. For the purpose of the standard master schedule format, all projected demand is stated on the forecast line of the master schedule.

For the purposes of the Master Planning exam, the forecast reflects the total projected demand for each period. The booking of customer orders does not affect the forecast quantity.

Actual demand, in the form of customer orders, is given on the second line of the master schedule chart. Note that, for purposes of the exam, the master schedule item is assumed to be a finished good which will be sold directly to customers. There would be no actual demand for this item other than from customer orders. And again, the booking of customer orders does not affect the forecast quantity on the first line of the chart. These two lines do not sum to produce total demand; rather, the forecast is the projected demand and the customer orders are the actual demand. Customer orders appear in the period in which they are scheduled to ship.

Two master schedule lines calculated by the computer are the **Projected Available Balance** and **Available to Promise** lines. The Projected Available Balance is a calculation designed to protect against making unreasonable supply plans. It quantifies the balance between the total expected supply and the total expected demand. The Available to Promise, on the other hand, is a variable calculated to protect against making unreasonable promises to customers. It quantifies the balance between the total expected supply and the booked customer orders. We will briefly review the process used in calculating these variables.

The Projected Available Balance is calculated in three ways, depending on the period being calculated. In the first period, the Projected Available Balance (PAB) is the sum of the on-hand balance plus the master production schedule (for period one), minus the customer orders. In periods two through the end of the demand time fence, the PAB is the prior period's PAB, plus the calculated period's master production schedule, minus customer orders. In the periods following the demand time fence, the PAB is the prior period's PAB, plus the calculated period's master production schedule, minus the greater of the forecast or customer order quantities.

The Available to Promise is calculated in two ways, again depending on the period being addressed. In the first period, the Available to Promise (ATP) is the sum of the on-hand balance plus the master production schedule (for period one), minus the sum of customer orders scheduled to ship before the next master production schedule receipt. In all later periods, the ATP is the master production schedule for the calculated period, minus the sum of customer orders scheduled to ship before the next master production schedule receipt.

The final line of the master schedule chart, the **Master Production Schedule**, is the anticipated build schedule for the item, including planned orders, firm planned orders, and released production orders. This line of the master schedule represents the total supply plan for the item. For purposes of the Master Planning exam, the Master Production Schedule quantity is shown in the period in which the order will be complete and the item becomes available.

Variations in the Master Schedule Format

The master schedule format designed for the APICS Master Planning exam is not intended to address all variations found in our professional literature, but we hope that it can be used by the student to better understand the professional literature, Master Planning exam questions, and the student's professional production and inventory challenges in the work environment.

Texts and articles use specialized master schedule formats to focus attention on critical points relevant to a particular discussion. Individual companies use specialized master schedule formats to address unique characteristics of their business environments or policies. We expect that the standard format developed for the Master Planning exam will expand to encompass many common master schedule variations in the years to come.

About the Authors

John J. Bruggeman, CFPIM, is a senior faculty member with the Corporate Technical Institute of IBM. He has 30 years' experience in virtually all areas of operations management. His primary interest is the role of logistics in corporate strategy. He currently serves on APICS' Master Planning Committee of the Certification and Curricula Council, and has served on other committees previously. He is a frequent speaker at local APICS chapter meetings.

Susan M. Haythornthwaite, CPIM, is senior consultant with the management consulting Services Division of Price Waterhouse. She has eight years' experience in production planning and manufacturing systems implementation. Her primary interest is in the implementation of integrated business information systems. She serves on the Master Planning Committee of the Certification and Curricula Council, and has previously held officer positions with local chapters.

Reprinted from the 1997 APICS Conference Proceedings.

A Vision Becomes Reality: The Eight Critical Steps to Successful Implementation of Sales and Operations Planning

James Correll, CFPIM, and Rory MacDowell

Sales and Operations Planning (S&OP) is a proven process for successfully linking strategies to ongoing operations. Information from all disciplines of the organization come together on a monthly basis so that management can take corrective action if goals such as profit, customer service, and cost are not being met. This paper outlines the main steps to successfully implement S&OP. Implementors will hear real-life experiences from several divisions of an international discrete manufacturing company. The company referenced here began the drive to Oliver Wight Class A at all major locations around the world several years ago. It has Class A S&OP processes at many of its operations and has begun a global S&OP process.

The specific implementation of S&OP depends on business issues such as markets, size, structure of the organization, and variability of product. Do not think that S&OP is a cookbook approach. The concepts are all the same, but implementation must be tailored to the specific business.

There have been many papers written on S&OP. This paper will discuss an eight-step approach to ensure a successful implementation:

- Getting Started
- Discipline and Data
- Pre-S&OP Process
- Business Decisions
- Financial Analysis
- Marketing Information
- Linking to Business Process
- Continuous Improvement.

Step 1—Getting Started

This is definitely the toughest part. S&OP requires substantial resources and is a never-ending process. Getting management to allocate the resources and demand discipline can be a real challenge.

If your company has decided to strive for Oliver Wight Class A, then getting the commitment may be easier because S&OP is a required step and key driver to achieve the results required by Class A. If Class A is not an objective, management buy-in is tougher, but the same results can be achieved. After all, it is about communication among the various functions of the organization and provides a vehicle for top management decision-making based on a single set of accurate and reliable data. Whatever your situation, getting top management to take the leadership role can be difficult. Here are some tips that might help.

Always approach management from a business perspective. Understand the business issues facing the company. Then

be a *solution provider*. A CEO/President who believes that there is adequate return on investment from an initiative will generally support and lead the way. One way to get the process started is to organize an informal discussion, maybe a lunch, with department managers or VPs about the business. At first, you may want to exclude the CEO/President because VPs may be timid to open up in front of the boss. Ask some questions about business priorities, markets, performance measures, statistics and definitions, forecasts, desired inventory, and backlog levels. If your company does not have an S&OP process, odds are the department heads will have differing opinions. This type of discussion will point out the lack of communication and misaligned activities. Some days later, suggest a solution—S&OP. Show how S&OP benefits all functions and the business.

Another approach is to visit other companies whose executives understand the benefits and requirements for S&OP. Make sure you visit the right level executive. The CEO will more likely listen to another CEO.

Talk to the CEO/President about the planning and control process in general. Focus on the fact that it all starts with forecasting—a best guess. Most of the rest is a numbers game. The software calculates when to order material, when to put orders on the shop floor, when to pick components from stock and so on. However, without a single forecast that everyone believes, most functions will second guess other function's motives and dependability.

Inundate the CEO/President with success stories about other companies' successes. Address the importance of leadership, communication, discipline, functional roles, performance measures, planning horizon, product family definition, and the importance of demand management. End with a basic cost-benefit analysis. For instance, ask how much it would be worth to the sales organization (in additional revenue) if delivery performance was at least 95 percent, and ask manufacturing how much cost savings could be realized by having stable schedules. Normally the benefits are conservative, but nonetheless staggering. When a CEO understands the process and hears the benefits, he will generally let the process go to the next step.

The best way to begin the process is through education. Get the management team off-site for a session presented by a qualified educator. Tailor the session to the company and its needs. An experienced S&OP educator will begin with a detailed explanation of the S&OP process, emphasizing the difficult and critical steps. Then the educator will use a generic worksheet that is easy to understand, showing how data relates. Next, use the same worksheet format with data from a real family within your company. This time let the CEO lead the discussion and let the educator become the consultant. Usually this starts a lot of discussion about the business, data, strategies, and plans. The CEO is now holding his first S&OP meeting.

Move quickly, start simply, and let the process evolve over time to the appropriate level of detail. Prepare a basic S&OP policy, identify product families, gather reasonable base data on each family regarding forecast, sales, production, inventory, and backlog, and conduct the first meeting. Do not wait until all the data is perfect and all the pieces are in place to have the first meeting; initial meetings will generally reinforce the need for S&OP even without perfect information.

Step 2—Discipline and Data

The S&OP meeting itself requires practice in scheduling, discipline, format agenda preparation, and team building. The first S&OP meetings at a European operation took two full days. Now they take one to two hours. The difference is discipline and data. The first meetings were totally undisciplined:

- no real agenda
- no preparation by participants
- lots of joking and arguing about the data
- several discussions going on at the same time
- no one really taking charge.

A proper S&OP session is a formal meeting, led by the CEO/President, with an agenda sent to participants well ahead of time and people well prepared with reliable data. It is a decision-making meeting, not a general discussion. Generally, the first S&OP meetings have too many participants because functional heads do not feel well enough prepared to answer the questions that may come up. The fact is that VPs should know what is happening in their respective areas and should present the information for their department during the meeting. If VPs need someone else to do their job at the meeting, then there is a problem. George Palmatier puts it best: "If two people are doing the same job, get rid of the highest paid one."

Meeting discipline is something that will come in time, but only if the team works at making it better. The CEO/President must lead. This is his meeting, and he should demand discipline:

- everyone must be present at meetings, no delegation without approval
- delegates must be prepared and authorized to make decisions
- start on time and return from breaks on time
- stick to the agenda
- ensure that discussions do not wander off from the issue and decision at hand
- ensure people are prepared
- no phones and pagers disrupting the meeting.

It is not unusual that the strongest personality of the group will tend to drive the meeting. In one location, the Demand Manager organized the initial meetings and became the de facto leader, making all the presentations based on his observations and analysis. This is wrong. It did not take long for the meeting to disintegrate into disputes between the Demand Manager and the department VPs. The CEO must lead the meetings and the VPs must represent their disciplines.

S&OP is the one meeting of the month where the top management teams decide what will be done to ensure business health—customer service levels maintained, financial forecasts met, and costs in line. This is not a time for pagers and phones, it is a time for managing the business. Done well, S&OP replaces the multitude of meetings held during the month. It is not another meeting, it is THE meeting.

Data reliability is generally one of the biggest obstacles to running a smooth and efficient S&OP. If the team does not work from one reliable/accurate set of numbers, S&OP will not be successful:

- how much inventory do we really have at all of our distribution locations or sales offices for this particular family?
- what is the forecast really going to be?
- how can production figures be higher than sales figures with inventory going down during the same period?
- how can the manufacturing manager be looking for parts to make when there is plenty of backlog?

One Regional President finally commented during initial S&OP sessions, "How can I make business decisions from this data?" Then he realized that he had been running the business for many years without it. From that point on, he was the biggest supporter of S&OP.

Gathering data and presenting it, in usable form in a timely manner, generally requires support from the Information Technology (IT) organization. Reports have to be written to allow analysis to ensure all data is accurate. In one operation, there were six computing systems, each with different data structures. The IT organization had to build a data warehouse to collect data from the various systems. Booking data, inventory data, backlog data, production data, and shipment data have to be collected and organized in standard format each month on schedule. Often, this is a nontrivial task.

The format of the data worksheet is also important. A suitable format should be established early in the process. In general, all S&OP worksheets have similar components and layout. But the worksheet should be tailored to the individual company. Also, do not put too much information on the worksheet. It is a normal tendency. Use supporting sheets if needed. Too much data on one worksheet is confusing and people will not read or analyze it. Start off simple.

Performance data cannot be overlooked or underestimated. If performance is not defined consistently and measured regularly, continual improvement will be almost impossible. If you don't measure, you will not improve. Gathering and reporting reliable performance measurement is a requirement for successful S&OP. Every measurement must be reviewed each meeting, even if the measurements continue at acceptable levels over long periods. If you take your eye off the ball, eventually you will miss. It only takes one to two seconds to look at a graph and say, "Yep, this one is OK." If measures are not at acceptable levels, then those responsible should be able to articulate when they will be and the plan to get there. The CEO/President will earn his stripes by demanding world class performance and by holding his staff accountable to make it happen.

Step 3—Pre-S&OP

As mentioned previously, the S&OP meeting is a decision meeting, not a discussion session. Decisions made at S&OP meetings are based on facts prepared at pre-S&OP meetings held individually by sales and marketing, manufacturing, and finance.

Sales and marketing begins the process by analyzing marketing and forecast data, evaluating ways to satisfy customer demand with existing inventory, recommending pre-order of material for potential orders with high confidence level, documenting assumptions and finalizing the forecast. The pre-S&OP Sales group should also review performance measures relative to forecast accuracy, identify improvements to the forecast process, and analyze accuracy of previous assumptions and identify ways to improve. In addition to sales and marketing department heads, the demand manager plays an important part in the pre-S&OP process. Output from the pre-S&OP sales meeting is a recommendation that, if accepted during the S&OP meeting, becomes a commitment to the company and a request for product from manufacturing. Usually, someone from manufacturing and another from finance attend the pre-S&OP sales meeting to understand how the forecast is developed. It is important, though, that the forecast is not influenced by either manufacturing or finance during the pre-S&OP meeting and also that the forecast is not changed during the other pre-S&OP meetings.

Sales and marketing then hands the forecast off to manufacturing (supply) as input to its pre-S&OP session. Manufacturing analyzes the data and, with the help of rough cut capacity planning, makes tactical decisions about how to provide product to satisfy the demand. Again, it is important that the forecast is not changed during the pre-S&OP supply meeting. It is the responsibility of pre-S&OP supply to define what it will take to satisfy demand as presented by pre-S&OP sales. If the forecast cannot be satisfied without adding resources, pre-S&OP supply should develop several alternatives with associated cost impact to satisfy the demand. Alternatives generally include the use of overtime, outsourcing, and the addition of capacity. Usually, representatives from sales and marketing and finance attend the pre-S&OP supply to understand the decisions or alternatives but do not interfere with the decision-making process. Recommendations are then passed to finance.

During the pre-S&OP finance session, forecast data and production recommendations/alternatives are analyzed to determine the overall impact on the annual business plan. "What-if" simulation tools are invaluable during pre-S&OP finance meetings. This analysis is then documented and presented at the monthly S&OP meeting.

Pre-S&OP analyses, assumptions, and recommendations are consolidated and readied for the S&OP meeting.

Step 4—Business Decisions

Some business decisions are easy and some are hard. All of them directly impact the success of the company. This is why senior management are the only ones to make these decisions. Too often, most companies cannot even make the easy decisions correctly. They do not have the necessary information, and experience and lack a solid decision-making process.

The MRP II process can be described as two different games: a guessing game and a numbers game. S&OP begins with a forecast—it is a guessing game. The output of S&OP is input to MPS/MRP which schedules and plans—it is a numbers game. Considered this way, who should be making the guesses that drive the company? Should the buyer guess what to buy and when? Should the planner decide what to build and when? Guesses should be made by senior management since it is responsible for improving shareholder value by successfully implementing the strategies of the company. This is why the CEO must lead the S&OP process and why the CEO must make the final decisions during the meeting.

Decisions must be made relative to sales plans, production plans, inventory, and backlog targets. Performance against the previous plan must also be reviewed each month and decisions made regarding ways to improve. During the S&OP meeting, the CEO must ask the tough questions and be willing to provide the resources necessary to achieve the plans that are adopted.

It is also important to implement the decisions of the meeting. One company decided to increase the production plan for one family and to reduce the plan of another in preparation for an anticipated swing in the market. To the president's anguish, he found out at the next S&OP that the previous decisions were not implemented. He not only lost orders due to inability to meet the demand on one family, but inventory increased in families that were produced but not sold. One way to help ensure that decisions are implemented is to prepare minutes of the meeting and forward copies to those that are responsible for their implementation. Department heads are responsible for decisions being implemented.

Step 5—Financials

S&OP data is usually presented in units because that is what marketing and manufacturing understand. However, business plan objectives are generally stated in financial terms like revenue, inventory turns, and operating income. The finance group must make it a practice to convert the S&OP worksheet from units into dollars and to link those dollars to the objectives in the annual plan. This is not necessarily an easy task, but it also does not need to be precise. The intent is to show trends; actual figures come directly out of the MRP system.

Most companies prepare some kind of monthly and quarterly financial forecast so that top management and the investment community can monitor progress. Sales plans and production plans stated in units, the S&OP worksheets, are what companies use to drive the business from a planning standpoint. If those plans are achieved, then the result can be predicted in monetary terms—the financial forecasts.

For a long time, one division held two separate meetings each month with the same people—one specifically to prepare the financial forecast and one for S&OP. When the S&OP worksheets were converted into dollars, the financial forecast meeting was discontinued because there was no need. All the information was available during S&OP. Moreover, when the CEO questioned the validity of the financial forecast, the division manager supported his projections with the S&OP worksheets, pre-S&OP analysis, assumptions, and performance measures.

Only when there is confidence in the S&OP data and the dollarized worksheets become the basis for financial forecast does the company truly begin using one set of numbers to run the business.

Step 6—Marketing Information

Marketing information is vital to a successful S&OP. It is listed here as a later step because when S&OP is first initiated there is a lot of change taking place in an organization, and some items must take priority over others. If a company feels it can or must consider marketing trends at the beginning of the process, then it should do so.

A formal process should be initiated for capturing, analyzing, and validating marketing information and for including trends, recommendations, and decisions in the SOP process. The purpose of market reviews is to identify opportunities for increased marketshare, revenue and profit. Generally, this review process addresses four main categories of information by major market: customer, competition, industry requirements, and distribution.

Typically market reviews identify and analyze the top customers based on items such as sales volume, products sold to those customers, top competitors and their approach to selling, main reasons for winning and losing orders, lead time versus competition, market share, and delivery performance.

Often market reviews identify new or replacement products that should be added to the company's portfolio. New product introduction must be addressed as a family during S&OP to ensure inventory targets are maintained during phase-in and phaseout. In addition, new product introduction has to be coordinated with sales training, customer notification, and advertisement programs. These are topics that need decisions during S&OP.

Several divisions of an international manufacturing company agreed to conduct "business review meetings" for each of their four major markets two times a year. The results are presented at their respective S&OP meetings. Moreover, findings are consolidated at a global business review meeting with results presented to the CEO during a global S&OP session.

Another company established a New Products Group of representatives from sales and marketing, manufacturing, and finance. Their charter was to plan the introduction of new products and to coordinate all activities to ensure a successful product launch. Too many times, a new product launch is unsuccessful because all the bases were not covered. A new products group can help ensure success.

Step 7—Linking to Business Strategy

Strategic planning generally spans a period of three to five years. It considers economic and industry trends and lists broad ways to achieve marketshare, revenue, profit, cost, and customer service targets. However, achieving these targets is not a matter of luck—it takes planning and adjustment along the way. The S&OP process is designed to link these strategies to ongoing operations.

With a planning horizon of at least 18 months, S&OP employs near-term strategies like promotions, new product introduction, and advances in manufacturing techniques, as well as opportunities created by changes in customer needs or competitor weaknesses to achieve interim goals. If interim goals are met, then odds are that longer term strategic objectives will be also be achieved.

While strategic plans are generally updated once per year, S&OP is updated at least once per month. As any point in the planning horizon comes closer, S&OP uses worksheet data, performance measures, and assumption versus reality analysis to determine if targets are likely to be met. If it becomes obvious that plans are not meeting expectations, and if the company is truly using at least an 18-month planning horizon, there will usually be time to react and to meet business objectives. The opposite is also true. During early days of implementing S&OP in one division, the president was getting disillusioned with the process because he could not see benefit in his decisions. The problem was that his group was using S&OP only to make decisions on a two-month window, when lead time was eight weeks. By the time he realized he was in trouble, it was too late. Once they started taking a longer view and measuring improvement over an 18-month horizon, he realized that he could adjust his plans in enough time to make a difference.

A solid S&OP process that uses at least an 18-month horizon realizes other benefits as well. At any time within six months of the end of a budget year, estimates for the following year are known. Bookings, sales, production, inventory, and backlog levels can be converted from units to dollars to support the budgeting process. Moreover, trends may indicate a need to increase capacity, and S&OP can be used to support capital and resource planning. Combine all this information with marketing reviews described in Step 6 and budgeting almost becomes a nonevent. In reality, the annual budget and supporting plans are updated monthly.

Step 8—Continuous Improvement

Like any process, the more S&OP is practiced, the better the results. As confidence in the data and pre-SOP recommendations improves, S&OP meetings begin to focus more on the long term. The planning horizon becomes a weapon. "What-if" analysis can be used confidently to determine business impact.

Also, as the S&OP meeting matures, the number of people attending the meeting can be reduced. At a specific European meeting, attendees have been reduced from 15 to nine.

One way to drive continuous improvement is to reference the Oliver Wight Class A Checklist on a regular basis and put plans in place to improve weaker areas.

Critiquing the entire S&OP process at each meeting is a powerful improvement mechanism. If attendees are honest, they will notice and list many ways the process can be improved. Reviewing recent performance measures and understanding the reasons they are acceptable or unacceptable will also help identify processes that could be improved.

In the end, continuous improvement is a culture. It is the constant drive to do better fueled by the excitement that comes with success.

Conclusion

It will be obvious that S&OP is working when top management considers it an integral part of overall planning process. Three different Division Presidents made the following comments after their S&OP matured:
- "For the first time in my career, I feel I'm in control of my business."
- "If I had this at my previous company, I could have done wonders."
- " I don't know how we ran the business before S&OP."

The key is to get it started and stay with it. S&OP is a proven process for successfully linking strategies to ongoing operations.

About the Authors

James Correll, CFPIM, held various management positions for several manufacturing companies early in his career and was the driving force behind Class A at two of them. As a consultant and educator with the Oliver Wight Companies, he has assisted more than 13 companies in attaining Class A performance. He is coauthor of *Gaining Control: Capacity Management and Scheduling* which was published in 1990. He earned a Bachelor of Science Degree in Industrial Technology from Southern Illinois University. He has served on the board of directors of the APICS Portland Chapter.

Rory MacDowell is Chief Information Officer of Keystone International, Inc., with headquarters in Houston, Texas. In addition to his duties as CIO, he heads up the global Class A reengineering activity for Keystone International. Prior to joining Keystone four years ago, he held several management positions at Schlumberger. He graduated from the University of Southern Mississippi with a degree in mathematics and computer science and is a member of MAPI (Manufacturers Alliance for Productivity and Innovation). He spoke at the APICS International Conference in Orlando, Florida in 1995.

Reprinted from APICS—The Performance Advantage, *April 1995.*

Inventory—Asset or Liability?
Richard E. Crandall, CPIM, CIRM

Accounting calls inventory an asset. However, some production and operations management (POM) authorities call inventory a liability, or at least not an asset (Sharma 1993). Is one right and the other wrong, or are they talking about different things? This article describes these apparent differences and explains how the positions between accounting and POM should be reconciled if a company is to manage its inventory effectively. It addresses the specific questions of:

- Why is inventory called an asset by accounting and never a liability?
- When is inventory considered an asset by POM? a liability?
- What is excess inventory? What are the causes of excess inventory?
- How can excess inventory be disposed of? prevented?
- What changes in management practices will be needed?

Managers who understand both the accounting and operations viewpoint of inventory will do a better job of inventory management for their company.

Background

Accounting views an asset as something a company owns, and a liability as something a company owes; therefore, inventory will always be considered as an asset by accounting. For POM purposes, an asset is something that has greater value than its cost, and is able to generate income for the company.

If inventory were always an asset, in both the accounting and POM sense, there would not be a difference in viewpoints. This ideal situation exists when finished goods inventory is readily salable and moves quickly through the distribution steps from the manufacturer to the customer. Agreement also exists when the work-in-process inventory is moving steadily through the manufacturing process without undue delays, such as in a Just-in-time environment. Finally, both parties believe that a raw materials inventory that is compatible with the needs of manufacturing is also an asset. In essence, inventory is an asset when it includes the right quantities of the right goods at the right place at the right time.

Conversely, for POM, a liability is something that has greater potential cost than value, or its presence prevents sales of other products, thereby causing it to generate a loss of income for the company. When and how can inventory become a liability in the POM sense? A simple answer is when a company has excess inventory at any point along the value chain from raw materials to customer shipment. Rosenfield (1993) defines excess inventory as existing when "the potential value of excess stock, less the expected storage costs, does not match the salvage value." If

excess inventory is viewed as a liability, there is a need to determine which inventory is excess and what can be done about it. Often a company doesn't recognize that they have excess inventory because the management reporting system (usually a part of the accounting system), does not adequately identify where and how much excess inventory exists.

Causes of Excess Inventory

How does a company end up with excess inventory? What, or who, produces it? The following examples are representative, but not exhaustive, of the causes of excess inventory.

- Marketing—Marketing may want to have inventory available for a fast response to the customer, or simply, to have product available for immediate sale. To do this, they must forecast demand for a variety of items and, no matter how diligent they are and methodologically sound their forecast method, the resultant forecasts are never perfect. Consequently, some finished goods inventory does not move as expected and eventually becomes unnecessary, or excess. Another possibility is that new products replace existing products, making obsolete the inventory of the replaced products. With the increasing emphasis on customer service and shorter lead times, it will be difficult for marketing to avoid generating excess inventories. Marketing decisions generally affect finished goods inventories.
- Production—Production may want to avoid unfavorable labor variances or to improve their labor efficiencies and machine utilizations. This can be done by producing at a level capacity load that also avoids fluctuations in the work force; however, it also produces excess inventories at times. Excess inventories also result when the manufacturing process produces good, but out-of-spec, products that can be sold only if a customer is found who can use them. The temptation is to keep and value these products even with no known customer. Finally, some processes require starting a quantity of parts higher than the order quantity to allow for process defects and assure having enough good units to ship. This often results in an excess of units that may not be shippable but are good units. Again, the inclination is to hold these units in expectation that a repeat order will make them shippable; often, however, they end up as slow-moving, or excess, inventory. Production decisions can affect both work-in-process and finished goods inventory.
- Purchasing—Purchasing may want to buy a larger quantity to get a price discount; this can easily result in excess inventory at the raw materials or purchased parts

stage. While this approach may look good in the short term, with favorable purchase price variances, it can generate excess inventories that will be costly in the long term.

- Production planning—Production planning may want to utilize available capacity in the shop. To do so, they schedule the production of standard products that are in constant demand. Eventually, some of these standard products become nonstandard, and excess inventory results. Another possible scenario is that a customer requests a manufacturer to produce and hold a certain amount of inventory, at any stage in the process, for that customer's exclusive use. While this situation implies that the manufacturer will not end up holding this special inventory, sometimes they do. Decisions by production planning can affect inventory at any stage of completion: raw materials, work-in-process, or finished goods.

The conditions described above, and others, can lead to excess inventories. Often, the different functions within an organization are in conflict about how much inventory to have. Top management may have to choose a compromise position with respect to inventory levels and product mix. Obviously, nobody wants excess inventory or sets out to create it. But what are the reasons behind its creation?

Why is Excess Inventory Created?

Sometimes, the performance measures used in a company cause the buildup of inventory to be attractive. For example, most companies use income, or costs, as a measure of performance, especially for production managers, purchasing agents and marketing managers. These groups tend to focus more attention on the income statement than on the balance sheet. If the level of inventory does not change, there is no effect on income. An increase in the level of inventory often increases income because it reduces the unfavorable labor and overhead variances that occur when there is erratic or less-than-ideal capacity levels of production. Conversely, a reduction in the level of inventory often causes a reduction in income by introducing variable work loads and unused capacity, causing unfavorable labor and overhead variances. Fry (1992) provides an excellent explanation of this effect.

While the increase in inventories generates income, it has the opposite effect on cash flows by decreasing available cash. A reduction in inventories has the reverse effect—positive cash flow. This presents a conflict in that managers in most companies use income more as a measure of performance than cash flow. However, the ultimate measure of a company's value is its cash flow—a position that accounting understands but does not always communicate to the rest of the organization.

Another cause of excess inventories is the mistaken idea that having inventory on hand is always desirable. Most persons view assets as something good, and liabilities as something bad. A better way is to view inventory as stored costs that will eventually be charged to the income statement. Inventory buildup, then, is a way of postponing the reporting of costs until those costs are, in theory, matched against the sales to which they belong. The Accounting Review Board Ruling 43 says that: "In accounting for the goods in the inventory at any point in time, the major objective is the matching of appropriate costs against reverses in order that there may be a proper determination of the realized income."

The present methods used to value inventory are limited in helping us to deal with excess inventories.

How Is Inventory Valued?

Two questions need to be addressed in deciding how to value inventory: (1) Is the individual unit of inventory correctly valued, or has excess cost been assigned to each unit? and (2) Does the inventory contain excess units that should have less than full value? The latter question involves evaluating the probability that the unit will be sold and when it will be sold.

These questions require a way to assign an initial value to the unit, and some way to revalue the units as the units remain in inventory unsold.

Initial Valuation

Accounting provides two ways of valuing inventory: cost or market value, whichever is lower. The lower value purports to provide a conservative value for the company and its reported income. While conservatism is the objective, it may not be the result. As pointed out below, full absorption costing is the least conservative way of valuing inventory of the methods described, yet it is the only one generally accepted by accounting practice.

Market value—Market value is not a practical way to value inventory, in most cases. It not only requires a way to determine the market value of inventory but also a way of adjusting the value of inventory as the market value fluctuates. Trying to develop a dynamic (adjusted through time) estimate of this factor is beyond the capability of most accounting departments. As a result, most companies do not attempt to use market value of inventory as an ongoing valuation method.

Cost value—One of the key decisions in valuing inventory is to decide which costs should be stored. These costs include direct materials, direct labor, and fixed and variable overhead expenses. Historically, accounting practice required that all of the above elements be assigned to the product and stored in inventory until the product is sold. In recent years, several alternative viewpoints have been proposed: activity-based costing (ABC), direct costing and theory of constraints (TOC).

- **Activity-based costing (ABC).** This supports the traditional approach of assigning all overhead costs to the product and storing them in inventory; however, it questions the methods of allocating the overhead expenses to the products. This approach allocates the overhead expenses differently, and goes beyond just cost allocation to emphasize a closer analysis of overhead to eliminate the non-value-added portion as unnecessary.
- **Direct costing.** Many management accountants like this costing method for use in planning, analysis and control; however, financial accountants have never accepted it as a method for valuing inventory. It advocates the assignment of fixed overhead expense to the period in which they were incurred, and not to be stored in inventory as a product cost. This means that inventory has a lower cost value, and therefore, less impact on the income statement. It also more clearly identifies overhead elements, offering greater opportunities to reduce them.
- **Theory of constraints (TOC).** As with direct costing, this approach advocates that all overhead should be a period expense. They go further to say that even direct

labor is more fixed than variable in today's manufacturing environments and should be a period expense. This means that only direct material purchase cost would be stored as costs in inventory, resulting in even lower inventory values than for direct costs. TOC also promotes the idea that only sold product that is sold (throughput) should be recognized as inventory (8).

FUNCTION	REASONS TO INCREASE	REASONS TO DECREASE
Marketing Finished goods	• Increase sales through immediate delivery • Reduce lead time to customers	• Change mix to have salable items available • Make cash available for other programs
Production Work-in-process	• Fill in low load periods to level production • Increase labor efficiency and machine utilization	• Reduce congestion on shop floor • Reduce lead times to provide faster service
Purchasing Raw materials	• Obtain quantity (volume) discounts • Reduce number of purchase orders required	• Shift emphasis from cost to quality and delivery • Reduce number of vendors to be dealt with
Production planning	• Reduce the number of late shipments to customers • Ship more from stock to meet shorter due dates • Reduce number of production orders	• Keep production capacity open for customer orders • Shorten due dates by wait times in the process • Increase flexibility to respond to customers
Accounting	• Reduce overhead volume variances • Increase working capital	• Reduce physical inventory task • Reduce cash requirements

Table 1. Incentives to increase/decrease inventory

Note: Although valuing inventory at the cost of materials may initially appear to be a very conservative valuation, it may not be. As manufacturers move more toward being final assemblers and increase their purchases of subassemblies or fabricated parts, the direct materials portion increases to a point where it represents 60-70 percent of the cost of sales (2). However, accounting practices can be misleading. Material costs to a final assembler are material, labor and overhead to a subassembler; material costs to a subassembler are material, labor and overhead to a fabricator; and material costs to a fabricator are material, labor and overhead to a materials processor. Figure 1 shows how the cumulative effect of this sequence could be to reduce the direct material content to a very low portion if one considers only the materials cost of the materials processor. The most conservative way to value inventory is at the scrap value of the raw materials used.

Each of the above positions is different from the traditional method of full absorption costing that assigns the maximum amount of cost to the product. The traditional approach stores the greatest amount of costs to be "matched" against subsequent revenue; the more recently proposed approaches store less for future release against revenue and, as a result, cause less distortion of the income statement during inventory buildup and reduction. Even more important, the three approaches listed above actively promote the analysis of overhead costs and the elimination of costs that are unnecessary. The full absorption method disguises overhead and discourages careful analysis; it is a financial accounting tool, not a management accounting tool.

The current thinking of many managers, including some accountants, is to store less costs in inventory and reduce the impact of inventory changes on the income statement.

Revaluation of Inventory

Most companies use full absorption costing to value inventory. This does not present a problem if inventories are low and goods are moving smoothly through the manufacturing and distribution process. In this situation, the overhead costs are not storied in inventory very long and do not seriously affect the income statement.

However, when inventories build up and become excess to the needs of the business (when the probability that they will be sold at a price higher than their accumulated cost is low), they become liabilities and the inventory valuation should reflect this through some reevaluation process.

Inventories that do not sell promptly fall into this category. However, most companies do not discriminate among inventories when assigning an initial value; they assume that all product will be sold, no matter why it was created.

Auditors attempt to assess such factors as age, potential obsolescence, damage and other degradation of inventory in assigning an overall reduction in the inventory value. However, they usually do this only during the annual audit and seldom do it in a way that would be of benefit to inventory managers in identifying the causes of excess inventory that could lead to preventing or reducing the buildup of excess inventory.

There is a need to develop a way to adjust, usually reduce, inventory values as time passes and the probability of sale diminishes. While this is logical, there are practical problems that must be faced, and most companies do not have a formal way of adjusting inventory values.

A more desirable solution is to prevent the accumulation of excess inventories, i.e., prevent the problem, not find a better way to report it. How can this be done? A company must first identify which inventory is excess; then it must sell or otherwise dispose of the excess inventory; and, finally, it must establish practices that prevent the recurrence of excess inventory. Rosenfield (1993) offers a way in which excess inventory can be identified, and White (1989) describes several ways in which a company can dispose of excess inventory.

Changes Required

To reduce existing excess inventory and prevent its recurrence, a company requires changes in attitudes, objections, performance measures, operating methods and accounting practices. It also requires the integration of various functions within the organization.

Changes in Attitudes About Inventory

Managers need to change their thinking about the desirability of having inventory versus the desirability of not having inventory. **Table 1** contains a comparison of the reasons for having inventory (the traditional perspective) and the reasons for not having inventory (the contemporary perspective).

These changes in attitude come from the realization that today's competitive environment requires attention on customer service, product flexibility and product quality, as well as product cost. White (1989) describes how customer service can be improved by removing the slow-moving inventory ("sludge") from the inventory base. Beddingfield (1992) also points out the competitive advantages of improved inventory management.

Changes in Objectives

Transition from the traditional way of thinking to the contemporary requires a combination of rethinking strategic objectives and changes in the performance measurement system. Both topics are important and several authors have discussed these issues, especially Dixon et al. (1970) and Vollman et al. (1993). Part of this change process involves establishing global objectives that can be translated into local objectives for each organizational function, such as marketing, production, materials management and accounting. As previously mentioned, the choice of inventory level and product mix may present conflicts among functions and requires a holistic approach to reach a common objective.

Changes in Performance Measures

It is necessary for the local (functional) performance measures to be closely related to the general financial performance measures, such as income and return on investment. As previously mentioned, building inventory is a way to show improved performance in income, which is used directly, or in some related form, as a measure of performance for functional areas such as marketing, production and purchasing. If other performance measures were used, such as customer service levels, the practice of building inventories, especially the less-salable, would probably decrease.

Changes in Operating Practices

Marketing, production and purchasing have to effect the needed changes to eliminate existing excess inventories and minimize the buildup of future excess inventories. To do this, they need help from the accounting function in identifying and measuring the status and causes of the excess inventories.

- Marketing—The burden of disposing of excess inventory usually falls to sales and marketing. This is not a welcome task and often has a lower priority than new product or key account programs; however, it must be done. Marketing should be among the most enthusiastic supporters of programs to prevent excess inventory. They can help by working more closely with customers to obtain better forecasts of customer demand; communicate with engineering and production about introductions of new products and phaseouts of discontinued products; participate in the reduction of production and delivery lead times to reduce the need for finished goods inventories; and become a closely integrated link in the company's planning and control system.
- Production—Several current movements in production and inventory management include a focus on reducing the level of inventories. Just-in-Time (JIT) includes a major emphasis on reducing the causes of inventory to reduce the absolute level of inventory. Materials requirements planning (MRP), when properly applied, will reduce excess and slow-moving inventory. Total quality management (TQM) attempts, among other things, to reduce the level of defects. Lower defects result in less uncertainty and fewer overruns on production orders. These

programs help to reduce the cycle time from customer to delivery and to improve on-time deliveries.

Changes in Accounting Practices

Accounting can help to identify, reduce and prevent excess inventory; however, they must change some of their practices, particularly about inventory valuation—changes necessary to make accounting information more useful to production/operations managers. These changes include how to value inventory, how to revalue inventory over tie, how to reduce buildup of excess inventory through proper financial performance measures, and how income and cash flow must both be considered in planning inventory.

Initial valuation—The initial valuation of inventory should be a discriminating process to separate the planned and readily resalable product in inventory from the unplanned product with uncertain resalability. This process also should be dynamic, in that the status of certain products will evolve as they move through the product life cycle. To show the extremes of this method, a regularly sold, standard product could be valued with full absorption costs, as done currently; at the other extreme, inventory of nonstandard product generated as the result of a production overrun, could be valued at the scrap value of the material.

A factor to be considered in the initial valuation is the probability that the unit will be sold. In the standard unit described above, the assumption is that the probability of sale is near 100 percent and the unit can be assigned full cost value. In the overrun unit, the probability of sale as a completed unit is near zero, and the unit value is only the revenue generated when sold as scrap. The values for these extreme groups of products are logical; however, how about units of inventory that fall between the end groups? How does a company value them?

When the probability of sale is less than 100 percent, one approach is to value the units at some cost less than full absorption cost, such as the direct cost or the purchased material cost. This is a way of reducing the average cost of the units in inventory and allowing some costs to flow through as period expenses during the production period. However, it is an expedient method of devaluing, and does not address the logic of the situation, namely, what is the probability of sale?

Another approach is to value the units at full absorption cost and then group them in a category of "25 percent probability of sale," "50 percent probability of sale," etc. This forces an evaluation of the potential salability of the product, but it requires extensive additional attention and record keeping; however, it reflects the reality of the situation. In addition, it offers a way to assign responsibility to the source of the excess inventory, thereby suggesting a way to prevent reoccurrences.

Revaluation of inventory—The total inventory should be classified by major product lines, and by method of initial valuation. It should be reviewed regularly (higher usage, or "A" items more frequently) to decide the need for revaluation. As with the initial valuation, certain guidelines could be developed. Some parameters to be considered include the age of the inventory, its physical condition and shelf life, the degree of obsolescence, and the number of sales days on hand. These adjustments could be handled in an "Allowance for Inventory Revaluation," in much the same way as an "Allowance for Uncollectible Accounts Receivable."

While this method requires judgment, this judgment can be systematically applied, and the process will identify major areas of concern or potential liability to the company. Adjustments in inventory value are not unheard of. Retail stores do it through the markdown procedure. This reduces the income when product is sold, and cost is matched with the sale. Wholesale companies, because of very narrow gross profit margins, sometimes revalue inventories higher when notified of price increases by suppliers. This has the effect of increasing income at the time of purchase, not at the time of sale, presumably because the inventory has increased in value. These adjustments make sense and are convenient; something similar should be done for manufacturing inventories, though it is less convenient and more difficult to determine the true value.

Clearly, the processes described above for valuation and revaluation of units of inventory would be time-consuming and an added expense; as a result, the emphasis should be on prevention of excess inventory, not accounting for it, or disposing of it. As with many problems, the best answer is avoidance, not correction.

Integration of Organization Functions

Identification, disposal and prevention of excess inventories requires a coordinated effort by all functions of a business, particularly marketing, operations and accounting. This coordinated effort starts with the strategic planning process and carries through to the day-to-day operations.

If all parties concerned were more aware of the effect of inventory changes on both income and cash flow, better decisions could be made about the best levels of inventory and the most desirable product mix. This requires better communications among the operating groups and accounting during the business planning processes and recognition of the responsibilities of the marketing and production groups in the cash management program.

Inventory is not an asset to a company if it is excess inventory. The sooner production/operations management and accounting recognize this and adjust their performance measures and operating practices, the sooner companies will be motivated to identify and reduce, or better still, to prevent excess inventory.

References

1. Beddingfield, Thomas W., "Reducing Inventory Enhances Competitiveness," *APICS—The Performance Advantage*, September, 1992, pp. 28-31.
2. Dixon, J. Robb, Alfred J. Nanni and Thomas E. Vollman, *The New Performance Challenge, Measuring Operations for World-Class Competition*, Dow Jones-Irwin, Homewood, Illinois, 1990.
3. Farmer, James R., "Re-engineering, Achieving Productivity Success," *APICS—The Performance Advantage*, March, 1993, pp. 38-42.
4. Fry, Timothy D., "Manufacturing Performance and Cost Accounting," *Production and Inventory Management Control Journal*, Vol. 33, No. 3, pp. 30-35.
5. Gaither, Norman, *Production and Operations Management* (Fourth Edition), The Dryden Press, Chicago, 1990.
6. Jenkins, Carolyn, "Accurate Forecasting Reduces Inventory," *APICS—The Performance Advantage*, September, 1992, pp. 37-39.
7. Lee, Hau L. and Corey Billington, "Managing Supply Chain Inventory: Pitfalls and Opportunities," *Sloan Management Review*, Spring, 1992, pp. 65-73.
8. Rosenfield, Donald B., "Disposal or Excess Inventory," *Operations Research*, Vol. 37, No. 3, May-June, 1993, pp. 404-409.
9. Schaeffer, Randall, "A New View of Inventory Management," *APICS—The Performance Advantage*, January, 1993, pp. 21-24.
10. Sharma, Ken, "Adding 'Intelligence' to MRP Systems," *APICS—The Performance Advantage*, March, 1993, pp. 53-58.
11. Umble, M. Michael and M. L. Srikanth, *Synchronous Manufacturing*, SouthWestern Publishing Co., Cincinnati, 1990, p. 28.
12. Vollman, Thomas E., William L. Berry and D. Clay Whybark, *Integrated Production and Inventory Management*, Business One Irwin, Homewood, Illinois, 1993.
13. White, R. Douglas, "Streamline Inventory to Better Serve Customers," *The Journal of Business Strategy*, March/April, 1989, pp. 43-45.

Reprinted from the 1996 APICS Conference Proceedings.

Production Planning for High-Performance Businesses: A Case Study

Tom Devaney, CPIM, and Michael Tincher, CPIM

W hat do you mean the customer service level hasn't increased? The new software and hardware installed last year was justified by telling the Board of Directors that the company could ship faster, be more reliable and predictable than ever, and would increase on time performance. Also promised were inventory reductions and productivity improvements. Well, what gives?

Are you hearing this dialog at your company? Did you install a new state-of-the-art software package, spend a lot of time and money, and expect the benefits to start falling to the bottom line? Well, you are not alone! Software is not going to solve any problems. It is only a tool that can aid in managing a business or a production facility more efficiently. If business practices do not change and the mindset remains the same, why would you expect different results? It sounds like you're expecting a miracle!

This presentation will describe the paths that A.W. Chesterton Co. took on its journey. It was a twofold journey: a path to new software and a path to excellence through the implementation of a sales and operations planning process.

The Company: A.W. Chesterton Co., Stoneham, Ma

A.W. Chesterton Co., a manufacturer of mechanical packings, industrial cleaners, coatings and lubricants (technical products), mechanical seals, pumps, and hydraulic pneumatic seal rings was founded in 1884 on the docks of Boston Harbor. The president and CEO is James D. Chesterton, grandson of the original founder. He was appointed to this position in 1988, after a long and successful career as international sales vice president. Mr. Chesterton's vision was to make A.W. Chesterton Co. a World Class organization and he is committed to this goal.

Chesterton began the Journey with a software installation. In the fall of 1989, the Board of Directors approved the funds to install new computer hardware (AS400) and software (BPCS) under the direction of Stephen B. Chapman, CIO and vice president and executive assistant to the CEO. The Board approved this endeavor based on the potential improvements the software would help Chesterton achieve: improvements in customer service, inventory reductions (25-30%), and productivity (10%) as well as enhanced purchasing potential.

A corporate Steering Committee was formed to oversee the implementation at the three Massachusetts sites; both a project leader and implementation team were appointed for each site.

Implementation

The implementation of new software and hardware can be extremely challenging to a business. For a successful implementation, a company must pick the best people in the organization to lead the project. Education and training in all modules, prototyping and, finally, a conference room pilot, not to mention the countless hours of user training and testing, are required.

Success

By the middle of 1991, 22 modules of BPCS were up and functioning. For the first time in its history, Chesterton was operating on a fully integrated software system. It took a few months for things to stabilize, but during that time Chesterton began to realize that its journey really had just begun. The software was functioning and the implementation was considered a huge success! Chesterton, however, had made the classic mistake of focusing solely on the computer path and had not in any way, shape or form changed its business practices. As Steve Chapman put it, "We paved the cow path." The benefits they expected would not come from the software. They would, however, come from using this tool as an aid to manage the business better by looking at the business processes that needed to be improved.

Breakout

In early 1993, a breakout strategy was developed for the Mechanical Packing Business of A.W. Chesterton Co. Under the direction of General Manager Greg Smith, Division Manager Dwight Bertozzi, and Operations Manager Harold P. Torrey, the entire facility accepted the challenge to manage the business by the principles of Manufacturing Resource Planning (MRP II).

A critical piece of the Chesterton success story was that management embraced the top management planning process of the MRP II business model, in particular, the Production Planning and Sales and Operations Planning process. For the typical company, 50% of the benefits of Manufacturing Resource Planning (MRP II) are achieved through implementation of a high performance Sales and Operations Planning process. A.W. Chesterton Co. was no exception.

Chesterton's business always had been difficult to forecast as their business materializes as a result of an outage or equipment failure at their customer's location. Some at Chesterton said business was impossible to forecast. The traditional approach which Production had taken over the years was to second-guess the Sales Department and only halfheartedly entertain the Sales forecast. Production would build its own forecast from history and an accumulation of bad experiences.

Steps to Success

The first step for A.W. Chesterton Co. was the creation of demand planning. Under demand management, Chesterton was able to create a process that allowed them to aggregate demand information by business and product line. A demand plan, with a monthly review of the forecast by Sales and Production, was critical to eliminate the second-guessing and finger pointing. The intent was to develop a one-plan process that linked all functions in a common game plan. The result was an integrated top management planning process for each business of Chesterton.

The second step was the monthly business review for the Mechanical Packing Business. This was conducted by Mechanical Packing Business management and reviewed Sales and Operations plans.

The business review is initially broken into three components:
(1) Review of operating performance from the past month—this review by product family is dollars and the unit of measure measures business plan, shipments, bookings, production, inventory and backlog performance to plan.
(2) Review of outlook for current month-end quarter—again, the outlook is by product line for the business plan, shipments, bookings and production plan. Inventory and backlog levels also were reviewed and compared with target or desired levels of each.
(3) Commitment by the Chesterton team to the production plan rates of output for each product family.

The third step on the road to success at Chesterton Mechanical Packing Business was an operational review of not just sales and production but a total of twelve key operational metrics.

At the first Monthly Operations Review meeting, all key members of the Woburn management team reviewed the business metrics. Any metric that was not at a 90%+ level of performance had a spin off team created around it to analyze the issues preventing its hitting this goal. Problem solving techniques learned allowed Chesterton to get at the root causes and improve the process. One such area was in production planning and scheduling. Because they did not do a good job of completing shop orders on time or rescheduling them if they became late, the production schedulers developed their own informal daily schedules that drove the factory. This was a major disconnect in the process. People did not believe the master schedule and the open order status in BPCS. By addressing and fixing this issue, the entire system became much more believable and formal.

By early 1994, performance in all operating areas began to rise into the 90th percentile. Equally important was that not only did the metrics get better, they also became more predictable and reliable. Chesterton no longer had measures that would be 70% one month, 90% the next, and 80% the next. The elimination of noise indicated that the process was now under control.

As the year unfolded, customer service was consistently in the mid-90th percentile while inventory began to drop. Satellite warehouses that once stored inventory were eliminated as were mezzanines that once held surplus inventory in the factory. Over a 15-month period, the Mechanical Packing Business' worldwide inventory dropped by 40%; housekeeping and workplace organization became the new focus. The total team was involved and each employee was required to attend a meeting where the business metrics were reviewed and discussed. In November 1994, the Mechanical Packing Business was awarded Class A status.

The Epilogue

Since achieving the goal of Class A MRP II at the Mechanical Packing Business, two other Chesterton businesses, Technical Products and Hydraulic Pneumatic, have achieved the same goal. Each has been able to maintain their Class A status each and every month. All three businesses are now exempt from physical inventory, customer service levels are at 95-100% each month, and there has been a 40-50% reduction in inventory.

About the Authors

Michael G. Tincher is President and one of two founders of Buker, Inc., a worldwide management education and consulting firm. Mr. Tincher works with companies from all types of industries implementing Manufacturing Resource Planning, Just-In-Time Production, and Total Quality Management to achieve Class A and World Class Performance.

Mr. Tincher has over 20 years' experience in manufacturing management. Prior to the founding of Buker, Inc., he participated in the development and conduct of worldwide Manufacturing Industry Client Education for Arthur Andersen & Company. During his career he served in a number of manufacturing positions for Dresser Industries.

Mr. Tincher is the author of numerous articles published in *Manufacturing Systems, Actionline* and *APICS—The Performance Advantage Magazine*. He is also the author of three books: *Top Management's Guide to World Class Manufacturing, The Road to Class A Manufacturing Resource Planning (MRP II)*, and *High Velocity Manufacturing*.

Mr. Tincher is Certified in Production and Inventory Management (CPIM) by the American Production & Inventory Control Society and is a member of the Association for Manufacturing Excellence. He is a graduate of Bowling Green State University with a degree in Economics.

Thomas E. Devaney has 20 years of experience in the field of Materials Control and Manufacturing Scheduling as a Materials Planner, Inventory Control Manager, and as a Materials Manager for a $60 million business. Recently he worked as the Manufacturing Area Manager on a software installation that ultimately led to the position of MRP II Project Manager at A.W. Chesterton Company. Two of Chesterton's four domestic businesses have achieved Class A status and a third has been recommended for the award. The process is also being pursued in the international business in Europe and Mexico.

Mr. Devaney has a B.A. in Business Administration from the University of Lowell and is certified in Production and Inventory Management.

Reprinted with permission of Congress for Progress 1992.

Getting Started with Sales and Operations Planning

John R. Dougherty

"What do you mean we've got to start planning sales and production?" said the general manager. "How do you think we've been running this company for the last 25 years?"

Of course, she's right. Every company does some form of Sales and Operations Planning already.

But hundreds of companies implementing or operating integrated manufacturing planning and control systems (MRP II) have discovered startling benefits to be gained by formalizing and integrating this planning process. This involves a monthly review process by top management and all functional areas of the company. Its ultimate goal is to always keep the detailed sales, manufacturing, purchasing and capacity planning systems in synchronization with the latest high level plans of management (the business plan).

This presentation assumes understanding of the basic philosophies, concepts and mechanics of Sales and Operations Planning, Master Production Scheduling and MRP. The purpose of this presentation is to provide a simple, step-by-step implementation plan to get it off the ground quickly and effectively.

Points of Emphasis

The italicized portions of the following *APICS Dictionary* (Sixth Edition) definitions highlight the key points for developing the Sales and Operations Planning process and involving the right people.

"*Business Plan*—A statement of *long-range strategy and income, cost and profit objectives* usually accompanied by budgets, projected balance sheet, and a cash flow (source and application of funds) statement. It is usually *stated in terms of dollars and grouped by product family. The business plan and the sales and operations plan, although frequently stated in different terms, should be in agreement with each other.* See manufacturing resource planning."

Implication—Top management usually plans in sales, profit, etc., but to run the factory, a production plan stated in units, and always equal to the dollarized business plan, is required.

"*Sales and Operations Planning*—The function of setting the *overall level of manufacturing output* (production plan) and other activities to best satisfy the current planned levels of sales (sales plan and/or forecasts), while meeting general business objectives of profitability, productivity, competitive customer lead times, etc., as expressed in the overall business plan. One of its primary purposes is to establish production rates that will achieve *management's objective of maintaining, raising, or lowering inventories or backlogs,* while usually attempting to keep the *work force relatively stable.* It must extend through a planning horizon sufficient to plan the labor, equipment, facilities, material, and finances required to accomplish the production plan. As this plan affects many company functions, it is normally prepared with information from *marketing, manufacturing, engineering, finance, materials, etc.*"

Implication—If top management wishes to truly control inventories, backlogs and employment levels, it must ensure that the level of manufacturing output scheduled recognizes current sales plans and backlogs. Concurrence from all company functions that can affect or be affected by the plans, is vital to ensure realism and commitment. The production plan must be stated in a unit of measure, by product family, that can be converted and reconciled to detailed end item schedules (the master production schedule).

"*Master Production Schedule (MPS)*—The anticipated build schedule for those *items assigned to the master scheduler.* The master scheduler maintains this schedule and, in turn, it becomes a set of planning numbers that "drive" material requirements planning. It represents what the company *plans to produce* expressed in specific configurations, quantities and dates. The master production schedule is not a sales forecast which represents a statement of demand. The master production schedule must take into account the forecast, the production plan, and other important considerations such as backlog, availability of materials, availability of capacity, *management policy and goals,* etc. Syn: master schedule. See: closed-loop MRP."

Implication—For the master production schedule to achieve management's objectives, it must exactly match the production plan (and reflect goals, constraints, etc.) and satisfy the sales plan.

"*Rough Cut Capacity Planning*—The process of converting *the production plan and/or the master production schedule* into *capacity needs for key resources: manpower, machinery, warehouse space, vendors' capabilities and, in some cases, money.* Product load profiles are often used to accomplish this. Syn: resource requirements planning. See: capacity requirements planning."

Implication—The production plan and master production schedule must match each other and be achieved for management's goals to be met. But, to be achieved, they require recognizing the physical constraints of budgets and cash flow plans. Rough Cut Capacity Planning allows production plans and master production schedules (and changes thereto) to be checked and adjusted for reality.

"*Time Fence*—A *policy or guideline* established to note *where various restrictions or changes in operating procedures take place.* For example, changes to the master production schedule can be accomplished easily beyond the *cumulative lead time* whereas changes inside the cumulative lead time becomes increasingly more difficult to a point where changes should be resisted. Time fences can be used to define these points."

Implication—When Rough Cut Capacity Planning, forecast changes, customer orders or the constraints of demonstrated capacity identify the need for rescheduling decisions, the procurement lead times of the various product families need to be considered. Top management and all affected functions must formulate policy that routinizes the proper decision making guidelines, participants and management approval levels.

General Implication—These definitions outline the mechanics necessary to integrate a good Sales and Operating Plan with the other functions of a closed-loop MRP II system. The implications noted clearly define the need for active leadership and participation by top management and all functional areas of a company. This is necessary during the design, implementation and ongoing operation of formal Sales and Operations Planning and full MRP II.

Who Must Be Involved?

Based on the company-wide impact of this process described above, it should be clear that the general manager, president or chief executive officer (CEO) needs to oversee this function. This process drives the planning and execution systems, which dictate customer service and profitability. Therefore, the executive responsible for the profitability and growth of the company needs to control Sales and Operations Planning.

The functional heads (vice presidents or directors) of marketing, manufacturing, design, finance and materials must also participate for the same reason. The master production scheduler, production and inventory control manager and marketing manager should also be present to propose needed plan changes and note and implement management decisions.

But often it is difficult to gain such an audience in the early stages, as represented by the general manager's quote that began this presentation. How can these vital participants be enlisted?

How to Get Started

1. *Educate the Participants.* Gaining interest and involvement is a laborious and slow process, unless there is a clear understanding of the goals, the impact and the process itself, involved in Sales and Operations Planning. The educational steps listed below are not interchangeable, but should be followed completely in sequence:

Type of Class	Participants	Purpose
MRP for Top Management (outside class)	Top Mgmt	Understand whole MRP II process, the role Sales and Operations Planning plays, Top Management's role, the payback.
MRP II—Full Detail (outside class)	Middle Mgmt	Same as above, but with more mechanical detail.
Sales & Operations Planning and Master Scheduling (outside class)	All	Understand how to implement and operate the system.
2-Hour In-House Educational Sessions (approx. 20)	Top Mgmt	Determine how the concepts will be applied at this company, set operating policies, assign implementation responsibilities.
2-Hour In-House Educational Sessions (approx. 40)	Middle Management	Same as above, but in more procedural detail for Sales and Operations Planning, Master Scheduling, and all other functions of MRP II.

Note: The balance of the steps outlined below can occur concurrently with the in-house sessions.

2. *Define Planning Families.* Most companies group their products into families or lines, but often based on the customer's perspective (i.e., products bought together such as a particular computer CPU with its matching printers, CRTs, etc.). It is vital to additionally or alternatively define families from a manufacturing viewpoint.

The basic rule to follow is that all products in a family must have a consistently proportional impact on costs, revenues and factory and supplier capacities. For example, a family could include knives, forks and spoons from a series of different patterns of silverware. Though knives, forks and spoons require widely varying manufacturing resources, a weighted average can be applied to the total number of pieces produced. Since knives, forks and spoons are sold in a consistent mix (place settings), if the production plan for the total pieces is changed, the impact on the critical manufacturing resources can be determined by multiplying the new plan times the weighted averages (load profiles) for each resource.

All products must be grouped in 10 to 12 families (a number capable of review in a 2 hour meeting). The units of measure in which the family production plans are expressed must also relate to the manufacturing process—pieces, sets, pounds, gallons, cases, etc. This allows the proper expression of rough cut capacity planning factors and demonstrated capacities.

These physical units of measure can then be converted back to dollars for financial analysis.

3. *Define the Format.* A standard format to display forecasts (sales plans), customer orders, production plans, backlogs and inventories needs to be determined up front. A suggested format is shown in figure 1. This format should be extended for the full planning horizon (12 to 24 months). Individual companies often expand this format to also include dollarization of the key unit data.

4. *Prepare Pilot Data.* A few families should be selected which will best demonstrate the benefit of the Sales and

Sample Sales and Operations Plan Worksheet

Family: Marketing

	−3	−2	−1	Curr	+1	+2	+3	+4
Forecast								
Actual								
Difference								
Cum. Difference								

Manufacturing

Planned								
Actual								
Difference								
Cum. Difference								

Inventory and Backlog

Planned								
Actual								
Difference								

Operations Planning process. These may include families subject to seasonal demand, marketing promotions, volatile sings in actual demand versus forecast and/or limited capability to adjust manufacturing output rates.

Forecasts, actual customer demands, production and inventory plans and actuals should be posted for the prior three months. Plans, forecasts and customer orders for at least the next three months (to start) should also be posted. The starting production plans can be derived from the current planning process or annual budgets or current master schedules, depending on what's available.

Any plans or forecasts that appear to require review or alteration should be highlighted. Marketing and planning personnel should jointly prepare suggested changes for top management review and approval.

5. *Develop a Proposed Sales and Operations Planning Policy and Meeting Agenda*. The police should include:
   a. *Objective* of the process.
   b. *Schedule* of future meetings.
   c. *Attendees* and their individual
   d. *responsibilities* (such as "VP Marketing—review of actuals versus forecasts/sales plans and changes to the future").
   e. A description of the *mechanics* of the planning process (how forecasts and sales plans, backlogs, inventory goals, production plans, etc. are to be considered, by product family).
   f. A description of how *demonstrated capacities* by product family will be maintained and utilized.
   g. A description of the *Rough Cut Capacity Planning* techniques to be used.
   h. A *guideline* for determining *which families* will be *reviewed* in the meeting, based on actual variances from forecasts and plans.
   i. A *guideline for* developing and approving various changes to the plans depending on the timing and impact of the changes (e.g., different approvals required for overtime, subcontract, new hires, etc.)
   j. A statement defining *how the plans* will be used to *establish financial plans*, budgets and detailed *Master Production Schedules* and line item forecasts.
   k. A *timed agenda* for a monthly review meeting, to last no longer than 2 hours.

6. *Begin Monthly Meetings*. The first few meetings often run longer since everyone is still becoming familiar with the process, formats, etc. It may take a few monthly meetings to fine tune the process and finalize the procedures and formats. Until everything is final, it may be advisable to just review the initial pilot families, or to only gradually add new families.

7. *Implement Full Sales and Operations Planning*. The following key issues need to be resolved to ensure that the full benefits of Sales and Operations Planning can be achieved:
   a. *Horizon*. Establish how far out you need to plan based on the cumulative product replenishment cycle (manufacturing and purchase lead times) and the visibility required for planning changes in capacity (internal manufacturing, new plants and suppliers). Near the end of the horizon, data may be grouped quarterly.
   b. *Rolling Forecasts/Sales Plans*. The shipment forecast and plan needs to be maintained continually through the full horizon, not just determined annually.
   c. *Bookings Versus Shipments*. The forecast and sales plan must be expressed by customer requested ship dates, not by when the orders are received. In make-to-order companies this may involve developing standard

lead time offset averages by product family, to convert planned booking dates into shipment dates. Some companies find it useful to track shipments *and* bookings versus the customer backlog, to provide early analysis by marketing of potential forecast changes.
   d. *Production Plans*. If the initial numbers used are annual budget figures or a summing up of current master production schedules, the process of maintaining a rolling, monthly-updated production plan, separate from the master production schedules, must be developed.

   Ongoing measurement of how closely the summary of the master production schedules matches the production plans, by month, within tolerances established by family, should be initiated.

   Appropriate adjustments to the plan, based on changing customer demands, forecasts and sales plans and inventory levels should then be implemented.
   e. *Measurements*. A set of standard measurements, by family, should be published and reviewed at each meeting. These should include:
      1. Customer service
      2. Sales versus forecast or plan
      3. Shipment $s
      4. Master production schedule versus production plan
      5. Actual production versus master production schedules versus production plan
      6. Level and frequency of schedule changes, within time zones.
   f. *Establish Demonstrated Capacity*. For each family, the number of units possible to be manufactured each month should be determined from recent past history. The historical averages should not be exceeded unless known increases in capacity are implemented. The plan should reflect the inevitable learning curve of introducing new people, suppliers or equipment.
   g. *Full Family Planning*. Once the pilot families are being effectively managed through the full horizon, all other families should be added to the process, for the full horizon, representing virtually all manufacturing activity. The use of "average product" planning items for design-to-order business is often required, in both Sales and Operations Planning and Master Production Scheduling. The use of planning bills of material will be needed at the master production schedule level.
   h. *Rough Cut Capacity Planning*. Key manufacturing and supplier capacity (and short term schedule change) constraints should be identified by family and expressed as load factors that can be multiplied by the planned quantities to produce expected resource requirements. These may include:
      1. Total people
      2. People by department or skill
      3. Key work center/lines
         • bottlenecks
         • fully loaded
         • proprietary (no alternates)
         • prone to break down
      4. Space
      5. Key suppliers (expressed in units or hours for key purchased materials)
      6. Inspection and Q.C.
      7. Design and engineering
      8. Dollar levels of inventories.

Key operating objectives should be similarly expressed and analyzed. These may include:
1. Shipment $s
2. Production $s
3. Inventory $s
4. Profit $s
5. Work force utilization
6. Work force stabilization
7. Inventory levels to support seasonal build-ups or safety stock for volatile products.

i. *Time Zones (Fences).* Depending on the lead times to procure and manufacture products within a given family, changing a schedule at different points in the future represents varying degrees of difficulty and cost. Exactly where these zones are for each family must be defined. Appropriate levels of analysis and approval should then be prescribed for proposed changes in each zone. Factors to consider include the amount of potential disruption in the factory and at suppliers, the potential extra cost (air freight, overtime, etc.), the impact on other commitments and the amount of increased inventory investment by delaying parts of the schedule already partially completed.

j. *Management Objectives and Policies.* A well functioning Sales and Operations Planning system will improve the ability to achieve objectives and follow policies. But it often also highlights potential for changing policies to better meet the objectives. Such opportunities include:
1. Make-to-stock versus make-to-order versus finish-to-order, by product line or individual product
2. Target inventory levels
   • amount
   • at what level in the product structure
3. Desired backlogs, lead times and customer service levels
4. Level labor loads
5. Seasonal build-ups
6. New product introductions.

k. *Style of the Meeting.* Several key approaches should be encouraged to maximize the benefits of this process. First, the various functions should avoid blameplacing and competitiveness. This causes defensiveness and less than optimal cooperation. The focus should be on how to change or better achieve future plans or forecasts, not on penalizing poor performance.

Second, the focus should be on future months' plans (generally 3 or more months into the future). Short term plans are very difficult and costly to alter. It is management's job to deal with the uncertainty of the future, and change forecasts and plans far enough in advance to better avoid short term emergencies. Third, a firm rule should be enforced forbidding time to be spent on "post-mortems" as to why a particular customer order was missed. The meeting should deal only with overall rates of shipment and production. Individual issues should be discussed outside this meeting. Specifics should be discussed only if there is potential impact on meeting future plans. Finally, this process and the meeting should evolve to a point where middle management identifies problems and formulates suggested solutions before the meeting, so that top management time can be preserved for only evaluating and approving the proposals. A "pre-meeting meeting" of middle management (manufacturing, materials, marketing, design, finance, etc.) often proves fruitful.

Final Result

A good Sales and Operations Planning process can start to produce benefits even before full MRP II is operational. It provides a single set of company numbers, maintained monthly and expressed at a summary level appropriate for top management review.

Good Sales and Operations Plans provide ready answers to:
• Why have inventory levels changed?
• Why have customer service levels changed?
• Why has profitability changed?

All of these questions can be tied back to performance versus the plans and forecasts, and the changes made to them. Price, cost and volume variances, from both a sales and a manufacturing viewpoint, are easily visible.

This process fosters an approach of Executive Consensus in running the business as opposed to one of Functional Selfishness and Competitiveness between manufacturing, materials, marketing, design, finance, etc.

Summary

Formal Sales and Operations Planning provides a single set of numbers and a routinized process to ensure that top management's objectives and plans are realistic and accurately reconciled to the detailed scheduling done in a company. The top executives and heads of all functional areas in the company must participate in this process, along with scheduling and marketing personnel.

Getting started first requires education. The next steps include defining families and formats, preparing pilot data, developing a policy and meeting agenda and finally, beginning the monthly meetings.

There are several keys to effectively implementing this process including: defining the horizon, maintaining a rolling forecast/sales plan, converting bookings to shipment forecasts/plans, developing the plans and measurements for all families, establishing demonstrated capacity, initiating Rough Cut Capacity Planning, defining time policies, and their potential alteration, while maintaining several key rules of style in making the meetings and the whole process effective.

The final results is plans, and a process to maintain them, that all functions commit to and can be held accountable for.

About the Author

John R. Dougherty, a Senior Partner for Excellence, has, since 1977, provided direction for manufacturers seeking to improve their management controls and productivity levels. John, with the partners for Excellence, instructs private, company-focused education sessions on the following topics: High Performance MRP II, MRP II Top Management Overview, MRP II Functional Detail, Sales and Operations Planning, Master Production Scheduling and Inventory Record Accuracy.

John has guided companies to successful improvements in their planning and control systems and approaches. Many of them have reached the coveted "Class A" level of achievement.

Areas of expertise and emphasis include:
• MRP II Implementation Projects
• Master Production Scheduling Policies and Approaches
• Inventory Record Accuracy in All Environments
• Issues Specific to Flow/Process and Repetitive Industries

- MRP II Techniques for Planning and Scheduling, Inventory Control and Analysis, and Purchasing
- Systems Effectiveness Audits Leading to Remedial and Fine-Tuning Approaches to Maximize System Benefits

John has taught and consulted to companies pursuing excellence via MRP II and JIT for 15 years. For 5 years he provided and managed consulting for two major software vendors. For 9 years he was a Principal of the Oliver Wight Associates. His experience spans the electronics, consumer goods, capital goods, pharmaceutical and chemical industries. Prior to that, the positions he held included: MRP II Project Manager, Materials Manager, Production and Inventory Control Manager and Corporate Planner/Master Scheduler.

John holds an MBA (Summa Cum Laude) from the Rochester (NY) Institute of Technology and a BS in Business Management from the University of Dayton (OH).

John is certified at the fellow level (CFPIM) by the American Production and Inventory Control Society (APICS). He is a frequent APICS speaker at international, regional and chapter meetings and has published numerous papers and articles concerning Management Improvement and control. John is co-editor of the Sixth Edition of the APICS Dictionary. He currently sits on the Master Planning Committee of the APICS Curricula & Certification Council.

Reprinted from the 1998 APICS Conference Proceedings.

Managing MPS Changes Despite Time Fences and Frozen Horizons

John R. Dougherty, CFPIM

MRP II/ERP/Supply Chain Management works only as well as changes are managed. The traditional, standard approach of time fences and frozen schedule horizons confuses the real issues, turns off top management and marketing, is basically ignored in practice, and rarely works effectively.

The rate of schedule changes is accelerating as customers and markets are more and more demanding and as manufacturing processes and supply chain partners (distributors, suppliers, etc.) become more and more flexible. Yet constant change seemingly leads only to chaos!

The question is, can a company profitably manage a higher level of change without firm adherence to time fences and frozen horizons, and can this be done while still providing competitive service, reliability, and flexibility to the marketplace?

First, let's examine where the change comes from.

Change Drivers

Too often schedule instability is always attributed to fickle customers. Though this represents some portion of the change experienced in a manufacturing company, there are many other sources:

- *Internal Sales and Marketing Initiatives*: Marketing promotions, product introductions, product changes, special packaging, sales incentive programs, and meeting monthly, quarterly, or annual revenue goals, etc. All of these (if not properly anticipated and planned for far enough in advance) can trigger demand changes that may require short-term, costly, and disruptive changes to the schedule.
- *Supply Chain Partners*: If a manufacturer is not shipping the product directly to the ultimate consumer, then decisions, programs, policies, or unexpected actions on the part of manufacturers, distributors, wholesalers, retailers, etc., can trigger demand changes when the ultimate consumer has not really changed their rate of product consumption. For instance, consider the case of prescription pharmaceuticals. Many such products are consumed at a very regular and predictable rate based on a number of patients with prescriptions. It's unusual to see the actual consumption of the product vary 10, 20, or 30% month to month. Rather, the consumption rates go up or down very gradually as the number of prescriptions change. (Obviously this would not hold true for "seasonal" drugs such as cough and cold, flu, and other seasonal or cyclical remedies. It would hold true for chronic problems such as high blood pressure, cholesterol, etc.) Manufacturers sometimes encounter unexpected, short-term shifts in demand when their supply chain partners make changes

in their inventory policies, take drastic steps to improve their cash flow, decide to promote certain products, etc. However, proper planning and communication far enough in advance could minimize the impact of these situations.

- *Competitive Marketplace Trends*: Here the changes can be driven by the demands of particular customers or groups of customers, or they may be initiated by your competitors who are offering improvements in flexibility that you must match. These could include shorter lead times, more customization, more flexibility with last-minute changes (even after the order is placed), more frequent deliveries, etc.
- *Transportation*: How and how often the product is moved from the manufacturer through the supply chain can affect demand patterns. If the approach is standardized and stable, little change will be noticed. However, if there are a variety of shipping modes, and a variety of frequency of deliveries which affect the economics of how a customer may order (and also affect the amount of inventory carried by the customer or supply chain partner), this could play a strong role in triggering demand changes.

In addition to demand-driven changes, many companies find a surprisingly high percentage of their schedule changes driven by supply side changes. These could include:

- *Quality Issues*: Product and process robustness could have a huge impact on schedule stability. Suddenly you can't make it "good" anymore. Yields fall, rework increases, reprocessing or replacement production is required. However, often the capacity or material to support this is not readily available, so the schedule must be changed. Or, capacity and material is used to solve the problem with one product, thus affecting the schedules of other products utilizing the same resources.
- *Manufacturing Flexibility/Mix*: Sometimes the combination, sequence, and interaction of different products that are scheduled to be made at the same time can affect output, efficiency, and productivity. In a World Class company, the impact of these factors is known most of the time, and schedules are laid out in light of them. However, as new products are introduced, new processes designed, new equipment or people acquired or assigned to make particular products, unexpected situations arise.
- *Supplier Reliability*: Sometimes formerly reliable suppliers suddenly start delivering late, less than the quantity required, or product that begins to experience a high reject rate. This then affects meeting manufacturing schedules. Sometimes it's just the "quality" (or physical or chemical characteristics) of the materials that lead to manufacturing quality or capacity issues.

- *The "Domino Effect"*: One company in the agrochemical business found that 50-80% of their schedule changes (often affecting as many as 20 or 30 items per week!) were a result of one or two problems that forced schedule changes to one or two key items, which then caused the rearrangement of many others. For example, a one-week late delivery of a key raw material could cause the rescheduling of several items using that raw material and then of several more items that have to be moved up in the schedule and run earlier to utilize the available capacity. This then could trigger changes in requirements for other raw materials or packaging materials, some of which will be short-term and lead to less than perfect performance from the suppliers. Those late deliveries lead to then yet another round of schedule changes affecting not only the items initially affected, but other items that need to be moved around in the schedule to utilize people and resources by making "the product that we can make."

- *Supply/Demand Balance*: In recent years, some companies have been "surprised" by their increasing inability to deal with changes, because "this never used to be a problem." They may have very reliable supply processes and sources which served them well in the past when customers ordered monthly deliveries with two weeks lead time. But as the demand parameters become more stringent (weekly or daily deliveries, more last-minute changes, lower field inventories, etc.), the manufacturing processes and supply chain relationships that were adequate to serve the marketplace in the past suddenly become too inflexible and stretched to the breaking point in this new, more competitive environment. Unfortunately, sometimes companies have to experience severe business problems (lowered service levels, lost customers, lower profit margins due to the expense of emergency manufacturing runs and emergency shipments to the customers, etc.) before they realize that they have to "reengineer" their supply chain and manufacturing processes to match the new demands of the marketplace.

Just Freeze It and Everything Will Be OK?

Over the past 30-40 years, companies have realized they needed to balance and manage supply and demand through the use of integrated resource management tools. Thus the evolution of MRP to MRP II, the addition of JIT, and currently, Supply Chain Management. Early efforts in these areas actually provide a computerization of real-time, constant adjustment of the production schedules to match the current demand patterns. For many companies this just meant that the schedules got changed as fast as transactions were entered and as often as the computer programs could be run. These companies quickly realized that it was easier to change the schedule on the computer than in the plant. In many cases, these early efforts resulted in no improvement and, in some cases, even degradation of performance.

From this emerged the important role of Master Production Scheduling as a process to manage change and carefully balance supply and demand. Rules and techniques emerged in the form of *frozen schedules* and *time fences*. Here companies attempted to set a period of time from the present in which no schedule changes would be allowed. Obviously Manufacturing, Purchasing, and Planning personnel were very much in favor of this approach. Instead of having to hit a moving target, they knew what their objectives were over some period of time and could deploy resources and break down activities and steps in a way to achieve the schedules at minimum cost. The time fences represented points in time in the future which defined how "frozen" the schedule would be. For instance, inside the first time fence, no schedule changes would be allowed. Between the first and second time fence, perhaps changes in product mix were allowed, but the total amount of production within a family or for a given resource had to be maintained at the same set rate.

From an Operations viewpoint, these approaches worked. With time fences set appropriately and schedules developed properly, plants could maintain 95%+ performance while improving cost and inventory management. In some cases, and for some periods of time, this also produced results that satisfied the needs of the marketplace and the customer. As long as the horizons and fences were set in a way that was realistic based on the inherent flexibility of the supply chain partners and the manufacturing processes, the schedules could be met and the changes accommodated.

But if the marketplace being served, gradually (or suddenly) required more flexibility than the manufacturing and supply chain process could offer, the process broke down. Sometimes it is not a change from what the marketplace requires, but rather the changing business environment that no longer allows the safety stocks, intermediate inventories, or premium labor and/or freight costs that are required to meet the schedules and accommodate the changes. In other words, as times get leaner and customers get meaner, the old approaches break down. As an increasing number of changes are requested and forced on the plant to keep customers happy, the rules start crumbling and being ignored.

In fact, precious few companies have been able to maintain the same lead times, horizons, and scheduling rules over a long period of time. If the company doesn't have enough foresight to work at streamlining their processes, shortening their lead times, and improving their agility, then the marketplace will inevitably point out the need for such improvement with falling sales and dissatisfied customers. **Yesterday's Class A process won't support tomorrow's World Class requirements.**

People on the operational side (Purchasing, Manufacturing, and Planning) in some companies tend to cling to the frozen horizons and fences long after they've lost their effectiveness. In some companies, an attitude of "we finally have got a set of rules in place, now we have to stick to them" takes over. Operational management doggedly measures the number of changes and sets as their goal a decreasing number of changes in the future. This philosophy or objective is the root cause of the problem. **Fewer changes is not good performance.**

In fact, over the long term, the more changes, the better! What this means is the ability to effectively change and still meet the schedule 95%+ of the time and the customer requirements 98%+ of the time should be the goal. Developing supply chain linkages, manufacturing processes, and planning and scheduling approaches that allow more change, less cost, and higher reliability needs to be seen as the ideal goal. Obviously, this can't just be accomplished by simply "trying harder." It means specific, focused improvement to manufacturing, planning, scheduling, and supply chain linkages in a way that makes it easier to change effectively.

Sometimes this involves changing stocking strategies, but the old rule that says "to improve customer service requires higher levels of inventory" is too myopic a viewpoint. This is true only if all other factors are kept the same.

If we change how we procure, make, move, combine, and ship product at its various stages of inventory, service can be improved *and* inventories lowered concurrently.

Another traditional approach says that you must maintain a firm master schedule covering the full cumulative lead time of a product (including each manufacturing step and each supplier's lead time). This is not necessary if you can maintain strategic inventories, adjustable capacity, and/or process or supplier flexibility on the longer lead time items. Changing requirements within the supplier's lead time is possible, if either you or the supplier has some extra inventory, or if you've identified points in time in which the supplier can adjust the mix and make more of one material, perhaps counterbalanced by less of another.

Master Scheduling

"Frozen schedules make cold customers."

The goal of master scheduling is to set up a series of material and capacity plans that can be executed 95% or more of the time. This should result in matched materials and resources that can be brought together in the final product to satisfy the customers 95% or more of the time. It is also vital to do this in a way that is cost effective so that good customer service is supported by profitable manufacturing execution.

The more variation there is in demand (inaccurate forecasts, customer order changes, unanticipated customer orders), the harder it will be to maintain a stable supply schedule to support it. Conversely, the less reliable the supply schedule is (quality problems, yield problems, supplier reliability problems, process or capacity reliability problems, etc.), the less confident the company will feel in working to the plan as a means of satisfying customers.

Demand variability occurs at different rates, in different industries, for different companies, in different marketplaces and indeed, on different product lines within any of these categories. Therefore, it is critical that reasonable guidelines be set to manage and continually synchronize the demand changes and the supply plans, product by product, to ensure that the manufacturer can reliably satisfy current customer demands. The use of "Time Fences" to identify "Rescheduling Time Zones" for this purpose is an increasingly important approach that every company needs to address.

The *APICS Dictionary* definitions (below) of **demand time fence** and **planning time fence** refer to how the computer operates in netting forecasts and customer orders and suggesting planned master schedule orders, respectively. In addition, each definition refers to management rules or approaches for guiding, analyzing, and approving changes to the schedule at various points in time.

Demand time fence: "(1) That point in time inside of which the forecast is no longer included in total demand and projected available inventory calculations; inside this point only customer orders are considered. Beyond this point, total demand is a combination of actual orders and forecasts, depending on the forecast consumption technique chosen. (2) In some contexts, the demand time fence may correspond to that point in the future inside of which change to the master schedule must be approved by an authority higher than the master scheduler."

Note, however, that customer orders may still be promised inside the demand time fence without higher authority approval if there are quantities available to promise (ATP). Beyond the demand time fence, the master scheduler may change the MPS within the limits of established

rescheduling rules, without the approval of higher authority. See: planning time fence, time fences."

You can see that the first part of the definition talks about a setting within a software package that causes the forecast and actual customer bookings to be properly combined and used in a way to best project total demand over the horizon. This helps clarify the effect of customer orders booked in a "lumpy fashion." (For instance, a monthly forecast of 400 would be shown on a master schedule as 100 a week. But if a customer ordered 150 in a week, this doesn't mean that the total demand for the month would be higher than 400, rather just that the forecast in the remaining three weeks may be lower as a result of the one large order or group of orders in a given week.)

The use of a "forecast consumption technique" typically happens just outside the set demand time fence. Inside the set demand time fence, forecasts are ignored and only customer orders are considered for planning purposes, since this represents the typical "backlog horizon" or "customer ordering lead time." For planning purposes it is assumed that no additional customer orders will be promised inside this demand time fence. This technique is critical for people in assemble-to-order, finish-to-order, or make-to-order environments where the ordering patterns from week to week are not always smooth and consistent.

Other people would use the demand time fence to identify a boundary inside of which only emergency changes to the master schedule will be approved. This does not mean that a schedule is ever "frozen," only that it is carefully controlled in the near term to ensure that the changes are critically necessary and feasible to execute. There are only so many emergency changes that can be made in the short term without affecting other items, other priorities, costs, quality and the overall reliability of the schedule. This approach ensures that the proper level of management gets involved in managing the number of changes that are possible, to the appropriate products to satisfy the customers.

Planning time fence: "A point in time denoted in the planning horizon of the master scheduling process which marks a boundary inside of which changes to the schedule may adversely impact component schedules, capacity plans, customer deliveries and cost. Planned orders outside of the planning time fence can be changed by the system planning logic. Changes inside the planning time fence must be manually changed by the master scheduler. See: cumulative lead time, demand time fence, firm planned order, planning horizon, planned order, time fence."

This time fence prevents the planning system from automatically adjusting or changing master schedules and driving down altered lower level requirements. This ensures that no schedules are changed at a rate faster and more drastic than the suppliers or manufacturing resources can cope with. This would lead to unreliable schedules and promises to the customers, and mismatched inventories and misapplied resources.

Sometimes companies will also utilize the planning time fence as a boundary defining the "future planning" time zone, where virtually all changes in master schedule product mix are acceptable as long as they fall within the monthly S&OP Production Plan rate. Before the fence is a "trading" zone where changes in the schedule inside critical manufacturing and purchasing lead times are carefully counterbalanced by equal but opposite changes to similar products. For instance, one product can be moved up in the schedule if a similar product is moved back by an equal amount. Or one product type can be increased if another similar product type, utilizing similar capacities or materials can be decreased.

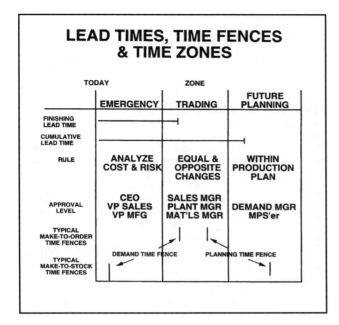

LEAD TIMES, TIME FENCES & TIME ZONES

As shown in **Figure 1**, it is very useful for companies to establish these three zones ("Emergency," "Trading" and "Future Planning") to help focus management attention on the level of change that can be accommodated over various periods of time on various products. Where these zones fall can vary by product line, as they should reflect the reality of what the current manufacturing and supply process can support in terms of schedule changes. Where the current supply approaches or processes cannot keep up with the requested changes triggered by the customers, changes in how you stock, produce or, in general, manage the supply process need to be pursued. For instance, this could trigger some companies to begin to stock extra amounts of long lead time raw materials or manufactured options, or move from a make-to-stock to a make-to-order environment. Too often companies make the mistake of assuming that their current lead times and planning approaches will just naturally support what the changing marketplace is requiring.

Fences vs. Zones

It's critical to point out that the rescheduling time zones described above *need not* exactly correspond to the software specific demand time fences and planning time fences described earlier (see Figure 1). There may be cases where the demand time fence represents the marketplace lead time or customer backlog that is longer or shorter than the time frame in which emergency changes can be accommodated in the schedule. For instance, an aircraft manufacturer may have a very long demand time fence because of a large backlog of orders. However, because this backlog of orders is constantly reshuffled, rescheduled and changed, often based on customer requests, the "emergency rescheduling time zone" could be much shorter or closer to the present than the "demand time fence."

Typically a planning time fence is set close to a cumulative planning lead time to ensure that constant changes inside of lead time are not triggered automatically by the planning system. However, through selective hedging or overplanning of the longest lead time materials (as mentioned earlier, perhaps through the use of planning bills, safety stocks, or option overplanning), the "trading zone"

may be significantly inside the software "planning time fence." In fact, by sharing future planning information with suppliers, a given manufacturer may be able to significantly shorten the trading time zone, since key suppliers with planning visibility can often react to schedule changes more easily and quickly. In these cases, often the boundaries between the zones vary from the demand and planning time fences or even within product lines. Then, the difference in how they affect the operation of master scheduling software vs. the human management of change to master schedules, should be clearly communicated to the organization.

Who Does What

Too often companies myopically "followed the rules" of frozen schedules and time fences, and the fact is, one set of rules doesn't fit all.

For instance, if schedule changes were driven by supply side problems, it's senseless to fill out forms, hold meetings, and gain approvals. If you're out of material, if production has been rejected, if capacity is overloaded, you simply must change the schedule. Whether or not Sales and Marketing need to be involved could vary on a case by case basis, depending on whether they could make some choices as to the sequence of products or how to allocate scarce material or capacity across various products or customer requirements.

Some changes are easier to make, regardless of the time frame. For instance, a last-minute change to package a common product in a different outer package (for instance, for a different market, with different labels, in a different size, etc.) is an entirely different question than changing from one product to another, which may involve hours of changeover time, clean-up time, etc. Yet too often, people try to apply the same analysis and the same approval levels for all these kinds of changes.

Sometimes the amount of change, whether it be a couple of days, or 10 or 20% of the quantity, is the key issue. Some level of change could be accommodated relatively cheaply and easily, where once a given point was reached, extra cost, confusion, and chaos is encountered. Identifying these break points and understanding that they may be different from product to product, resource to resource, or even over different times in the year, is critical to making sure the rules are followed and effectively used.

"Sales and Marketing are too liberal and Manufacturing is too conservative!" This represents the conventional wisdom. Sales and Marketing ask for anything and everything, not worried whether every change can be accommodated. Manufacturing says no to everything because they're worried that if they say yes once, then they'll have to say it again and again past the point of their being able to support it. But when emotions run high and problems run up the chain of command, management mandates often trigger changes that *are* met. The customers are satisfied and Sales and Marketing are reinforced in their approach of "asking for everything" because they usually get what they want, and Manufacturing, though they complain all the time, in the end usually deliver. This scenario is often reinforced, repeated, and exaggerated over time. Sometimes what's missing is an understanding of the cost and impact of satisfying a few customers at the expense of others. The "special requests" are usually met, particularly when there's a director or vice president asking for them and monitoring the results. What often goes unnoticed is the extra cost, disruptions, and performance problems on other products and/or customers, which get "pushed out of the way" in the effort to satisfy the high priority reschedule requests.

The fact of the matter is that the truth lies somewhere in between. Sales and Marketing need to understand the full, true business impact of trying to accommodate every change in the short run, while Manufacturing needs to be realistic and not conservative. They need to understand exactly how much and what kind of change can be accommodated, and not be negative or reluctant to accept it. The emotion needs to be removed from the decision-making process. It should be more a matter of "if you want one more change, here's what else may suffer or may need to be altered to accommodate that change." It's strictly a matter of Top Management, Sales, and Marketing deciding how best to allocate scarce resource and material in way to satisfy the most important customers, markets, and business objectives, while understanding what has to give, to support these objectives.

And the Final Solution Is

There is no one right way, no final best approach. Everyone must understand that balancing supply and demand is an on-going and ever-changing process. As supply reliability varies, how we schedule, what we stock, etc., must change. As customer demand patterns change, how we schedule and what we stock must change. As lead times shorten and the rate of change increases, how we manage the schedule must also be constantly adjusted. You can't set horizons and time fences once and for all, and stick to them. They must be constantly reviewed and adjusted to match the current state.

But the rules for managing change need to reflect how well the current supply chain linkage and manufacturing processes match what the customer's expecting. If the original business was one of long efficient runs of finished goods inventory, held in multiple warehouses across the country, where customers could buy from a short product list, at a price that covered this level of inventory, it's naive to believe that this situation will last forever.

If customers start to require more frequent, smaller deliveries, more product customization, shorter lead times, and last-minute changes, a manufacturing company often finds itself faced with having to redesign its supply chain and manufacturing processes. Different equipment, different plant layouts, different stocking points, and retrained employees may be needed to run smaller batches quicker, customized to each customer's specification and shipped direct to the end customer.

The competitive marketplace may drive the price of the product down, thus forcing the manufacturer to either cut costs and/or find a way to satisfy the customer without holding large inventories of finished or semi-finished goods. This also could force changes to, and reengineering of, the supply chain and manufacturing processes.

There needs to be a continual comparison of the cost of manufacturing vs. the cost of holding inventory at various levels (raw materials, semi-finished, finished goods, distribution warehouses close to the customer, etc.) vs. the cost of changing the manufacturing process in a way that actual production can be more closely linked to individual customer demands (make-to-order or at least finish-to-order).

Managing schedule changes is, in fact, the "tip of the iceberg" that is the challenge to most manufacturing companies today. Short-term schedule pressures are often indicative of shifting trends in the marketplace that indicate that reengineering and realignment of manufacturing processes

and resources is required to more cost-effectively and flexibly satisfy the changing desires of the customer.

The question is **HOW?** Described below are some of the most effective ways of reengineering your supply chain/manufacturing process in a way to make it easier to accommodate more changes.

Muting the Impact of Change ("Getting Agile!")

Here is what World Class companies have proven will help profitably and effectively accommodate the ever-increasing demands for flexibility and agility.

- *Shorten Cycle Times*: Much of this comes from attacking set-up, queue, move, administrative, planner, and other "preparatory" portions of the time it takes to make product. If you can "turn it on and turn it off" easily, quickly, and cheaply, then you can lower lot sizes and make very close to what each customer wants. This means you can cycle through making all of your products more frequently and be able to respond to changes more easily.

- *Improve Quality*: If processes are more predictable, you can carry just enough inventory, again shortening runs and improving how quickly you can cycle through all your products. In addition, any changes triggered by quality problems can be minimized.

- *Shorten the Journey*: This is all about synchronous flow and cellular manufacturing. Rearrange the resources so it takes no time at all to move product from one step, one operation, one work center to another. This will also help shorten the lead times and diminish chances for quality problems during storage or movement.

- *Finish- or Make-to-Order vs. Make-to-Stock*: This helps lower order quantities, since you'll just make what a customer ordered. Again, cycling through the products will be more frequent and you'll never waste time, material, or cash resources on the wrong configuration of a product. The lead time to the customer may not be as quick as shipping from stock, but in combination with the other changes in this list, many companies can finish or make-to-order in a matter of a few days.

- *Rethink Stocking Strategies*: This goes hand-in-hand with the point discussed above. Instead of finished goods, carry semi-finished or raw materials. This cuts down on transportation and stocking costs, since you won't need inventory moved to warehouses across the country, made in large lot sizes, and held in warehouses. What inventory you hold should be a function of how fast it takes you to finish or customize the product for the customer vs. how long they're willing to wait. If you can get from raw material to finished product very quickly, only stock raw materials. If early manufacturing steps take too long, stock semi-finished. In some cases you could stock a combination to hedge against the forecast variability of how you predict what the customers will be ordering. Many factors enter this equation, as shown in **Figure 2**.

- *Standardize Product Offerings*: Too many companies fall into the trap of trying to be all things to all customers. Every time a customer wants something special, they not only make it and continue to offer it but, in some cases, attempt to stock it. As they add new products and new features, they never trim back the old ones. Little consideration is given to the cost of maintaining multiple inventories, multiple processes, and expanded data to support the variations. In some cases, customers will accept a different version of the product (perhaps a higher

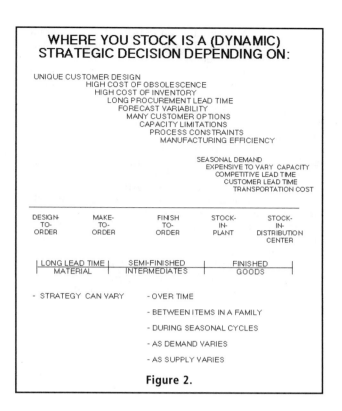

quality, more powerful version) if you negotiate price. Lowering the price sometimes is more than offset by reducing the cost of having to maintain and manufacture a wide variety of slightly different products. With fewer things to make and stock, it's easier to improve quality, streamline processes (you're making each product more often, rather than a few of them only occasionally, and reclimbing the learning curve each time) and pursue all the other tactics on this list.

- *Streamline Transportation*: As customers want more frequent shipments in smaller quantities, does freight enter the picture, because you now cannot ship trainloads, truckloads, etc.? How about consolidated shipping schemes? How about milk routes, where you ship to particular regions on particular days and have customers order in a way that facilitates regional consolidation? How about flying instead of trains or trucks? It may be more expensive, but if you can carry lower inventories, the cost may be more than offset, as many consumer goods manufacturers (pharmaceuticals, etc.) have discovered. How about working to outsource all of your warehousing, shipping, and transportation issues? Many of the transportation companies have expanded their services vertically up and down the supply chain and can provide expert, cost effective services.
- *"Dig Up the Fences and Put 'Em on Wheels"*: Instead of firm and frozen schedules and fences, look at each product, each customer, perhaps even each region or market separately. Design scheduling and schedule change rules to match the needs of each market, while supporting it with the appropriate level of flexibility in your procurement/manufacturing process. Sometimes these rules will change with the time of year, particularly in seasonal industries. For instance, in the high season you may make something to stock and hold it in regional warehouses close to customers. Out of season, some items may be declared "finish- or make-to-order" once the customer is understanding and supportive of this change. As mentioned above, don't have the same level of analysis or approval for every change. If it's a minor change that can be accommodated easily, then don't slow it down with rules and regulations. If it's a change that's inevitable (quality or process problems), then just make it and don't go through meaningless bureaucratic approval steps.

Whose Job Is This Anyway?

The steps mentioned above cannot be unilaterally implemented by Planning and Scheduling or even Manufacturing and Materials Management. Cross-functional teams from Marketing, Sales, Customer Service, Purchasing, Finance, Shipping and Distribution, Manufacturing, Planning, and Scheduling need to look at each product area and customer situation individually. First identify ways of streamlining the supply chain processes as mentioned above. Then change the rules for managing changes to the schedule as the process and the schedule flexibility actually change.

The rule from the 1970s was to get Top Management to sign off every change inside the "frozen" time fence. This rule was hardly ever followed, and often dropped when it proved to be impractical and insignificant. Only changes that truly impact overall cost, customer service, reliability, or other operational issues should be brought to a Top Management level. Sometimes it's simply more important to just have Top Management audit the number of changes and the type, rather than approving each individual one. Some of the changes may not need immediate, day-to-day approval and can be reviewed in weekly Master Schedule review meetings or monthly Sales and Operations Planning meetings. Day-to-day decisions that require higher level approval need to be practically assigned to managers who are accessible and have the time and interest to delve into the right level of detail.

The rule of "lowering the level of decision-making" applies here. The only time Top Management has to be involved is if lower level management cannot enforce or stick to the proper decisions, or need better support from other departments to have them followed.

"How's It Goin'?"

From the very start it's key to have at least weekly measurements tracking how well you're doing. Customer service (against customer request date as well as acknowledgment date), family production performance by month, master schedule performance by week, master schedule stability, and any other supporting measurements that affect meeting these key measurements need to be published and monitored throughout the process of changing, improving, and streamlining your supply demand balancing act. Other metrics that could be important include manufacturing on-time performance, supplier on-time performance, forecast accuracy, and inventory accuracy.

Summary

- This needs to be a **company-wide effort** with full understanding and involvement from Top Management, Marketing, Sales, Technical and Development, as well as all the other operational functions.
- If you can't change fast enough, or if change costs too much—**attack the process!** Streamline, reengineer, make it easier, quicker, more reliable.

- **Set realistic rules and then change them!** Make sure the rules for a feasible level of change and an appropriate level of analysis and approval matches your current environment. As you improve the environment, change the rules.
- **Attack the accuracy and reliability of all data.**
- **Finish or make-to-order**, don't stock it.
- **Make transportation a non-issue.**
- **Lower inventories and costs** at the same time **while improving flexibility!**
- **Rationalize and standardize products** by understanding the customer's true needs and satisfying them with a streamlined product line.

About the Author

John Dougherty, CFPIM, has, since 1977, provided direction for manufacturers seeking to improve their management controls and productivity levels. With the Partners for Excellence, he instructs private, company-focused education sessions on many topics, including Logistics, Supply Chain Management and MRP II Top Management Overview; Logistics, Supply Chain Management and MRP II Functional Detail; Sales and Operations Planning; Sales Planning and Demand Management; Distribution Resource Planning; Master Production Scheduling and Inventory Record Accuracy.

Mr. Dougherty has guided companies to successful improvements in their logistics, resource management and planning and control systems and approaches. Many of them have reached the coveted "Class A" or "World Class" level of achievement. His experience spans the electronics, medical products, consumer goods, capital goods, pharmaceutical and chemical industries.

He is certified at the fellow level (CFPIM) by APICS. He is a frequent speaker at international, regional and chapter meetings of many professional and industrial groups and has published numerous papers and articles concerning management improvement and control. He was co-editor of the sixth edition of the *APICS Dictionary*. He was a six-year member of the Master Planning Committee of the APICS Curricula and Certification Council.

Reprinted from the 1996 APICS Conference Proceedings.

Scheduling to Keep Your Customers Happy
John R. Dougherty, CFPIM

Introduction: The '90s—The Era of the Customer

Today every company needs and wants to be demand and customer driven. Everyone wants to get "closer to the customer." The universal goal is to "delight" the customer. Now more than ever "the customer is always right." Customers—we must be focused on them, linked to them, constantly communicating with them, more responsive to them, more flexible for them, more open to their requests and inputs, etc., etc., etc.

These are exciting ideas. But how do we measure how well we achieve them? Is it simply a matter of increasing our customer service performance measurements or line item fill rates? That alone wouldn't be particularly hard to accomplish if companies could carry larger inventories, rely on redundant equipment and personnel for ultimate flexibility and scheduling, and absorb costs for last minute product rework, schedule changes and the like.

No company can afford to ignore that the 1990s is also an era of streamlining, restructuring, downsizing, rightsizing, fine tuning, cost containing, profit improving, etc. Increased customer satisfaction has to come concurrently with improved cost and asset management. **This means that short-term fixes, the latest program, process or acronym will not be enough to get the job done.** These dual challenges have forced companies to drastically rethink the way they manage their assets, the flow of materials and their supplier and customer partnerships in a way that produces better long-term value for themselves, their customers and their supply chain partners.

With such a heady challenge, the temptation is strong to seek new approaches, new tools, new initiatives and new programs. However, true breakthrough changes in how we manage things don't happen very often. In fact, historically we can see that bigger challenges usually motivate companies to find better and more effective ways to take advantage of the tools and technologies that were already there. There are many World Class companies using the tools we already know about in different, better and more rigorous ways to achieve the benefits and goals described above. These approaches and tools include Manufacturing Resource Planning (MRP II), Just-in-Time (JIT) and Customer Linking. It's important to beware of the many consultants, software companies and practitioners that rename old processes to emphasize or describe their improved use of them. Thus we have Enterprise Resource Planning (ERP) or Supply Chain Management as opposed to MRP II. Thus we have Reengineering, Demand Flow Planning or Continuous Flow Manufacturing as opposed to Just-in-Time. Thus we have Customer Connectivity vs. Customer Linking or Customer Communications. Much of this new terminology is more appealing and attractive because it better describes the tools and how they're used in today's companies. But it's critical not to be blinded by the new name and think that the proven, established principles and approaches are no longer applicable. Rather, they're being expanded, enhanced and in many cases being used in ways that more closely resemble their original intentions.

Given the challenges described above, it is particularly crucial that all three of these areas be addressed concurrently and integratively. For instance, MRP II alone will not produce the desired results. Even Class A MRP II only ensures that supply and demand are balanced and that current processes are managed in an optimal fashion. MRP II helps companies substitute forward-looking **information** rather than holding redundant inventory or capacity in anticipation of dealing with supply and demand changes. Class A MRP II would lead a company to significant decreases in inventory and increases in reliability, flexibility and cost competitiveness. But that simply isn't enough to compete in the 90s.

JIT is a philosophical challenge to how we do things. It doesn't settle for optimizing current processes (as MRP II does) but instills a mindset and methodology in which everyone is always looking at changing and improving processes. Implemented by itself, it would significantly improve company flexibility, significantly lower costs and somewhat lower inventories. However, unless every one of a company's suppliers and every one of its customers had similar systems, it wouldn't provide the optimum supply demand balancing and forward planning that MRP II would. Therefore, most companies have learned the valuable lesson that MRP II and JIT both work best when integrated and used together to very effectively compete on a cost and flexibility basis.

However, the third leg of the stool is Customer Linking. Here we're not talking about just simplistic use of Electronic Data Interchange (EDI) to more quickly and efficiently transmit requested customer delivery changes and rescheduled supplier acknowledgments. Rather, we're talking about truly linking the information, planning and scheduling of the customer with the supplier through every step of the process. This would include customer participation in product design, process development and much more detailed and timely communication of customer long and short-term requirements, inventories and the like. In some cases, companies have found that they have actually eliminated the need for forecasting by using their customers' planned requirements to directly drive their manufacturing schedules! Pursued alone, this process would help. But its true power comes when done in conjunction with the aforementioned MRP II and JIT processes. In fact, the three should be worked

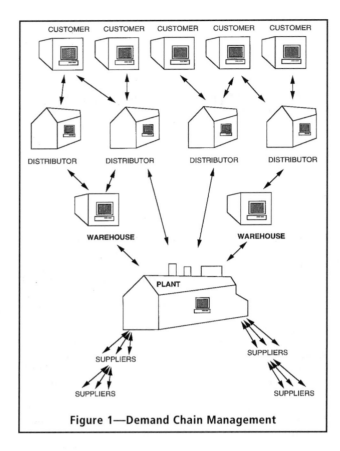

Figure 1—Demand Chain Management

on concurrently. JIT improvements should be prioritized and focused by customer requirements. MRP II planning approaches should match and facilitate the dynamics and choices that the customer demands.

This paper will describe how some leading edge companies use specific scheduling approaches or techniques to integrate these three key processes and achieve remarkable results.

"Demand" Chain Management

Figure 1 shows a relatively deep "supply chain." It shows a plant buying components or raw materials from suppliers who in turn have their own network of suppliers one or more levels deep. It also shows the plant distributing product through both distributors and warehouses. Some of the warehouses then supply smaller distributors. The distributors in turn move the product through a dealer network to the ultimate customer. For purposes of simplicity, we have not added to this diagram cases where the plant may ship direct to large customers or direct to large dealers, but certainly that happens in many cases. Whether a particular company's environment is similar to this or twice as complex or only half as complex, the issues remain the same. At each step of this process decisions need to be made about purchasing, manufacturing, scheduling, building and holding inventories. In other words, how much "supply" is needed and will be needed to support the demand of the next customer in the chain?

As suggested by the title of this figure, we believe the focus has been on the wrong question. The first question is not "how much to supply"; rather, the first real question is how much will be "demanded." If as much energy was put into managing demand as we have put into managing

supply over the last 30 to 40 years, we'd find that the complexity and costs of our supply processes could have been greatly reduced.

When we think of demand management, we often think of forecasting and customer order management. Why does anyone forecast? The answer is simply because their customers don't give them a long enough horizon of orders, commitments or requirements that allow them to do all the supply planning and execution necessary to have the product ready when the customer wants it. In other words, simplistically, it takes the plant longer to buy and make than it takes the customer to order.

But is the customer always insensitive to the lead times of their suppliers? Though this often seems to be the case, many businesses have improved their ability to establish, review and maintain longer range plans. In fact, in many cases individual levels within a demand chain operate excellent MRP II, Forecasting, Customer Management and Distribution Resource Planning (DRP) systems. Often what's missing is linking these various systems together over the planning horizon to better share information. However, one of the challenges this presents is handling massive amounts of detailed data from hundreds of customers on hundreds or thousands of items stretched out over weeks and months of time.

The fact of the matter is that the key to effective demand planning in the 90s is not **mathematical sophistication**, but rather **practical segmentation**. A more refined mathematical formula which seeks to predict the future based on the past will render far less benefit than the ability to manage, combine, sift and summarize the future demand data that customers can provide.

There are various forms of segmentation that will help. For instance, segmenting sales history by **customer** so that you can identify trends for major customers or groups of customers in like industries. Additionally, historical segmentation could be done by **regional areas**, **types of market** or by **particular product features or options** such as color, size, package, label, etc. The key here is to identify major segments of demand so that they can be pursued for more individualized forecasting. For instance, some companies attempt to get forecasts from those customers that represent 80% of the product volume. They then add a factor to those numbers to come up with a total forecast by item.

Time segmentation is also significant. Here you're asking questions such as why does demand change over time? Are there promotional activities instigated by you, your customers or other levels of the demand chain? Are there price changes that are announced at typical times of year that affect demand? Do price changes necessarily have to cause a spike in demand? Could price changes be announced but the supplier reserve the right to ship under the old price 30, 60 or 90 days after the order was received to smooth the flow of material and, in effect, not deliver it any sooner than the customer wanted it anyway?

Should the **level of detail** be segmented? Does the final packaging or labeling of the product need to be known 12 months in the future? Is it just enough to know the total volume of base product that will be required? This could lead to asking customers, for instance, for a detailed line item forecast for the next 13 weeks by product size, package, label, etc., then just a monthly demand forecast by type of product for the following six months and then just a quarterly forecast for the next five quarters for an entire product family.

In all cases this segmentation of data has to be done in light of the **availability of data** and its **significance**. For instance, if you had a highly flexible manufacturing process where it's very easy to change product mix within the month, less detail would be needed, even if it was available. Conversely, in situations where you need a lot of detailed data but it simply is not available, either through historical records or through customer information, the choice there may be to begin to collect and segment the data now for use in a year or two.

Finally, segmenting the effect of **new product introduction, product design changes, product label changes** and the like is also important. Making all this information easily identifiable in an attempt to analyze past historical trends by market, customer, segment, etc. and to use it for validation and evaluation of future planning data can be critical.

Probably none of the ideas expressed in the previous paragraphs would totally surprise the reader. However, how many standard, off-the-shelf forecasting or demand management packages provide for this kind of segmentation and organization of information? How easy is it to inquire a pre-existing database to get this information and analysis? Certainly the power of the computer is not what stands in the way, but the design of databases and software programs may be a hindrance. This challenge is being overcome by leading edge companies by the upgrade of both their own and their customers' demand management systems.

Type of Customer Input

The segmentation should lead a company to determine what type of detailed information is desirable from customers. In some cases the customer can simply download the output of their planning system and feed it direct into the supplier company's database in the form of individual, line item forecasts. This would represent the actual output of their MRP II or DRP systems which take into account their forecasts, plans, current inventories and hedge factors.

Where this is not available or too voluminous, different approaches need to be taken. For instance, the customer could forecast total volumes by month, by major product group and highlight only those cases where product mix changes within a group are anticipated. Or the customer could simply express future demand as a percentage of past demand, showing increases or decreases by month over time and showing any variation in cyclical or seasonal demand patterns or promotion or pricing impacts. The farther into the future, the less detail the supplier companies should need since they're generally only planning broad levels of internal and supplier resources required, not the detailed, weekly product mix.

What does the supplier company do with this information: how is it stored, displayed and utilized to make detailed planning decisions? In some cases customer demand information is converted into long-term contracts or blanket delivery agreements. These may take the form of guaranteed annual amounts in annual, quarterly or monthly detail. Various agreements could exist as to the amount and frequency of change to these delivery amounts. Obviously the dynamics of these numbers will vary depending on the marketplace and planning skill of the customer in question. What's important for the manufacturer to understand is that the quality of these data will vary and data should be used and monitored in light of that quality. In other words, segment the data into parts which have varying reliability. **Figure 2** shows an expanded version of a traditional planning spreadsheet often used by master schedulers or planners. On the bottom are the traditional MPS, projected inventory and available-to-promise lines. Please note that the segmented demands are displayed and then summed in the line marked "Total Demand." In this way, a demand manager or scheduler could actually look at the detailed demand information, item by item, and determine where the total demand is coming from in making decisions on how to best cover it in the master schedule.

		Weeks								
		1	2	3	4	5	6	7	8	Total
FORECAST										
PRODUCTION (OPTION) FORECAST										
WAREHOUSE DEMAND										
REGIONAL OR MARKET SALES PLAN										
CUSTOMER #1 SALES PLAN										
CUSTOMER #2 SALES PLAN										
BLANKET ORDER DELIVERIES										
ACTUAL (CUSTOMER) DEMAND										
INTERPLANT DEMAND										
PRODUCTION REQUIREMENTS										
TOTAL DEMAND										
PROJECTED AVAILABLE INVENTORY BALANCE										
AVAILABLE TO PROMISE										
MPS										

Figure 2—Total Demand Management

The Production (Option) Forecast would be the system calculated prediction of the amount of this product to be sold as a percentage of a family or product group forecast.

The warehouse (DRP generated), regional customer and blanket demands represent segments planned separately from the overall forecast. That forecast line should be "consumed" or lowered by these segment demands and then combined with interplant and production requirements to dynamically maintain total demand.

There may be very few items that would have demand tracked in every one of these segments. But tracking whatever different sources of demand that do exist would facilitate supply demand problem resolution by enabling selective communications with different segments to validate their reliability or make suggested changes.

This simple diagram shows only eight weeks of information. The database would certainly hold much more than this and should be able to store and display it in monthly or quarterly totals as time goes out in the future.

Inventory Chain Relationships

There are some cases when the finished product inventory is held at various steps in the "demand chain." For instance, a dealer is holding inventory as well as a distributor, a warehouse and the supplier. In these cases, the forecasted demand should be that over and above what is

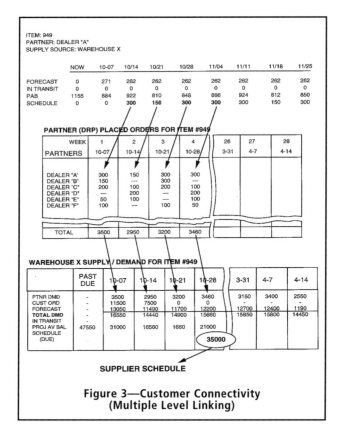

ITEM: 949
PARTNER: DEALER "A"
SUPPLY SOURCE: WAREHOUSE X

	NOW	10-07	10/14	10/21	10/28	11/04	11/11	11/18	11/25
FORECAST	0	271	262	262	262	262	262	262	262
IN TRANSIT	0	0	0	0	0	0	0	0	0
PAB	1155	884	922	810	848	886	924	812	850
SCHEDULE	0	0	300	150	300	300	300	150	300

PARTNER (DRP) PLACED ORDERS FOR ITEM #949

WEEK	1	2	3	4	26	27	28
PARTNERS	10-07	10-14	10-21	10-28	3-31	4-7	4-14
DEALER "A"	300	150	300	300			
DEALER "B"	150	---	300	---			
DEALER "C"	200	100	200	100			
DEALER "D"	---	200	---	200			
DEALER "E"	50	100	---	100			
DEALER "F"	100	---	100	50			
TOTAL	3500	2950	3200	3460			

WAREHOUSE X SUPPLY / DEMAND FOR ITEM #949

	PAST DUE	10-07	10-14	10-21	10-28	3-31	4-7	4-14
PTNR DMD	-	3500	2950	3200	3460	3150	3400	2550
CUST ORD	-	11500	7500	0	0			
FORECAST	-	13050	11490	11700	12200	12700	12400	1190
TOTAL DMD	-	16550	14440	14900	15660	15850	15800	14450
IN TRANSIT	-							
PROJ AV BAL	47550	31000	16560	1660	21000			
SCHEDULE (DUE)					35000			

SUPPLIER SCHEDULE

Figure 3—Customer Connectivity (Multiple Level Linking)

already held in inventory at each location and should be reflective of the lead times and lot size rules being followed at each. But perhaps just as important would be the need to be able to communicate and summarize the total inventory in the system, so that in times of supply demand imbalance, a planner knows what opportunities there are for translocation of the inventories or suggested changes in safety stock levels or lot sizing policies.

Figure 3 shows an example of this kind of linkage. Dealer A holds Item 949 in stock and sells it to the ultimate customer. The detailed line item forecast by week for the months of October and November represent how much Dealer A expects to sell. Dealer A currently has 1155 units in inventory and based on a weekly demand delivery pattern, Dealer A is passing requirements down to Warehouse X of 300 in the week of October 14th, 150 in the week of October 21st, etc. This planning into the future would be done by DRP. The total demands placed on Warehouse X

	WEEKS					
	1	2	3	4	5	6
ACTUAL DEMAND (SCHEDULED)	240	254	182	140	70	
AVAILABLE TO PROMISE	0	-14	58	140	210	280
MPS (CAPACITY)	240	240	240	280	280	280

Figure 4—Capacity Booking

by Dealers A through F and all other dealers totally 3500 in the first week of October, 2950 in the second, etc. This total "partner demand," (coming from a linked "partner" DRP system) is then added to other individual "customer orders" and a "forecast" of those orders, where the warehouse is shipping directly to customers, not through the dealer network. Thus the total demand for Warehouse X of 16,550 in the first week of October (or any other week) can be analyzed by its segments if problems occur. Inventories, lead times, lot sizes and safety stocks for each dealer can also be accessed where appropriate.

Capacity Booking

As shown in Figure 2, an "available-to-promise" (ATP) calculation can always be kept up-to-date for a given item at a supply point. The traditional calculation is beginning inventory plus schedule minus any booked demands. In other words, it's that portion of the on-hand and on-order which has not been committed to customers. Its use becomes much more sophisticated when you segment the demand, as we have done in Figure 2. For instance, would future blanket requirements and future warehouse demands lower ATP? There's no right answer to this question, but each company must decide for itself what it wants to treat as "firm commitments" (those which lower ATP) vs. what would be used for planning purposes only. The resulting ATP can be used for making commitments to customer or warehouse requests when they occur. In companies with relatively few products, this can be done by item number, as Figure 2 implies.

However, in some environments there are many, many items to be promised and many of them have similarities in that they are made from common subassemblies or intermediate manufactured products and utilize common capacities or resources. In such businesses (which often are primarily make-to-order or finish-to-order), it often makes more sense to summarize the ATP for a given family of items and relate it to its impact on available capacity. **Figure 4** shows such a summary where the current total committed demands for a family of products is summarized by the amount of the critical capacity required to produce them. In this example, a fixed capacity of 240 per week is available. Currently customer commitments have been made that totally sell out Week 1 and actually oversell Week 2. Weeks 3 through 5 are partially sold out and the ATP indicates how many units of capacity are left to promise to the next customer that wishes to order. This order promising technique slots demand by capacity limitations and ensures that promises are made to customers in a reliable fashion. However, it presumes that a forecasting and planning process is used to set the original schedule and ensure that all proper materials and resources are available.

Redefining Where Supply Meets Demand

Figure 5 displays major activities that occur for a product to be designed, produced and shipped to a customer. The answer to the question, "Where do you meet the customer?" is a function of the lead time the customer gives vs. the amount of time it takes to do all of these supply functions. If you drew a vertical line down this chart at an order date that represents a typical customer lead time, where it intersects each of the other lines describes "where in the supply process you meet the customer." Anything to the left of that vertical line indicates things that need to be done in advance of receiving a customer order and therefore based on a forecast or customer contract or commit-

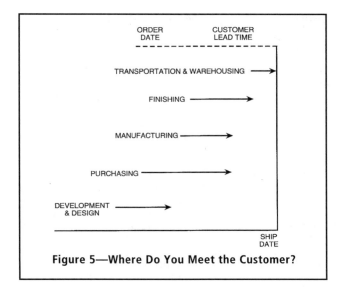

Figure 5—Where Do You Meet the Customer?

ment. Anything to the right of the line indicates things that could be done after the customer order is received. The longer the customer lead time, the more things can be put off until the order is received; and similarly, the shorter the lead times for the various supply functions, the more that can be put off until the customer order is received.

Of course, customer lead times in and of themselves are dangerous. A long customer lead time generally means that the customer also has more time to change their mind before final shipment. Customers would generally believe, with a long lead time, that the supplier should be able to accommodate changes inside that lead time. The changes could be in quantity or ship date, but sometimes could also be on the actual design of the product. So fighting for a longer customer lead time or bigger customer contract period in and of itself doesn't eliminate all potential short-term changes.

The better solution is to work on shortening the lead times for all the supply side functions. This is where Just-in-Time or Continuous Flow Manufacturing techniques come in. Eliminating set-up or changeover times, simplifying processes, shortening cycle times, eliminating queue and move times represent true, permanent improvements in flexibility, regardless of changes that the customer asks for.

World Class companies are finding it productive to challenge their assumptions about where they meet the customer. For instance, some are developing multi-tier supply approaches. For certain items for certain prices they guarantee delivery within one or two days. But for certain other items, and for cheaper prices (and in many cases with a lot of different options available to the customer) they tell the customer that they'll deliver within several weeks. Thus, in this case some items in a product family are make-to-stock and some of them become make-, finish- or package-to-order. It may sound like heresy, suggesting that customers be asked if they're willing to wait longer, but there may be some products supplied to customers where it would make no difference to them whether the lead time is one day or two weeks. Thus the Customer Linking is not just sharing planning data, but also getting to better understand how the customer uses your product and what dynamic forces are at work that would change their requirements for that product over time. By shortening supply cycle times and also redefining customer expectations, in some cases the customer can be better served and the supplier can do it more productively and profitably in a longer lead time.

Some companies redefine the make-to-order (or package-to-order) vs. the make-to-stock rules by time of year. For instance, with a very seasonal product, it might be planned such that it will always be in stock during the heavy season but be handled on a make-to-order basis (at least beyond a certain quantity) out of the season. This could be true for products such as toys (Christmas), agricultural chemicals (planting or growing seasons) and the like.

Think of your local McDonalds. The Fillet of Fish sandwich is make-to-order at 10:00 in the morning, but it's make-to-stock at noontime. They set their schedule and inventory policies that way and it becomes part of the routine.

The approach to this entire question can also affect how products are designed. For instance, a new product can be designed in a way that makes it easy to alter its final packaging, form, strength, color, size, etc. at the very end of the manufacturing process. In other words, design a product and a process to make it easy to finish, assemble or package to order. Then offer it to the customer, with the lead time needed to do this and sell them on the benefit of their ability to specify more product choices.

The terms make-to-order vs. make-to-stock can be very misleading. The fact of the matter is that most companies stock something. It may be raw material or may even be "capacity or resources." It could be semi-finished material, subassemblies, finished goods or some of all of the above. **Figure 6** shows some of the many factors that contribute to a company's choice as to where they should stock. The factors, starting with "unique customer design" and ending in "transportation costs" are arranged on the page to represent their impact on lead time. The ones listed to the left and top of the page tend to push suppliers to a design or make-to-order approach. Those on the bottom right tend to move companies to a make-to-stock or finish-to-order strategy. For instance, on the fourth line it says "Long procurement time." Below it would intersect with make-to-order. In an environment with long procurement

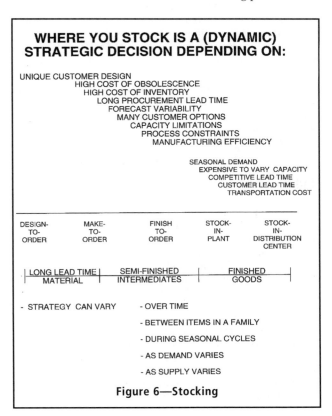

Figure 6—Stocking

times but with a lot of "forecast variability," many customer options and some "capacity limitations" as listed, generally companies can't afford to build all the variations or products and hold them all in finished goods stock. Therefore, the combination of these factors would move them toward the make-to-order approach, where long lead time materials are stocked along with a few semi-finished items.

It is most important to consider that this is a decision that an individual company can make differently for different items and product lines. It's a trade-off of the various factors vs. the costs and risks of carrying inventory at various levels. That strategic decision can vary, over time, between items in the family, between times in the year and as demand or supply reliability or variations begin to change. For instance, as the demand stability or forecastability of items becomes much firmer, it is affordable to commit to finished goods but, in fact, keep less of them because there's less demand variation to cover. Or, as a process begins to exhibit variability with increasing scrap rates and unpredictable cycle times, additional stocks, before and/or after that step in the process may be needed to hedge against that variability.

In environments where many different options or choices are offered to the customer, the use of planning bills, common parts "kits," option bills or option "kits" and two-level master scheduling should be utilized. The complexity of these techniques are such that they can't be covered in this paper, but they are documented in many other articles. It should be noted that the use of such approaches for planning will grow as customers are offered more choices and as the lead times shorten, thus allowing companies to make more and more products in a finish- or assemble-to-order fashion.

Supply Side Improvements

Having a Class A MRP II system operating as a starting point adds reliability, balance and inventory and cost optimization to any business.

Then aggressively pursuing Just-in-Time and Continuous Improvement activities that attack set-up times, cycle times, inventories, levels in the bill of material, process complexity, distances that materials travel throughout the manufacturing cycle, etc. will further optimize a company's ability to adjust supply to match demand when that is necessary. Below are described some techniques that leading edge companies have used to further enhance their supply management capabilities.

Underloading

Ironically, maintaining a schedule that represents less than 100% of full capacity can be a way of building flexibility into a process to allow for last minute changes to accommodate supply or demand variation. It is much easier to move a product in and increase quantities when the schedule is underloaded and other products don't have to be moved out. The key here is to assure that you are planning for enough of any long lead time or upstream purchased or manufactured materials so that they will be available to support the last minute schedule increase. This can be accommodated through the use of planning bills where a master schedule of a planning bill drives down dependent demand requirements on the materials and in the mix specified. Then when the actual item is moved into the schedule, the amount of the overplanning in the master schedule for the planning bill is reduced by a similar amount.

Improving Supply Management

Upside Planning

Some companies have developed some clever approaches to using the system to help them simulate the impact of a "range of outcomes" or a "high and low plan." First they pick a base forecast and a base plan against which to establish their live planning system. These forecasts and master schedules are used to then drive the execution of the day-to-day purchasing and manufacturing activities. However, in parallel (again often using planning bills of materials), they will plug in a forecast and a schedule that would represent a potential upside or incremental amount of business that they're not yet sure of getting. These schedules are run through the MRP II system in a simulation mode to calculate how much more of key materials or capacity would be necessary to support them and when.

The planning bills would include only those key materials that have traditionally been a bottleneck and only those key resources that traditionally have been capacity bottlenecks. This high side plan and what it would cost is then analyzed and sometimes leads companies to make decisions such as to strategically order more of given materials, find subcontract sources for upside capacity, build inventories up to a particular level in the upstream processes in anticipation of them, etc. Typically firm planned orders are used at the appropriate level to schedule the additional amounts to cover this simulated, upside potential. Only when Sales and Marketing are willing to fully commit to the upside potential is the actual live forecast and full master schedule then updated. But when it is, many of the materials and capacity needed to support the increases will already be built into the plan as a result of this upside planning.

This is a particularly useful technique in seasonal or cyclical businesses where the opportunity of capturing a significant amount of extra business is very time sensitive and occurs only on an occasional basis. During the off season, the upside planning can be done to anticipate what will be needed to support the high plan and also to set milestones or time targets when final decisions need to be made to commit to procuring or hiring or acquiring additional resources. A multi-level planning bill could give warnings based on lead time offsets of when extra materials and resources need to be ordered. These milestones and decisions should be tracked and reviewed in monthly Sales and Operations Planning (Production Planning) meetings.

Master Scheduling Approaches

Some companies are able to shorten the planning horizon for their detailed master schedule. They are able to do this (especially once their cycle times and lead times have been reduced) by making a lot of the longer term material and capacity planning decisions from the Sales and Operations Planning production plan or from of a master schedule at the family level utilizing a planning bill. This is a particularly good approach if there are a lot of minor variations within a family. There may be only four to thirteen weeks of detailed master schedules by line item. The balance of the cumulative lead time planning horizon may be by family or product groupings (again using planning bills) that explode down dependent demands only for materials and capacity with lead times greater than the four to thirteen week horizon or ones that have potential bottlenecks and need to be constantly monitored.

Option Overplanning

This term is normally used in conjunction with two-level master scheduling and the use of planning bills. It refers to the idea that the plan will accommodate mix variation. For instance, if there were two customer options and the typical ordering pattern is about 50/50, the plan would support 60% of either option. This option overplanning would use firm planned orders with increased quantities scheduled at the typical customer lead time. Extra optional material would then be ordered as a result.

The idea of overplanning options, though, can be applied even without two-level master scheduling (for instance, on make-to-stock items). Planning bills can be constructed whose sole purpose is to generate additional demands for optional components. For instance, a company that provides the same product with many different labels in many different languages due to regulatory requirements, may master schedule the end products based on the forecast. But a planning bill encompassing all the different labels and packaging variations with the typical product mix specified could then be scheduled to drive down extra requirements for the packaging materials. Thus, if customer order demand shifts and a master schedule change needs to be made in the short term, the additional packaging materials will already be on order or in inventory as a result of the overplanning done through the option planning bill of material.

Summary

Manufacturing and distribution are similar to the construction industry. The basic type of materials, tools and people hasn't changed much over the years. However, the level of automation and the approach to doing the job have. Therefore, the end results are different.

For instance, today's buildings and homes look much different than they did years ago. The construction materials are similar: wood, stone, brick, etc. The quality, strength and form of these materials has improved, thus enabling and fueling the change in customer preference for the style of buildings. The shapes and the sizes of what is possible have grown as well. The types of tools used to turn these materials into buildings are also quite similar: mixers, saws, hammers, screwdrivers, etc. The tools are now more automated and powerful, but they do basically the same work.

Obviously what's changed most is the vision of the customer and the ability of the workers. That analogy also holds true in our manufacturing and distribution industries.

Most of the techniques talked about in this paper have been used by companies over the last 30 years. They've been refined, automated and improved, but the approaches are basically the same. Even in the area of Just-in-Time we could arguably say that it represents a broad scale formalization of techniques that formerly were used to expedite a given order through a plant (streamlining changeovers, cutting cycle times, making lot sizes matching the demand quantities, etc.).

The moral of the story is this: as customers become more demanding, suppliers must become more creative. But the first line of creativity is to ensure that everyone working in the business understands and optimally applies the use of approaches, tools and techniques that already exist in the body of knowledge. A trained, thinking, empowered worker making the best use of the tools available is the true formula to Class A or World Class benefits. True breakthroughs are rare and infrequent. World Class companies don't pursue them at the expense of ensuring that they're getting the most from what is already available.

About the Author

John has, since 1977, provided direction for manufacturers seeking to improve their management controls and productivity levels. John, with the Partners for Excellence, instructs private, company-focused education sessions on the following topics: MRP II Top Management Overview, MRP II Functional Detail, Sales and Operations Planning, Master Production Scheduling and Inventory Record Accuracy.

John has guided companies to successful improvements in their planning and control systems and approaches. Many of them have reached the coveted "Class A" level of achievement. His experience spans the electronics, consumer goods, capital goods, pharmaceutical and chemical industries.

John is certified at the fellow level (CFPIM) by the American Production and Inventory Control Society (APICS). John is co-editor of the Sixth Edition of the APICS Dictionary. He currently sits on the Master Planning Committee of the APICS Curricula and Certification Council.

Reprinted from the 1996 APICS Conference Proceedings.

Integrating Vendor-Managed Inventory into Supply Chain Decision-Making
Mary Lou Fox, CPIM

What Is VMI?

Effective use of vendor-managed inventory, or VMI, leverages advanced technology and trading-partner relationships to enable the flow of information and inventory throughout the entire supply chain. It provides visibility into demand at the trading-partner level—often where the consumer or purchases is—to improve the flow of products, eliminate inefficiencies, and lower costs. When done well, VMI improves customer service by eliminating stockouts, decreasing inventory, and ensuring that the right products are in the right place at the right time based on consumer demand.

VMI is also known by several other acronyms: CRP (Continuous Replenishment Program), QR (Quick Response), and ECR (Efficient Consumer Response). Traditionally, these programs have been designed by large retailers who have required their vendors to participate, although ECR was jointly developed by grocery distributors and manufacturers.

The following benefits of a rapid replenishment program to a retailer, distributor, and manufacturer are clear and will be explained in further detail:
1. Improved service to stores, which reduces store out-of-stocks and leads to higher sales.
2. Reduced distribution center (DC) inventories.
3. Reduced administrative costs, as more transactions are handled electronically.
4. Reduced operating costs.

Some manufacturers feel they do not benefit from replenishment programs, because they are forced to incur the additional costs of managing the retailer's replenishment simply to retain the retailer's business. Under pressure to "get something going" to satisfy the immediate needs, the manufacturer passes up the opportunity to reap significant rewards from the program.

How Does It Work?

VMI incorporates demand planning and distribution planning to provide integrated, enterprise-wide answers to problems in the supply chain. A consumer-driven forecast for demand is compared to inventory on hand and in transit, and this determines the net requirements at the customer DCs. Then, shipment amounts can be determined, as well as grouped into specific orders. An efficient VMI system should work with traditional transaction systems already in place. The transaction system will feed data into the VMI system, providing actual demand for a specific forecast period and additional inventory information. By using an inventory plan in this manner, the user can generate a replenishment order, which becomes a purchase order for a trading partner.

At Johnson & Johnson, for example, a Customer Support Center was founded in 1991 with the challenge of meeting the demands of all its customers—mass merchandisers and grocery and drug retailers. Today, by using an integrated supply chain management system with a robust VMI module, Johnson & Johnson supplies more than 15 external customers, and is expected to double that number within 12 months.

Black & Decker implemented an advanced demand planning solution as part of its VMI program and obtained outstanding results. Customer-service levels to one of the company's largest retail customers reached 98 percent, and returned goods from that same customer decreased from $1 million to $75,000.

Schering-Plough implemented a VMI program to meet standards set down by one of its largest customers: Kmart. Schering-Plough received a Top 10 vendor performance award in its first year in the giant retailer's Partners in Merchandize Flow program. Through its use of an advanced supply chain system that includes VMI, Schering-Plough has since increased service levels to nearly 99 percent and reduced inventory levels at its Memphis facility by 25 percent.

How Manufacturers Benefit from VMI

A manufacturer analyzing rapid replenishment programs must assess the value of these programs to future success and the need to take a comprehensive approach to their implementation. In the grocery, consumer products, apparel, and automotive manufacturing industries, these programs are a competitive necessity.

From an operations perspective, the customer information used for ordering in the rapid replenishment program is integrated with information used for planning inventory and production in the manufacturer's planning processes, providing a single supply chain view into demand and supply.

There Are Four Key Benefits to the Manufacturer:
- Improved Customer Service. The obvious area of improvement comes from the ability to respond quickly to the needs of retailers' distribution centers. A more substantial improvement results when the manufacturer integrates the retailer's information throughout its replenishment planning process. Then, the manufacturer is more efficient at moving products out to the retailer and at stocking the right products in its own DCs, so they will be available when the retailer's orders materialize.
- Reduced Demand Uncertainty. A common occurrence for every manufacturer is the large, unexpected customer order. Demand is uncertain under most circumstances, but the lack of visibility beyond current, open

customer orders increases the need for DC buffer stock and necessitates expediting when the unexpected occurs. A rapid replenishment program based on time-phased planning uses forecasts at customers' DCs to provide needed visibility to future customer orders and allows the manufacturer to plan and to have inventory to meet the demand when it occurs.

- Reduced Inventory. When the manufacturer succeeds in using the demand information provided by the retailer in its planning process, the manufacturer can use the forward visibility inherent in the demand information to position inventories in the supply chain when needed and to reduce excess stocks used to buffer uncertainty. Essentially, the manufacturer trades information for inventory.

- Reduced Costs. Adding the rapid replenishment ordering process to the existing customer service function typically increases the level of effort committed to a customer. The way for the manufacturer to achieve cost reductions is to use replenishment programs as an opportunity to reengineer the customer demand fulfillment process to include both fulfilling customers' orders and replenishing DCs as a single business process, rather than as the isolated work of two departments.

The Importance of VMI in the Supply Chain

The increasingly competitive environment in many industries is requiring companies to implement interenterprise processes, such as VMI. Collaborative processes like VMI are the future of trading relationships across the supply chain, which means that any demand- and supply-planning processes must be modified to account for these collaborative efforts. A company's role in the supply chain as a carrier, retailer, wholesaler, or manufacturer then becomes another factor that adds complexity to demand and supply.

A manufacturer, for example, would want to establish VMI relationships with its large customers. Some customers will simply provide a forecast of orders and will ask to ensure delivery of those orders. Other customers may provide daily shipment data expecting replenishment based on the data. Still others may provide point-of-sale (POS) movement data across stores, asking that the manufacturer use this data when planning replenishments. Finally, some may actually provide store-level, accounting-quality POS movement data and not only ask to replenish to this demand stream, but accept payment of goods based on it as well.

These increasing complexities are requiring that companies take a new look at planning supply and demand to meet their customers' needs and to rise above the competition.

The computerized planning tools currently used to manage the supply chain tend to fall into two categories: point solutions and conventional supply chain solutions. Point solutions are planning tools that address one particular business function, such as forecasting, manufacturing planning, or load building. These solutions are often feature-rich, but address a limited scope of business processes.

The integration limitations of point solutions are overcome by conventional supply chain management systems. These systems are built by the vendor from the ground up, with the aim of enabling a comprehensive supply chain management process that includes and integrates demand planning, distribution planning, manufacturing planning, and transportation planning. For example, if a planner is looking at a supply planning screen and sees a shortage, he can do a few quick clicks to "peg" into a demand planning screen. The planner can evaluate whether the demand

is caused by forecast or customer orders, whether it is an estimated or statistical forecast, whether the forecast is consistent with history, and whether an event such as a promotion is causing the demand. This information is crucial to a supply planner trying to determine whether expediting is justified to relieve a projected shortage.

This type of pegging is not possible without an integrated system. Users of interfaced point solutions must go through a cumbersome process of opening two applications and selecting the same data twice, rather than simply pegging up the planning chain within an integrated database.

Current supply chain solutions also give a planner the ability to integrate the supply chain across enterprises. Users of supply chain systems employ techniques like POS data and VMI to integrate their vendors and customers into a holistic supply chain model.

By giving the replenishment program demand information to all planners—up and down the supply chain—more planning can be performed more effectively. The resulting reductions in expediting premium freight and transshipments are significant.

With the number of rapid replenishment initiatives increasing, it is important to create a vision of how these programs are best implemented instead of rushing to "get something going." The best and most cost-effective approach is to take the long-term view, which is the integrated supply chain approach.

If the manufacturer incorporates the replenishment program into its customer service, fulfillment, forecasting, and distribution functions, and uses the information passed through Electronic Data Interchange (EDI) for planning as well as order fulfillment, it can achieve maximum benefit while still implementing individual programs in a timely fashion.

Customer Case Study

In its 106-year history, Johnson & Johnson has never posted a loss. And there's good reason. As the world's leading healthcare products maker, the company is renowned for its product lines—including TYLENOL® Acetaminophen, MONISTAT® Cream, and BAND-AID® Brand Adhesive Bandages—and for quickly adapting to the many market changes of the past century.

Consistent with this reputation, Johnson & Johnson is proving to be a leader in continuous replenishment—a process that has been lauded as the way of the future for effectively managing the transfer of products between manufacturers and retailers. Continuous replenishment improves customer service by eliminating stockouts, decreasing inventory, and ensuring that the right products are in the right place at the right time based on consumer demand.

Johnson & Johnson's continuous replenishment efforts were initiated in 1991. Responding to the market's increasing emphasis on customer service, the company set up a unique organizational structure focused on a new type of "Customer Support Center." Designed to provide customer service for all of Johnson & Johnson's Consumer Sector operating companies—including Johnson & Johnson Consumer Products, Inc., McNeil Consumer Products Company, and Advanced Care Products—the Johnson & Johnson Consumer Sector Customer Support Center is a separate company within the organization. It handles order management, distribution, and accounts receivable functions while offering the added benefits of a totally committed project team and a single point of contact for all customer service activities—including inventory replenishment requests.

It wasn't long before the Customer Support Center's continuous replenishment capabilities were put to the test. By the end of 1991, QR requests were knocking loudly on Johnson & Johnson's door, prompting the Customer Support Center to quickly develop an approach to continuous replenishment that could meet the demands of all its customers—including mass merchandisers and grocery and drug retailers.

To help support the onslaught of Quick Response requests coming from some of the company's largest customers, Johnson & Johnson selected Manugistics, an integrated set of supply chain management applications. Using information from EDI transmissions, Manugistics links the Customer Support Center with Johnson & Johnson's customers and distribution centers. The system is tied directly to the company's order management system—which includes order processing, transportation load building, and sales reporting systems. Information from these systems is fed downstream to each of the separate operating units to provide decision support throughout the organization.

It took less than three months for Johnson & Johnson to implement Manugistics and begin running multiple QR programs for each of the organization's operating companies. Today, Johnson & Johnson is supplying more than 15 external customers using what is now referred to as the "Efficient Consumer Response" project.

To accommodate its customers, Johnson & Johnson had to develop one standard method for managing its continuous replenishment processes in-house. "We've had to accommodate more than 15 different interpretations of the same inventory replenishment model," said Joe Bakunas, manager of logistics and replenishment for the Customer Support Center. This exposure has provided the project team with an in-depth understanding of diverse customer needs. Bakunas believes this knowledge has enabled them to roll out the program to new customers at a very quick rate. "Manugistics is a very flexible system, allowing us to quickly recreate information every day based on the latest piece of data we get from the customer," he explains.

"We're rewriting our own book in terms of how we do logistics with our customers."

Jeffrey Gora, replenishment planner for the Customer Support Center, stresses that although rolling out a replenishment program to one customer is a large accomplishment, "If you don't have the flexibility to roll it out to others, the method can't accomplish enough. It's a nice gold star, but you're extremely limited in what you're really able to do. The larger your program, the larger your benefits."

Johnson & Johnson can certainly testify to the benefits. According to Gora, Johnson & Johnson now has a very thorough way to generate customer requirements based on warehouse withdrawal. "That puts us one step, maybe two steps closer to the end consumer. And the flexibility we have with Manugistics gives us the capability to look further down the pipeline and mange demand."

In the future, Johnson & Johnson plans to add as many customers as possible to the program. "We see this as a strategic advantage for Johnson & Johnson," says Gora, "because it is significantly increasing our ability to supply products to our customers." To continue the forward momentum, the company is steering toward the client/server version of Manugistics and further improving processes to provide even better continuous replenishment to its customers.

Because its customers are holding the reins on the future, Johnson & Johnson has no way of knowing what's around the next bend. What it does know for sure is that two and a half years ago the company found itself at the entrance to a new way of doing business and in eight weeks had built a strategic method for continuous replenishment. With a record like that, there is little doubt that Johnson & Johnson will remain at the top of its industry—whatever the future holds.

About the Author

Mary Lou Fox, CPIM, is senior vice president of professional services for Manugistics, Inc., Rockville, MD. Her expertise is in helping companies implement integrated logistics software in the areas of demand, distribution, manufacturing, and transportation planning.

Reprinted from the 1999 APICS Conference Proceedings.

Keeping the Promise of Available to Promise: Sales and Manufacturing Team Up

Jack Gips, CFPIM, and Nancy Schultz, CIRM

Master scheduling is the meeting point for sales forecasts, order entry, and manufacturing planning in most manufacturing companies. One feature contained in the master scheduling modules of many MRP II and ERP software packages is a calculation that is descriptively named "available to promise." Its purpose is

- to provide information for promising valid delivery dates to customers
- to reserve or allocate products for customer orders in advance of delivery
- to provide warnings that supplies are getting low so remaining products can be allocated to satisfy the greatest number of customers or the most important ones
- to prevent unusually large demands from reducing inventories unexpectedly to levels that cause stockouts for customers who have placed steady demands and/or provided good projections of their needs
- to provide sales organizations with information about what is available based on previously planned product schedules so they can sell what has been planned rather than take orders at random levels
- to differentiate quantities of products that have been produced to satisfy the forecasts of different markets, customers, or sales organizations and ensure that each gets its fair share.

ATP must be applied differently to products that are make-to-stock, assemble-to-order, and make-to-order. In all cases it compares current and future supplies against existing customer orders to determine what supplies are not yet allocated. When a new order is entered or reviewed, the customer's request is matched with the unallocated supplies to determine when it can be satisfied.

On make-to-stock products, ATP can be used to determine the following:

- if products are available at the time of order entry
- if all line items can be shipped immediately or at the customer's requested date
- when every item on an order will be available for a single shipment
- when partial shipments can be made.

On assemble-to-order items, ATP can be used to determine when a configured product can be promised based on the availability of the options and features that have to be assembled.

Deliveries of make-to-order products can be promised based on ATP for critical raw materials, components, or capacities of critical work centers.

Obstacles to the Use of ATP

In truth, many of the companies whose systems are capable of calculating available to promise information have failed to use it in actual practice. For some, available to promise does not fit the dissociation that exists between sales and manufacturing. Sales may forecast to give manufacturing a driver, but has no obligation to sell into that plan. Customer orders are often accepted and promised with "standard delivery lead-times" or simply entered for immediate delivery without any comparison to the plans or available to promise. Sales people may in fact be rewarded for overselling the forecasts or for selling the dollar volume even though the mix bears no resemblance to the forecast. If this approach continues to exist once a system is installed, available to promise is usually switched off or ignored.

Some companies would like to use their available to promise information, but it is not accurate enough to use or not presented in the right form to use it. If the supplies (on-hand inventories or supply orders) cannot be trusted or the demand data contains errors or false demands, available to promise information calculated from these will also be untrustworthy. If many customer promises based on these data are not met, available to promise will not be used for very long.

If available to promise is not presented to the people who enter the orders in an easily usable form, the same will be true. Sales and customer service people usually do not want to see available to promise as one line on a multiline master scheduling worksheet. They want it to appear on their order entry and quotation screens. If the orders call for multiple line items, they usually want to enter the whole order and review available to promise for the entire order rather than one line at a time.

ATP Calculation

Calculating ATP is relatively simple. The formula is as follows:

AVAILABLE TO PROMISE = Total Supply − Total Actual Demand
where, Total Supply = Quantity On Hand + Quantities On Order
and, Total Actual Demand = Quantity on Customer Orders

The quantity on hand includes any safety stock, since safety stock is not allocated to any particular customers and is therefore available to promise. The total actual demand excludes sales forecasts, since they are a prediction of future demand and the inventories to cover them are not allocated to any customers. **Figure 1** shows the calculation of ATP for a make-to-stock item.

There are some problems with the ATP calculation in some of the newer ERP software packages. Several of these packages deduct safety stocks from the on-hand quantities before calculating ATP. Their argument is that safety

---

| On Hand = 2900 | | | | | | | | Safety Stock = 1200 |

Period	1	2	3	4	5	6	7	8
Rem. Forecast	0	600	1000	1100	800	1100	900	1000
Cust Ords	1500	100	100		300		200	100
Proj On Hand	1400	4700	3600	2500	1400	4300	3200	2100
MPS Supply Orders		4000				4000		
A-T-P	1400	3500				3700		
A-T-P (Accum.)	1400	4900	4900	4900	4900	8600	8600	8600

Figure 1.

stocks are for emergency use only and not normally available for sale. Since most of these safety stocks have been calculated based on the variability of demand against the forecasts, they are planned to cover those expected variations and not just for emergencies. The users of those packages can often be found either manually adding back the safety stocks to the ATP or ignoring ATP altogether.

Another common problem is the exclusion of system planned orders from the calculation. These systems only consider released and firm planned orders. The argument in this case is that system planned orders change frequently and are therefore not reliable enough to base promises on. The result for companies that take orders now for delivery at customer requested dates in the future is that the calculation runs out of supply before it satisfies all the demand. Manual calculations show that the order can be covered by the planned orders that are being ignored. In fact, the planned orders are the plan. The system will always cover demand if there is demand to be satisfied. They should become firmed as they approach the item's time fence and released at the lead time. This problem becomes much more serious if the software does not provide for time fences and firming messages when system planned orders cross them. If the system is allowed to plan orders inside the time fence and in the first few weeks of the horizon, available to promise will show very little, if any, supply to satisfy the customers if these orders are excluded. It will show ATP that is impossible to meet if it includes planned orders when the system is allowed to plan them inside the time fences.

There have also been arguments that supply order deliveries often cannot be trusted because the components to produce them are frequently not available. Or, if a supply order is to be pulled up to an earlier date, it is important to be able to drill down to see the availability of the components before moving it. There has been much ado about the need for "drill down" capabilities in the software. In reality, however, only a small percentage of companies are in a position to use this kind of information. As an example, take a company whose product has 100 components and four levels in its bill of materials. A customer requests a quantity greater than is currently planned. We drill down to look at all these components and find 20 of them would be short if the next order is pulled up to satisfy this request. This is to be expected since the order is greater than the original plan. What do we do now? Call 10 suppliers and check on availability? Analyze the work centers for capacity and the raw materials for the manufactured items to see if it can be done? Do we do all this before promising delivery to the customer? And what if this scenario happens many times every day? Is all this detail really better information than we can receive from ATP? Do we have time to analyze it?

It may be practical to drill down to the details in companies whose products have small bills of material and

whose processes have a few short paths. We learned a long time ago that it was not practical in many companies to manage our plants at the detailed component levels. It was one of the reasons we emphasized the need to manage our master schedules and drive the decisions made there to the component levels. Having the technology to manipulate the details does not necessarily make it the right thing to do.

ATP Scenarios

When a customer order is ready to be entered, there are a number of situations and decisions that ATP can prompt. The actions taken and decisions made may vary by company or product. One factor may be the degree of importance of the item to the customer (such as a lifesaving drug). The fierceness of the competition or the importance of controlling costs may also come into play. Available to promise does not make products available. It simply tells you if they are planned to be available when a customer requests them. If not, there are usually two options: change the plan and make them available or promise delivery at a different time when they will be. Anything else is wishful thinking.

Scenario #1. The customer asks for 100 units of an item at a particular date and there are 100 or more available.
Action: Promise the delivery as requested.

Scenario #2. The customer asks for 100 units of an item at a particular date and only 50 units are available to promise.
Possible Actions: Ask the customer if a partial delivery at the requested date and a second delivery when ATP shows more available will be acceptable. If this is not acceptable, contact the master scheduler to see if there is a way to adjust the schedules to satisfy the customer.

Scenario #3. The customer asks for 100 units of an item at a particular date and the system shows that there are exactly 100 available to promise. However this is a new customer and the 100 have been planned based on forecasts from important existing customers. After checking with the master scheduler, it is determined that if they are given to the new customer, the replenishment cannot be available for several weeks.
Possible Actions:
1. Give them to the new customer and take the heat from the rest.
2. Call the existing customers and check on their needs. Negotiate with both to split the quantity until more can be made available.
3. Buy the product from another customer who has it or from a competitor to satisfy both customers.
4. Save the product for the customer who gave you the forecast and turn down the new business.

Scenario #4. The U.S. marketing organization has worked diligently to provide a reasonably accurate forecast for the domestic demand. The international marketers provide a very inaccurate forecast and sometimes forget to forecast at all. They assume that the plant can make whatever they need. So the manufacturing planners forecast international demand based on history. There are 100 units available to promise. They were produced to satisfy a U.S. forecast of 80 units and an international forecast of 20. An international order comes in for 75 units. A replenishment order cannot be available for several weeks.

Possible Actions:
1. Give them to the international customer and hope U.S. marketing understands the situation.
2. Call the U.S. marketing and ask them if they are willing to share. Negotiate with both to split the quantity until more can be made available.
3. Have international marketing call U.S. marketing and ask them if they are willing to share. Let them negotiate and keep manufacturing out of the middle.
4. Save the product for the U.S. customer who gave you the good forecast and tell international that it is important to provide a good forecast if they want product availability at short notice.

Scenario #5. There are 100 units in inventory in the finished goods warehouse. A customer requests 65 but the system shows only 50 are available to promise. This is because another customer previously ordered 50 but requested delivery three weeks later. The next supply order is not due until week 5.

Possible Actions:
1. Ship 65 on the new customer order and assume that manufacturing will be able to respond.
2. Call the master scheduler before shipping and ensure that manufacturing can respond. Then ship the 65 on the new order.
3. Try to make a partial shipment on the new customer order and deliver the remainder in week 5.

The Changing Business Model

The scenarios above are based on the traditional customer service model with a customer on the phone talking to a customer service representative (CSR) during normal business hours. However, this model is changing quickly, especially in a make-to-stock environment. Industry consolidation and information technology is mutating customer service processes at the speed of light. Three trends will force us to reconsider how our ATP "tool kit" should be deployed to engage and inform customers in the future.

The first trend is customer segmentation. No longer does one set of service rules apply to every customer. The level of responsiveness required of your business may vary based on the industry your customer serves, or the importance of that customer to your business strategy. For example, if your customer serves one of the mass merchandisers like Home Depot or Wal-Mart, rest assured that you will be required to adjust to variations in their demand with very little lead time. If you want the business, the mass merchandisers and the mass merchandisers' customers set the rules of the game. Your only decision is whether to play or not. However, you will not likely plan on offering Wal-Mart-type lead times to all your other customers. Customer service is becoming an increasingly strategic discipline, counterbalancing the other critical procurement variables, price and quality. For each customer segment the business leaders, not operations, must define the level of service and service features that will give your business competitive advantage. Over-serving with no clear goal is a waste of shareholder value. So is under-serving if there is market advantage to leverage. Differentiating customer service strategy by customer or customer group will impact the way you manage many factors: standard lead times, inventory, capacity, and logistics. Available to promise is a means of managing these differentiated strategies.

For example, you could create a group of megacustomers with their own dedicated available to promise to ensure that they get preferred access to planned supplies over nonmembers of that group. Within that group, however, the megacustomers who place their demands first will get priority access to that supply over their fellow megacustomers. Probably business rules will cause whoever provides the best forecast to earn the right to a preferred level of service over their short lead time peers.

The second trend is a synchronous communication enabled by advances in information technology. Much service activity that used to be conducted by telephone and fax is migrating to other communication channels like true EDI and Internet. The term "true EDI" implies real data interchange between supply partners' information systems, not "mock EDI" that needs to be rekeyed. Customer-limited access to their order information through the Internet, often referred to as an Extranet, is evolving to include computer-to-computer communication that is mutating and merging with our traditional definition of EDI. The benefits to both the customer and the supplier are enormous. Customers can access up-to-date information any time of the day or night, a particularly powerful advantage as the sun never sets on many global industry leaders. Suppliers benefit as well, as the costs of serving customers drop dramatically as proportionately fewer staff are required to process orders and distribute information.

Again, there are profound implications for available to promise. While the traditional scenario suggests that customer service wants ATP info to appear on order entry and quotation screens, or after multiple order lines have been entered, what are the ramifications if the customer is now in the driver's seat? All of the ATP user issues mentioned earlier are intensified when you visualize your customer accessing the information directly without the filter of a customer service representative deciding whether they can trust, and how they should present, the information.

- Is the inventory accurate?
- Will the supplies really appear when planned?
- Do planned orders provide a sufficient picture of supply into the future?
- Does the demand data contain false demands like safety stocks?
- What are the business rules for dealing with unusual spikes in demand?
- How can you assure that ATP adapts to differentiated service levels among customers?
- How should the information be presented to the customer in a user friendly way?

An additional issue arises as well. What happens if the customers' requested lead times cannot be met? Probably your Web site will need to allow the customers to indicate their preference by noting whether they will accept the alternative promised dates, whether they want to trigger a human intervention to expedite the delayed item, or whether they want to cancel the request for that item.

The third trend, vendor-managed inventories (VMI), takes the customer out of the picture altogether for routine supply chain management. In a VMI environment the supplier has access to the customer's inventory and usage data and is responsible for maintaining the inventory level required by the customer. Now ATP technology comes full circle, as the supplier's customer service representative or planner becomes a surrogate buyer. Technology and business rules developed to support trend two, true EDI and Internet commerce, will greatly enhance the efficiency of handling the customer's purchasing activity in house.

Conclusion

Available to promise has proven to be a very effective tool to coordinate the efforts of sales and manufacturing in both make-to-stock and make-to-order environments when it is used correctly. As we look into the future, we see that it will become even more important because it is exactly the type of information required to streamline the supplier-customer interface our high speed world will demand. It is usually discarded quickly if the right conditions are not in place when it is started up. This means that we must get it right the first time. Our inventories must be accurate and our supply orders must be delivered on schedule. We must clearly define the target levels for customer service and the rules for prioritizing our customers and for handling the scenarios. We have to determine the roles of the customers and the suppliers in utilizing the systems and ATP if we are to eliminate middlemen and bureaucratic delays. Once this is accomplished, ATP promises to link manufacturing and sales to a single plan, reduce unnecessary schedule changes, improve the quality of promise dates to the customers and on-time delivery to those promises, and simplify our customer relationships. It will help create an environment in which our customers will not be inclined to look elsewhere when they need our products.

About the Authors

Jack Gips, CFPIM, is president of Jack Gips, Inc., an independent firm specializing in manufacturing education and consulting. He has spent 30 years in manufacturing management and as a consultant to a wide variety of companies and industries. He is a member of the board of advisors of the Prentke Romich Corporation, a manufacturer of electronic communication aids for people with disabilities.

Mr. Gips has been active in APICS as a chapter programs chair, member of the PAC and JIT certification subcommittees, and chairman of the 1977 International Conference. He has been guest speaker at hundreds of APICS chapter meetings and seminars, as well as at many other professional societies, software users' groups, and corporate management meetings.

Nancy Schultz, CIRM, established her consulting business, Nancy Schultz Consulting, in 1989. Her firm helps manufacturing and service companies, government, and educational institutions gain competitive advantage through effective customer support processes.

Before establishing her business, Ms. Schultz spent 17 years with General Electric's innovative Plastics Division in the areas of inventory management, production control, and customer service. She was a key contributor to the customer service restructuring project there highlighted in Tom Peters' *Thriving on Chaos*.

She has helped a number of organizations establish cohesive customer support strategies, clarify business rules, redesign processes, identify world-class practices, and install new business information systems. She has also managed implementation projects, documented procedures, and coordinated functional and skills training.

Reprinted from the 1997 APICS Conference Proceedings.

Sales and Operations Planning: A Process That Works

Joseph Brad Gray

For most manufacturing companies, the main objective today is to cut cost through work process implementation, thus improving and standardizing the way they do business. To accomplish this end, most large manufacturing corporations spend millions of dollars on I/S platforms and MRP II software packages that require consulting firms to educate, train, document, and implement the software. From an MRP II perspective, the basis for the software purchase is to reduce the effort put forth to develop a feasible production schedule and facilitate the balance of supply and demand at the least possible cost.

However, during the reengineering phase of these projects, very little effort is placed on the elements of the planning process that feed the million-dollar MRP II functionality. Like most endeavors, preplanning eliminates countless hours of waste and avoids critical mistakes. Because of this neglect, most companies ultimately spend relentless hours in meetings to determine why the production schedule does not meet the demand being realized in orders. After years of this agony, committees are again formed to look at the latest software packages that will now meet the needs of the company and save it from its costly state….the cycle begins again!

The problem is not the software; the problem is the planning preparation phase where top management wrestles with the hard decisions of supply and demand, balancing the abilities of their manufacturing facilities with the demand plan. The old saying, "Poor planning on your part does not constitute an emergency on my part" is not true as most plant managers will tell you. The lack of a supply/demand balancing process in a company will render the most expensive and sophisticated MRP II software useless and create emergency order after emergency order for the manufacturing community. The problem: the lack of a formal Sales and Operations Planning Process that demands decision making of executive management long before the customer order is ever realized.

The Beginning

Like most challenges that face a process, the success and failure of Sales and Operations Planning (S&OP) is based on a few fundamental truths that must be observed. Failure to play by the rules, results in failure. The actual balancing of supply and demand is not the challenge as it is based on a very simple mathematical formula subtracting demand from supply impacting inventory levels. The success and failure of S&OP starts from the very beginning on how a company structures S&OP in its organization. The critical components (truths) of S&OP are:

- Top Management is involved and must make the decisions based on the outputs of the S&OP process

- There is only one supply number
- There is only one demand number
- One multifunctional team balances supply and demand, identifies, raises, and resolves the conflict. When conflict cannot be removed, upper management breaks the tie.

The four principles outlined above are to S&OP what oxygen is to a human: without it, the organism will die. The principles are not in order of priority as they must happen simultaneously. Failure to implement each element will result in failure as each "truth" feeds off another "truth."

Team Formation

Most top managers assign the responsibility of balancing supply and demand in materials management/supply chain organizations, chartering the manager of this group with the impossible task of ensuring product is always available for the customer. However, we can all agree that no one function completely owns the supply chain process so why do we continually assign the responsibility to one person? S&OP demands that representatives of each function involved in the process of getting goods to customers represent their function with a common objective of balancing manufacturing capability and market demand. The usual makeup of an S&OP team is

- Manufacturing
- Sales/Marketing
- Customer Service
- Materials Management (Coach, Team Leader)
- R&D/Technical Service.

This team, known formally as the *Partnership Team*, is chartered with the responsibility of balancing supply and demand (that is, demand can NEVER exceed supply in the planning process) through the raising and resolution of conflict(s). Conflict is the essence of S&OP and it is the identification of conflict (transformed in planned/unplanned plant outages, competitive responses in the market place, new product offerings etc.) that brings life to the process. The resolution of conflict from a multifunctional team enables the S&OP process as each function now has ownership for "the plan." In the old world, manufacturing or materials management owned the plan…in S&OP, the business owns the plan.

One-Number System

The one-number system is utopia but like utopia very few find their way. Imagine an organization/process where everyone agrees with the demand number put forth by Marketing and Sales and the capacity number identified by manufacturing. Unfortunately, too many companies spend far too much time (therefore money) listening to arguments from manufacturing on why their demand number is better than the sales forecast or sales and marketing arguing that they know the plant's capability better than the plant manager. These petty and inefficient debates have more to do with "control" than with getting the customer product.

In the one-number system, each function has a responsibility. Marketing and Sales own the forecast. Although easy to say, implementation is key. By owning, we mean that it is the job of Marketing and Sales to forecast demand in the planning period outlined by the Partnership Team. The task assigned to Marketing and Sales is to identify the tools (i.e., regression analysis) necessary to forecast demand. Once identified, the Partnership Team members can issue challenges to the number but at the end of the day, the Marketing/Sales functions owns and is responsible for the forecast and the improvement of the forecast over time. Likewise, manufacturing community owns the capacity number. Again, debate and data-oriented challenges to the capacity numbers are welcome, but in the end, the plant manager and his staff are responsible to bring credible, data-driven capacity numbers that can and are achieved when demand is placed against the plant in the form of a detailed production schedule.

Executive Management Involvement

Perhaps the most written about, most difficult to implement, and key to the success of all processes is the support and involvement of upper management. The words support and involvement are the most overused terms in business today as we typically fail to define them in terms of actions or behaviors for management. When left to their own, executive managers will normally define support and involvement in terms of delegation and not actually use the delegated process in their own decision-making processes. In S&OP, we define support and involvement as that mechanism/tool used to make and guide decision making relating to short- and long-term capital expansions/decreases within the organization. Stated another way, support and involvement is the ability of upper management to participate in the process at the conflict resolution phase using the output of S&OP (i.e. percent of capacity, inventory to target, percent of forecast accuracy) to guide decision making and setting functional goals (with supported resources) to improve the S&OP process (i.e., forecast accuracy, production to plan accuracy, improved working capital turns, etc.). In S&OP, executive management manifests itself in several forms but perhaps the three most visible are

- The Partnership Team results (outputs of the meeting include production to plan, forecast to plan, short- and long-term supply/demand balances, and relative inventory impact) are placed on the executive meeting agenda.
- All conflict/disconnects that could not be resolved at the Partnership Team level are brought to the executive team for resolution.
- All capacity expansions and/or closings are based on the results of S&OP.

Many confuse the Partnership Meeting as the S&OP process, but it is not. The process ends with the presentation and participation of executive management to either support the plan, refute the plan, and resolve any conflicts. Failure to perform the above by upper management means that one does not have a healthy S&OP process. The process only

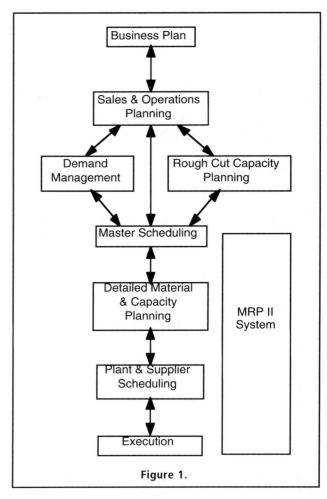

Figure 1.

works when all levels of the company are working in conjunction with the process.

Application of S&OP

Having covered the base components of S&OP and some of its key attributes (one-number system, executive management participation, etc.), we will now focus on the model outlined in **Figure 1**. Our goal at this point is to show what actually happens in the application of a formal S&OP process.

One will note that S&OP begins with the Business Plan. Again, we see a process that begins with executive management as they are the ones in most companies that set "the plan."

After the Business Plan is defined and the formation of the partnership team is complete, the coach begins the S&OP process. The coach assumes the role of defining the purpose, desired outcomes, and agenda for all Partnership meetings. The meetings usually take approximately 30 minutes to 1.5 hours and should be scheduled at regular frequencies at least one year in advance. Prior to the Partnership Team meeting, marketing/sales present to the team leader the forecast requirements and manufacturing presents the capacity data for the same time period. At this point, each does not worry what the other has stated. Upon receipt of the supply and demand data, the team chairman prepares the spreadsheets outlining the supply side, demand side, and inventory side. From this standpoint,

---

the math is very simple so we will not spend time on this part of the process.

Having prepared the worksheets, the team leader distributes the results to team members prior to the meeting. During the actual partnership team meeting, it is best if the team spends several minutes on the actual results of the previous month versus the plan. By taking the time to review the results of the plan (both forecast to actual and production to plan, inventory to target) the team criticizes its efforts, identifies failures/disconnects, and puts in place the necessary corrective actions to avoid making the same mistakes/errors in the next S&OP cycle.

After completing the review, the team then addresses the output from the forecast and capacity inputs. The consequences of the math are realized and discussed. The fundamental rule is that one never plans to operate a plant at greater than 100 percent of its capacity. Remember, the goal is to achieve balance, thus producing a credible master production schedule. When demand exceeds supply, the team must develop solutions to solve the problem (i.e., import material, purchase on the outside, increase inventory in slack months, etc.); however, it is imperative that before the team adjourns, agreement is reached on the plan and a balanced plan is obtained. If a balanced plan cannot be achieved, the team must prepare a list of needs, or "Issues," for executive management review.

After the Partnership Team has identified all the barriers, constraints, and issues, it is now prepared to create a formal "Issues" list with a corresponding list of solutions and cost. The Issues List will be one of the items to be reviewed with the Executive Management Team. At the management team meeting, the Partnership spokesperson will review the historical performance with associated corrective actions, as well as the output of the new cycle. Instead of using numbers it is found that graphs better identify the areas of opportunity and provide management with a quick look at the situation. It is at this point in the presentation that the Issue's List becomes important. Once the issues have been identified and the cost and associated benefits/consequences are realized, the executive team is in a position to make its final decision (i.e., build capacity, decrease demand, purchase on the outside, etc.), thus providing the input necessary for the next cycle of the S&OP process.

At this juncture, all levels within the company are focused on the issues at hand, the available options, and the cost to remove the barriers. In addition, one can clearly see

that the one-number system is honored with discussions centering on the results. Challenges made to the supply side or demand side numbers (which can and do occur) are legitimate but go back to the function for resolution and not to other functions to develop their set of numbers. In the end, the cycle is reviewed each month at the Executive Management Review. At this point Management has now seen the total balance over the planning period and knows that obstacles and constraints are being removed outside the critical time fence (S&OP is not done within the critical time fence). As a rule of thumb, the options available decrease and cost increases as one approaches the critical planning period.

Summary

Balancing supply and demand has long been a challenge to all organizations, as it in itself is not an exact science. When faced with what is sometimes deemed unscientific data, organizations spend countless hours and money to "purchase software" and force a process that is by design not an exact science. S&OP is a process that recognizes the variability of the forecasting process and at the same time facilitates a formal agenda to remove barriers far in advance to achieve a rough cut capacity plan. In addition, S&OP can and does provide executive management with a process to focus the organization on corrective actions and results, as well as found the company on the fundamental principles of MRP II. But, perhaps the greatest contribution of S&OP is the process's ability to produce a feasible master plan, thus facilitating the ability of the Detailed Production Scheduler to produce a credible detail schedule based on a formal plan. Without a formal, credible, and feasible master plan, the detailed schedule is doomed to fail, rendering the million-dollar software useless.

About the Author

Joseph Brad Gray is the North American Supply Chain Manager for Dow Chemical's Emulsion Polymer's Business. He serves on the Emulsion Polymer Commercial Management Team as well as Dow's Global Supply Chain Management Team. He has 14 years with Dow Chemical in various material management jobs. He graduated from Stephen F. Austin State University with a BBA in management and marketing.

Reprinted from the 1996 APICS Conference Proceedings.

Demand Prediction: More Than Statistical Forecasting

Philip F. Helle, CPIM

The purpose of this presentation is to describe a process for predicting demand that will reduce the dependency on Statistical Forecasting, Estimating, and Historical Data. This age of information and communication offers tremendous opportunity to acquire data about marketplace activity and develop profound information about future demand that is far superior to statistical calculations as a sole means. The inference is not that statistical means of predicting demand are inadequate, only that there are more precise methods for many categories of demand sources.

Situation Analysis

Performance in the following key company areas: Forecast Accuracy, Customer Service (Order Fill Rates), impact on Manufacturing Capacity and Scheduling, Suppliers and Inventory Management, has been less than desired in most firms. Many of the past attempts to address these issues have been traditionally reactionary, in that there has been an immense effort to correct an occurrence such as a "stock out," by replanning, changing schedules, and expediting suppliers with little effort directed toward the root causes of the problem. This proposed process intends to focus primarily on eliminating or minimizing the root causes of the problems as they relate to demand.

The present method of projecting future sales of a product is often applied in a "top down," aggregate manner by using the total history by month to statistically calculate future usage for a product. If the only contributing factor to total historic usage was consumer "take-away," this approach could result in a reasonably accurate prediction. The flaw in this approach is that the Root Causes of the major reasons for demand have not been identified and analyzed.

In reality, there are a number of factors that influence (month-to-month) sales that are independent of consumer sales, such as:

- Retailers Response to Promotions
- Wholesalers Response to Promotions
- New Product Introduction
- Gross Factory Sales Quarterly and Year-End Objectives
- Developing New Markets, i.e., International Sales
- Requirements Originating from Distributors, Both Large and Small
- Requirements Originating from Company Owned Distribution Points
- Demand as a Result of Special Discounts
- Fulfilling Various Government Requirements
- Demand Directly from Mass Merchandisers
- Estimated Needs from Brokers
- Demand as a Result of Inventory Replenishment
- Demand for Newly Opened Territories
- Requirements by Location
- Demand as a Result of increased Market Share

The recommended approach requires that the total demand be analyzed to determine the various sources of that demand. Once segregated, each demand source will be researched to determine what the demand drivers (Root Causes) are, and how they affect the aggregate demand.

The constant pressure on either or both Manufacturing Flexibility and Additional Inventory as the solutions to unpredictable demand is not wrong or in any way a strategy that needs to be stopped. However, demand volatility should not be totally addressed by requiring Manufacturing to react or by stocking large amounts of inventory, to meet the delivery requirements. These solutions are often cost prohibitive.

Businesses must learn how to improve accuracy of Demand Prediction substantially through the application of information gathering, filtering, analyzing and calculating through the application of this innovative approach to the development of a Demand Prediction Process.

Assumptions About Current Conditions

- The demand for products in total, including all customers, is too difficult to accurately predict using only statistical models based on history from previous years.
- Developing forecasts from the "Top Down" using aggregate history will often produce inaccurate forecasts by month.
- Statistical forecasting models can be developed for some products for some elements of demand. However, a percentage of customers' demands cannot be reasonably predicted using statistics.
- Most businesses introduce activities that affect the real demand on the manufacturing process and suppliers, but do not represent actual consumption of the product.

Assumptions Concerning this Innovative Approach

- Developing various demand prediction methodologies is best accomplished by generating forecasts, estimates, and collecting known facts by customer, by product, by territory, by market segment, etc., from the "Bottom Up."
- Attempting to analyze the demand patterns of all customers for all products will likely be too complicated to accomplish and would not be an efficient use of analytical resources. The approach must remain practical.
- Analyzing the demand patterns for predominant customers for the primary products is an appropriate manner to start the "Bottom Up" approach to achieving an acceptable means of predicting demand.
- Grouping customer demands by product group, territory, market segment, or other categories or types of

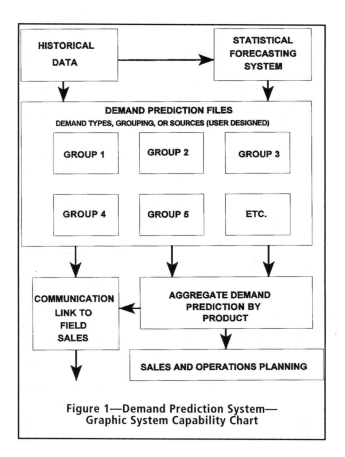

**Figure 1—Demand Prediction System—
Graphic System Capability Chart**

demand patterns may minimize the variety of demand patterns.

- Acquiring demand information directly from key accounts that have demonstrated erratic and unpredictable ordering patterns rather than calculating demands statistically is a far superior way to achieve an acceptable level of demand prediction accuracy.

Recommendation and Rationale

- Forecasting systems, Sales History programs and even spreadsheet systems can be used to develop product demand patterns for "Key" customers, market segments, and groups of customers. The major point is that the reasons (Root Causes) for demand need to be understood.
- A system would contain the demand prediction information separately from the statistical forecasting function. This separate demand prediction capability would have the ability to store unlimited sets of data representing the various types of demands that are in evidence. The system or database would be called a "Demand Prediction System." See Graphic System Capability Chart, **Figure 1**.
- The Field Sales department will use the product by customer demand patterns for key or impact customers to determine if they are representative of projected demand or if they should solicit demand information directly from the customers.
- Marketing will use the individual Customer Demand Patterns to develop common patterns to determine if standard statistical forecasting computations are applicable for groups of customers.

- The top-down, aggregate forecasting method typically used cannot effectively incorporate individual customer high impact demand in specific weeks, months, or any short-term period. These high impact demands contribute extensively to "stock outs," unplanned inventory fluctuations, misuse of valuable manufacturing capacity, and disruption of supplier schedules.
- A bottom-up, product-by-demand source approach will enable businesses to identify and predict high impact demand more accurately, either by using demand history of products by customer to directly forecast future demand or identify demand patterns that are too difficult to forecast and recommend direct communication between the customer and field sales to establish demand quantity and frequency.
- Predicting demand by customer provides the basis for developing closer relationships with "key" customers. This leads to supplier-customer partnerships and the establishment of a smoother, more level flow of product to the customer. Such an approach will support the well-accepted concepts of VMI (Vendor Managed Inventory) and ECR (Efficient Consumer Response), which will strengthen the relationships further.
- The demand prediction effort will be integrated with the Master Schedule, (Plan to Produce) to facilitate a plan into the future that predicts:
  —Future Inventories
  —Potential "Stock outs"
  —Capacity Requirements
  —Lower-Level Demands
  —Supplier Impacts
- The Demand Prediction Process will be an integral part of a Total Sales and Operations Planning Process which will Include Sales Planning, Production Planning, Inventory Planning and New Products Planning.
- This process will inherently improve customer service while maintaining minimum inventories in finished goods and components.
- Field sales would have continuous access to the demand patterns of products by customer and would provide demand information on an exception basis based on their knowledge of current activities. It is important to note that the intent is to abolish current monthly forecast development cycles that typically exist. They, in effect, would be asked to identify conditions that would significantly deviate from past demand patterns, only by exception.

A factor that also contributes to forecast error, stockouts and inventory fluctuations is the end of month, quarter, or year shipment emphasis motivated by financial goals. This approach would propose to prepare in advance for the impact by planning to have specific inventory, intentionally allocated for such occurrences.

Vision—How the System May Evolve

- This system may become the primary tool for the field sales people, in that, it would be an interactive, daily means of referencing and updating key customer demand information.
- The system would be capable of linking customers to distribution centers to predict demand by DC and, therefore, integrate the distribution planning directly to the product master plan, noting that territory may be a demand source segregating factor.
- It is recommended that the business develop or purchase a forecasting and demand management system

	1997												1998		
	JAN	FEB	MAR	APR	MAY	JUN	JUL	AUG	SEP	OCT	NOV	DEC	JAN	FEB	MAR
Predicted Demand															
Current Plant Schedule															
Planned Plant Schedule															
Actual Plant Production															
Actual & Projected Inventory Balance															
Optimum Inventory Level Range															
Variance															

← FULL LEAD TIME →

Figure 2—Product Master Plan Format

that will be more efficient than using spreadsheet technology to develop demand patterns.

Identification Of Key Accounts

- The primary approach to identifying "Key Accounts" is generally directly related to the dollar volume of business of customers with the business. However, any other criteria for designating a customer "Key" is a matter of company policy.
- While overall volume is important, another meaningful factor in identifying "Key Accounts" is the degree of variability in their ordering patterns for specific products. The most important criteria in separating accounts is to provide for analyzing "impact" orders for a product.
- A customer may be designated as "Key" if their demand variation on any one product is significant enough to impact inventory levels or potentially cause stock outs.
- The method for determining those customers that should be identified as "Key Accounts," and if the demand can be statistically forecasted and if future demands can only be established through direct information from the customer is as follows:
1. Retrieve demand history for high-volume customers by product by month for the preceding 24 months from Sales history.
2. Present those demand patterns in a graphic format using a demand management system as roughly described in Figure 1 to encourage proper significance to the degree of demand fluctuation.
3. The demand pattern graphs will also indicate all promotions, by week, to provide some level of understanding of the reasons for demand variation.
4. Nontraditional patterns will be captured and analyzed to determine applicability to projected demand.
5. Analyze the degree of month-to-month variation in demand and determine the cause of variation, i.e., promotions, special packs, coupons, inventory stocking changes, etc.
6. A process of grouping similar demand patterns, customer by product, can begin with the objective of establishing:

a. If all Product/Customer demand patterns (profiles) are consistent enough to be predictable.
b. How many predictable demand patterns exist for a product.
c. If some customer demand patterns for given products are unpredictable and, therefore, the demand can only be developed via direct information from the customer.
d. Grouping of Market Segments

Implementation Plan

- Demand patterns will be developed for key customers within the major product lines and will be analyzed by the Implementation Team using data from the Forecasting and Demand Management System and displaying demand patterns for analysis.
- The intent is to continue the process by analyzing major product data in the same manner for smaller and smaller customers and continue with other products as the information becomes available from the Sales history, until the impact potential for customers is deemed low.
- The next step will be to form the organization around this process, which is usually somewhat different than the typical organization.
- The implementation of the process would necessitate education and training of all those who would be affected as this process will involve changes in both tasks and thought processes.
- The method of analyzing the demand patterns currently being used in most firms is slow and cumbersome, as it involves transferring data from system to system for display and individual manual comparisons and analysis. A more efficient means of analyzing the data would necessitate a more comprehensive system to replace the spreadsheet systems. Two alternatives exist to address the issue:
—Develop a system,
—Purchase a system.

Purchasing a system is typically more practical as development is a time-consuming process.

The team would begin to review software packages. A designed or purchased system would have to contain these primary functions.
1. Statistical Forecasting and Override Capability.
2. The Ability to Collect and Maintain a Substantial Number of Files for Numerous Demand Sources.
3. Demand Segregating and Aggregating Capability
4. Demand Management Files to Monitor Current Predicted Demand.
5. "What If" Capability
6. Product Master Plan Format (See Figure 1) for Efficient Transfer to a Master Schedule.
7. Grouping by Code
8. Demand Pattern Development
9. Data Storage Flexibility

10. Use of Statistical Calculations and Acquired Data
11. Direct Input from Demand Source
12. Multi-Level Relationships
13. Ability to Aggregate on Command
- A detailed, explicit procedure must be developed to describe the steps, sequence of events, responsibilities, and how to use the system(s) involved.

In summary, it must be understood that this Demand Prediction Process requires a significant amount of data storage, analysis and manipulation, depending on the number of and types of customers a business maintains. Firms considering this approach will usually change organizational structure and functional responsibilities to assure that adequate resources are available.

About the Author

Philip F. Helle is a principal of Helle Associates, a consulting firm specializing in Enterprise Resource Planning and Business Engineering related consulting and education.

Mr. Helle has guided manufacturing firms of all sizes successfully through Manufacturing Excellence, Demand Management, Plant Layout, Group Incentive, and MRP II programs during his many years of consulting and educating. His experience has included metal working, chemical, pharmaceutical, electronics, aerospace, furniture making, and textile environments. The variety of sizes of companies includes Divisions of Fortune 100 and range to privately held small firms.

Mr. Helle has an A.S. in Industrial Engineering from Central New England College, a B.S. in Industrial Management from Northeastern University, and is a graduate of the SIM Management program at Worcester Polytechnic Institute.

He is a certified practitioner in the field of Production and Inventory Management and has been active in APICS for over twenty years, serving as President in 1970–1971 and on the Board of Directors for the Worcester County Chapter for 19 years.

He has been an instructor for Worcester Polytechnic Institute in the Continuing Professional Education Program for many years, offering a number of seminars for the business community.

Mr. Helle has been a frequent speaker and educator at local meetings and workshops and has spoken at regional chapters for many years. He has presented a variety of topics at International APICS conferences and Region I APICS conferences. In addition, he has presented at Regional Purchasing Society conferences, local Industrial Engineering conferences, and Finance/Accounting conferences.

Reprinted from the 1998 APICS Conference Proceedings.

How to Build Your "Knowledge Chain" for Success Through to Your Customers: A Case Study

James G. Hutzel, CPIM

The objective of this presentation is to demonstrate how to implement Vendor Managed Inventory (VMI) with key Customer Partners to ensure the proper flow of finished goods to your customers. Among some of the elements that will be covered are how to incorporate EDI, Internet capabilities, Demand Management techniques and processes, and Agile Manufacturing techniques to facilitate an overall Customer/Supplier Partnership which is required to successfully implement VMI.

What Is VMI?

The concept of VMI is to manage your finished goods throughout the Supply Chain into your customers' plants and processes. Some companies also call this process Efficient Customer Response or Continuous Replenishment. It serves to minimize lead times since you receive "early warning" information concerning significant demand pattern changes at the point of sale or distribution for the customer. You want to obtain the demand stream as early in their process as you can in order to obtain the most timely and accurate information on an SKU by SKU basis. Not all of your customers will be candidates for this process and some may not be interested when you introduce the subject to them. However, for those that do commit and when the project succeeds, you can become "indispensable" to your customer.

Overall Scope of Project

The VMI process is one of close coordination between links in the Supply Chain. In fact, it serves to change the "link" in the Supply Chain to a "pipe" with a flow process for all resources and material. We will be presenting how our company went about implementing the VMI process with some of its key customers. We started out by identifying demand patterns for the product that we produce for these customers. Concurrent with that, our sales people were making contacts with customers who we had analyzed and thought to be candidates for this type of process. We will cover this process in more detail later on.

Some of the work done to analyze demand patterns for the product was part of the selling process to convince our customers that we could continue to manage our items in their inventory. We had a meeting to introduce the demand patterns for selected items in order to convince them that the process added real value to our relationship and to the Supply Chain process. The item we picked is displayed in **Figure 1**. This item was a high demand item (an "A" item), and as soon as we completed the analysis, we saw that we had a significant demand drop over the last several weeks. We discussed this issue

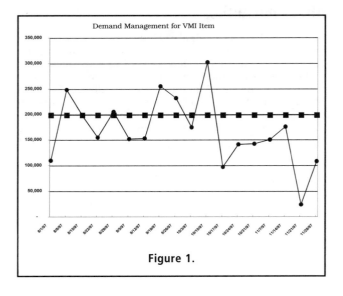

Figure 1.

with our customer during the initial meeting a few days later. We asked what was happening concerning demand for this item. They thought for a few moments and then replied, "We were promoting another item during that time frame and it moved demand from this item (the one we were analyzing) to the one being promoted." We had then reinforced one of our points that VMI required regular, frequent communication of this type of change so that we could proactively plan the correct flow of materials for all items. We also reinforced the statement we had made about being able to handle and respond to Demand Management information once we had dedicated ourselves to dealing with it on a routine basis.

Our company was introduced to the concept of Vendor Managed Inventory through the consultant who was leading our Agile Manufacturing project. VMI is a great complement to your World Class Manufacturing initiative.

Why Do VMI?

- Shorter Lead Times
- Less Inventory
- Improved Customer Service
- Better Overall Response to End Customer Demand
- Less Time Involved In Planning Processes
- Improved Communication.

Let's discuss each of these in a little more detail. Lead times are reduced since we are able to eliminate time-consuming links in the Supply Chain and get advanced information about usage of items in our customer's inventory.

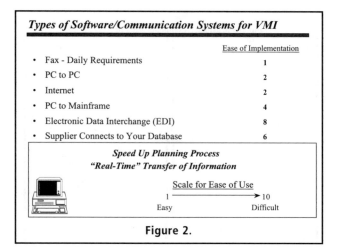

Figure 2.

We can be very proactive in Master Scheduling these items when we see changes in the demand for them. If we have long lead times for critical components, we can release a MPS requirement or a Firm Planned Order (FPO) to cover that critical component based on early demand information from the VMI process. A long-lead-time item for our company is paper, and some paper mills quote lead times of 30 to 40 days for some of the types of paper we use. We need to shorten that lead time however we can and the VMI process offers us a way to do just that.

The VMI process results in less inventory for both the customer and the supplier since it reduces lead time and eliminates non-value-added activities (primarily communication links) which comprise most administrative and planning lead times. One of my favorite expressions describing the effects of VMI is to "exchange information for inventory." When we have uncertainty of information about demand in the Supply Chain or when it takes too long to move and respond to information, then we need inventory to cover our response time. Inventory, of course, can be the wrong inventory since the longer the time span we are covering, the less accurate our forecast or guess will be. Also the more likely that the item could go obsolete or be damaged in handling in the warehouse. So, VMI, in conjunction with other world class initiatives like Agile Manufacturing, helps to eliminate the need for unnecessary inventory.

Since we are getting the demand information directly from point of use in our customer's distribution channel, we are reducing lead times throughout the replenishment process. This improves accuracy of forecasting since we are forecasting a shorter horizon; therefore customer service levels improve dramatically. For the reasons listed above, we have much better response to end-customer demand. A week reduced out of the Supply Chain results in shorter lead times, less inventory, improved customer service levels, as well as less time involved in the planning process. Purchase orders become unnecessary for individual items since it addresses replenishment as a continuous process, not one that is batch oriented. We have negotiated time periods that are covered by our customer so we can start our manufacturing processes, cover our long lead time raw materials, and allocate work center capacities based on the desired product mix. Our Master Production Schedule also plays a key role in providing the right information at the right time. We will cover that in more detail later on.

As a result of improvements in all of these areas, communications are improved. Not only is communication a "result," it is also a "driver" for these processes. As we improve communications of demand for our product throughout the Supply Chain, we eliminate non-value-added activities.

Management Commitment, Investment, Resources Required

The project requires management commitment from both partners. Both your company and your customer must have full management commitment and "buy-in" for this project to be successful. Commitment means understanding what is required over the life of the project and the resources required to initiate and maintain this process. It is especially important for you to identify key decision-makers within your customer's organization and ensure that they are committed and involved in the VMI process. They must understand the benefits as well as the resources required to implement VMI. Education is also critical to the overall success of the project, both for implementation as well as for the ongoing, maintenance phase of this process. Your sales staff plays a key role in this initial identification as to whether or not a given customer is a good candidate for VMI.

Investment of time and resources within your company is also necessary to keep this project vital until it becomes a way of life. Dedication of personnel from Demand Planning, Master Production Scheduling, Customer Service as well as Sales is required to make this program successful. After the initial commitment, it is important to educate those who will be involved in any aspect of the VMI process. People on both sides need to fully understand how the process will work and what their role is to make it successful. The education can be tailored to the individual way that VMI is being installed at that particular customer. Rough-cut evaluations of communications software are also recommended at this time. That helps define the scope of the project in terms of size, investment, and the number of people required. If you elect to go with a full Electronic Data Interchange (EDI) project then you will need much more involvement from your IS department and the IS team from your customer. This obviously adds cost and can increase the lead time for the project. (See **Figure 2**.)

As you can see, the scale for ease of use allows you to tailor the project to your budget as well as your timetable. The ease of implementation scale addresses the aspect of time, cost, and the number of people required on the project team. Many times, the VMI initiative results from a directive by one of your customers, especially one of your larger customers. They may have a sense of urgency to get this process started and they obviously have a great deal of leverage with the top management team of your company. My first exposure to VMI was on a project like that and the customer went so far as to set up the communication systems and computer systems that they wanted us to utilize. It gave them a common system, which improved their efficiency and gave us a baseline to start with.

The factor of primary importance for success with VMI is communication. That means verbal communication in addition to just the transfer of files or planning data. This is not an automatic computer system; it is rather a people-based system. You need to stress the open and free exchange of information in all aspects of your implementation of VMI. This is true of the project portion of VMI, during implementation, as well as later when the system

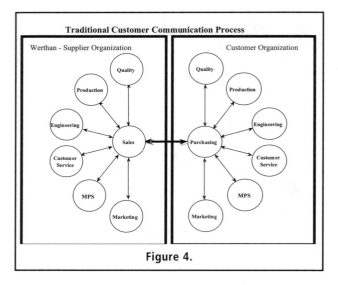

Figure 4.

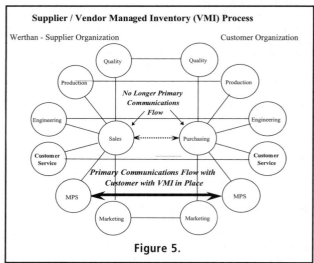

Figure 5.

is up and running. This information includes, but is not limited to, promotions, product phase-in/phase-out, opening of additional distribution channels, promotions by competition, and so on. Basically, we become an extension of our customer in terms of obtaining, analyzing and responding to demand information.

Organizational Issues

As you set up the VMI process you must address organizational issues within your company. (See **Figure 3**.) The primary contacts are between your sales force and the purchasing agent or buyer within the customer organization. When initiatives such as VMI are initiated, it is important to:

- Dedicate personnel to the project and for support on an ongoing basis.
- Educate all of those who are involved (see **Figure 4** for a short list of functions).
- Provide the proper justification for top management so that you get the required commitment.
- Realign customer and supplier organizations and contacts to enhance the communication and minimize the links of communication (see **Figure 5**).

Let's take the first point and discuss it in more detail. One of the things we have done is to combine the traditional Customer Service Representative position, the Master Production Scheduler, Material Requirements Planner, and Shop Floor Scheduling positions into one position. This position is dedicated to performing all aspects of the job in regards to planning product for our customer. This minimizes the number of communication links internally within your own organization and improves communication of issues to customers as well as to suppliers as required. This vertically integrated position requires the types of skills acquired through association with APICS. One of the job requirements we have set for this position at Werthan Packaging is CPIM or CIRM certification. APICS certification-level skills are put to use by our VMI associate every day in the dynamic marketplace we live in. This is required in order to maintain and improve the VMI process and serve our customers better.

Concerning the second point, the educational process has been ongoing and comprehensive in nature. We focused a lot of the initial education with the Sales force at the beginning of our project since they were the ones on the front line, talking to the customers on a frequent basis. They did a lot of the preliminary evaluation to see if a particular customer fit our criteria for VMI and to determine if that customer was interested in participating

in the VMI process. At this time, we are getting an excellent acceptance rate from our largest and most repetitive customers. As our sales force has increased in their knowledge of what this process is all about, they have become quite effective at explaining to our customers that the process adds value to the Supply Chain.

The third point is about justifying to our top management that the VMI process will strengthen our relationship with those customers who agree to VMI, it helps to reduce lead times, it reduces inventory, it is cost effective, it is a priority for us as well as our customers, and it makes us "indispensable" to those customers who partner with us in VMI. The 'bottom line" is that VMI is a good business decision. We had some help in this category thanks to our Agile Manufacturing consultant, who has helped convince our top management that VMI is a worthwhile business objective.

The fourth point covers some essentials that are required to enable the VMI process to operate at peak efficiency. As shown in Figure 5, the primary communication between companies moves to a direct link with Master Scheduler communicating to Master Scheduler/Material Requirements Planner, rather than our Sales person to the customer's Purchasing Agent and then through the rest of the customer's organization. This eliminates unnecessary

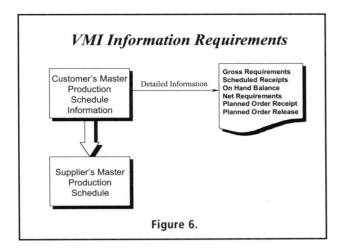

Figure 6.

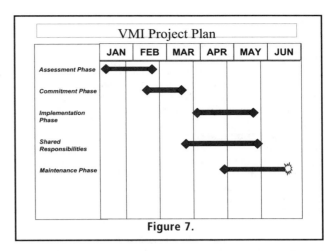

Figure 7.

communication links within the Supply Chain and speeds up the process. In our case, our primary VMI person is a Customer Demand Management Representative. This individual has APICS-level experience in the following areas: Demand Management, Forecasting, Master Production Scheduling, Capacity Planning (Resource Requirements Planning and Capacity Requirements Planning), Just-In-Time practices, Shop Floor Scheduling, and Production and Inventory Control.

Vendor Managed Inventory Process

VMI needs to be set up to provide you with all the information you need to schedule your plant and to replenish your items in your customer's facility with very little intervention from personnel at the customer's site. To do this we need demand information for the customer's product, on-hand balance information for our items in their warehouse and forecasted demand information for the end product that consumes our item. The rest of the traditional Master Production Scheduling information we already have at our disposal: scheduled receipts (shipments that have left your facility and are in transit to your customer's facility), ECN changes, and other pertinent information for good inventory control (see **Figure 6**).

In addition to these items, we developed a "run strategy" for the VMI items within our Master Production Scheduling system, a planning bill of material to group these items and separate planner codes to help us keep these items from blending in with the rest of our ERP database. While performing the demand analysis for the items, we also developed lot sizes based on current demand, safety stock levels where appropriate, and time fence dates. These were all formalized and loaded into our ERP system. This made the overall Master Production Scheduling process an integral part of the VMI effort with this customer and made it difficult for our planners to forget what we were doing on a given item. (Some of these items are shown on **Figure 7**.) It also fully integrated these items into our ERP system through the MPS system.

I cannot stress the importance of this step enough. You need to have a strong, well-functioning Master Production Scheduling process in order to develop the disciplines and practices that will lead to a successful VMI process. This is about balancing supply and demand, and that is Master Production Scheduling's forte.

We are using our Master Production Scheduling process and software to directly implement the actions required to effect changes as suggested by the dynamic

demand information. Once we developed the planning bill and planning parameters such as lot size and appropriate time fences, we put them into our Master Production Scheduling system. We began initial requirements several weeks out in the future; that way we didn't have significant changes to our existing Master Production Schedule.

We began seeing immediately that the system was telling us that we had to do things differently than what we had been doing. We have had some problems with some customers not allowing us adequate lead times to process our orders within full lead time. We started this Master Production Schedule process with lead times in line with where they were previously. Our company has two major steps in the production of paper bags. The first is the printing of the outer wrap of the bag; the second is the actual tubing and bottoming of the bag. Production run rates are high for both of these operations, but at this time we still have substantial setup times in both printing and tubing. This compels us to produce product with larger lot sizes, and of course this is passed along to our customers as well.

Some of their plants also have large run quantities; it is not unusual for us to run 500,000 to 1,000,000 bags in one production run. Our longest element of lead time is typically for paper for the printed sheet. This can be as long as 30 to 40 days. Obviously, we need to cover or offset that lead time with some amount of forecasting and the planning bill of material also serves us well in that regard.

One of the first things we encountered as we were starting the system up was that the it was telling us to start producing product by telling us to release planned orders at the Master Production Schedule level and also at the printed paper level. Under the old system, which we were running parallel at our customer's request, we had not yet received an authorization for production. This was the beauty of the new system. It was recommending that we start production now in order to avoid expediting problems and this is just what we needed. We had just been through a period of time where we had been having problems supplying this customer consistently and on time. In the case of VMI, the system was being proactive and telling us to commit to production in order to avoid a potential problem. It was doing exactly what we had designed it to do and was trying to keep us out of trouble. We then communicated with our customer that we needed commitments earlier in the process so we could proceed with production. As we improved this process we were able to reduce lead times to shorter time frames. We were also able to drop the parallel system and the redundancy of effort by relieving our customer of immediate replenishment planning responsibilities for our items. We now monitor and plan replenishment when it is required based on the numbers in our VMI system.

I must stress that this system is not an automatic one. It requires regular, frequent attention to details and investigation of some messages that sometimes do not always make complete sense. It requires the attention of trained people who know our business, our customer's business and the dynamic marketplace. It requires monthly maintenance of the planning bills to ensure that they still reflect the product mix that is current for the future, as well as the present. Master Production Scheduling also must regularly and frequently review planning parameters, such as lot sizes, lead times, ordering patterns, shifting mix issues, Resource Requirements Planning, demonstrated manufacturing performance, and others. This also requires APICS-level experience to maintain and enhance the effectiveness of the VMI and Master Production Schedule processes.

Computers/Hardware

As was mentioned before, there are several types of software or computer systems that can serve as a vehicle for the communication process so vital for VMI. Some specific VMI packages are available. However, you need not invest in a specific and possibly expensive package. Many companies start with a VMI setup that can be handled with a fax machine. The KISS principle applies to this process in terms of the time required as well as the resources required. The primary goal is to get the process started as soon as practical and to communicate demand management information between supplier and customer.

The human interaction is the most important element in the VMI process; the computers serve to help link up information flow between individuals. With the falling cost of computer hardware and software today, cost is no longer a significant factor. A good VMI setup should cost each partner less than $5,000. A PC spreadsheet or PC database program may be all that is required for users on both sides to freely exchange information on a daily basis. Internet capabilities continue to provide new options once security issues are resolved. Most IS personnel have legitimate concern about sending proprietary company data across the Internet today. It is extremely cost-effective and fault-tolerant since the Internet is comprised of so many different networked computers; when one node goes down, another takes its place.

Implementation Plan

The project was detailed in Gantt chart format as seen by referring to Figure 7. The major phases of the project are as follows:
• Assessment Phase
• Commitment Phase
• Implementation Phase
• Shared Responsibilities
• Maintenance Phase.

Assessment is extremely important since it proceeds the commitment phase. If the customer is not assessed as a good candidate for VMI, then the investment of time and effort should stop at that point. Until the customer is ready to provide the needed support and resources for the project, save your time and effort for other projects that are viable.

Once the customer is assessed as a good candidate for VMI, then the top management of that company should commit to the project. Commitment means more than verbal support. It must be supported and the management must understand what must be done to make this work. Demand information must be shared, promotional information, changes in items (ECNs), phase out of an item, and so on.

The implementation phase is the start of the actual work in putting together the system, starting to work as partners. A project team needs to be put together so that common deadlines can be established an worked on. The project team needs to be empowered so that they make the VMI process work. The process is initialized, typically with a few, significant items that both partners agree to. This way, the process can be piloted and refined without burdening everyone with a lot of items and a new system to implement.

During this time, shared responsibilities are defined. These include but are not limited to communications required by both partners. The definition of a communication process including both verbal and computerized formats. When files are to be transferred, when there are meetings or conference calls, all must be defined so that communications take place when expected. Information flow can be piloted and this improved flow will quickly communicate promotions or spikes in demand. In addition, an "anticipated delay process" is put in place to communicate changes in the supply side.

The maintenance phase is fairly self explanatory. World class initiatives such as VMI need regular review and scrutiny to ensure that all elements are functioning properly and at peak efficiency.

Benefits Obtained from Implementation

The benefits of a well-functioning VMI process are as follows. Lead times and finished goods inventory will be reduced in the Supply Chain. This is facilitated through the tighter control of, and quicker response to, changes in demand for these items. Savings of up to 20 percent are not unusual for those items that are being handled with VMI. This percentage will result in savings of $1 million of on-hand inventory for our company. Customer service levels will rise to all-time highs. Vertical integration of planning, customer service duties, demand management, and other functions results in faster turnaround on orders and less communication snafus. Other less tangible benefits are smoother production flows, fewer interruptions to the Master Production Schedule, and improved quality of work life for those involved in a company utilizing VMI. My advice is—start evaluating your customers to see if they would be good candidates for a partnership with you utilizing VMI.

About the Author

James G. Hutzel, CPIM, has been involved in manufacturing management for more than 25 years in positions including first line supervisor, general foreman, manager, director and group director. He also has consulting experience specializing in ERP and DRP implementations. Other positions held include materials manager, director of production planning and inventory control, and group director of materials for various other companies. He is experienced in repetitive manufacturing, job shop, flow manufacturing, and JIT environments. Company experience includes General Motors, Jenn-Air Company, Esselte Pendaflex, Frigidaire Company and others. He has been the driving force for MRP II and

ERP implementations as well as JIT initiatives at several companies.

Mr. Hutzel is recognized by APICS as CPIM and is currently a certification class instructor for the MITE Chapter of APICS. He is also on the APICS book review board. He is currently employed with Werthan Packaging in Nashville, Tennessee, and leads the production inventory control, customer service, demand management, and master planning functions. Werthan Packaging is currently implementing VMI, ERP and Agile Manufacturing practices simultaneously.

Reprinted from the 1999 APICS Conference Proceedings.

Transportation! The Hidden Gold Mine for Small Business

James P. Knechtges and Michael J. McAlpin, CPIM

The objective of this presentation is to provide small businesses with the opportunity to see real-world results from two different companies' successful transportation plans. We will show how these companies directly improved profitability through transportation management.

In most small and mid-sized companies, transportation is considered a necessary evil. We view it differently. We look at it as an untapped gold mine. Its potential to add profit to a company's bottom line is significant. As a starting point, we will present an overview of essential transportation concepts, including modes, terminology, and freight classifications. Next we will cover key points to negotiate with carriers and examples of quantifiable cost savings achieved through these negotiations.

When we are finished, participants will be able to develop and implement a transportation plan based on these concepts. They will learn how to evaluate and measure the degree of success with respect to the plan and how to continuously assess and improve the plan.

Modes of Transportation

There are a few terms we would like to discuss.

LTL: LTL stands for "less than truckload," meaning a shipper is not giving a carrier a full truckload worth of freight. The size of a full truck may be compared to a 48' truck carrying no more than 45,000 lbs. per load. The carrier makes money by putting multiple LTL loads together and combining a full truckload and taking it to the final destination area.

Truck Load: That is where you are buying an entire truckload from point A to point B.

Intermodal: Where you use a combination of trucking and rail service to move a load to its final destination. It could also be extended to ocean and then back to ground again for final delivery. Intermodal has many possible combinations, not just one.

Air: Moving freight via air is the most expensive mode and also the quickest. Two-day and 3-to-5-day air options can help minimize the costs. Shippers also tend to pay a premium for this service.

Small Parcel: This is a mode of transportation used to move product that does not have enough weight or size to warrant being shipped via truck. There are many small parcel carriers in the United States that can accommodate these needs. We are all familiar with those big brown trucks.

Ocean and International Freight: Product is moved in containers that are 20' or 40' long. Material is packed to maximize the utilization of the cubic space or weight depending on product density. Ocean and international shipping require another entire presentation. We are simply mentioning it here.

Own Fleet: Moving your product using your own trucks and drivers.

When any of these transportation modes are used in conjunction with finding the best way to serve your customer at the most reasonable price, then you have tapped the hidden gold mine.

Concepts and Terminology

NMFC: "The National Motor Freight Classification is a pricing tool that provides a comparison of commodities moving in interstate and intrastate transport. Based on an evaluation of density, stowability, ease of handling, and liability, the commodities are grouped into one of 18 classes. The NMFC provides both carriers and shippers with a standard by which to begin pricing negotiations and greatly simplifies the comparative evaluation of the many thousands of products moving in today's marketplace." (http://www.erols.com/nmfta)

The National Motor Freight Traffic Association, Inc., (NMFTA) is a nonprofit organization with thousands of members throughout the United States and Canada. Its members are primarily motor carriers in the LTL transportation market. NMFTA offers a variety of transportation services to both shippers and member carriers. In conjunction with the National Classification Committee (NCC), NMFTA publishes the National Motor Freight Classification (NMFC). Their phone number is (703) 838-1810.

Freight classes range from class 50 to 500. They are in sequence: Class 50, 55, 60, 65, 70, 77.5, 85, 92.5, 100, 110, 125, 150, 175, 200, 250, 300, 400, and 500. Generally, higher freight classes have higher transportation charges since they have less density and more mass.

It is important for a shipper to understand the freight classifications for all inbound and outbound product. If you are uncertain, ask your carriers, a third-party logistics provider, or the NMFTA for help.

Keep in mind that a carrier and shipper need to figure out what to charge and pay for a shipment. What should a carrier or shipper charge or be willing to pay in order to ship a truckload of steel or a truckload of feathers? Shippers and carriers both needed help on these issues as they related to volume versus weight. This is why the NMFC was developed.

FAK (Freight All Kinds): One way you can get additional discounts from a freight carrier is to have all of your freight classified as one generic classification. This is called a Freight All Kinds (FAK) tariff. This simplifies freight management for the shipper tremendously.

FOB	Freight	Who Pays	Who Owns Freight in Transit?	Where Does Title Pass?
Origin	Collect	Buyer	Buyer	Seller's Plant
Origin	Prepaid	Seller	Buyer	Seller's Plant
Dest	Collect	Buyer	Seller	Buyer's Receiving Dock
Dest	Prepaid	Buyer	Seller	Buyer's Receiving Dock

Figure 1. FOB in Plain English

Additionally, a FAK may give you a discount off another commodity. For example, if you are moving a light class 150 product and you have in effect a FAK of class 70, you are receiving a discount on the cost of the shipping for the product. This type of tariff logic can reduce substantially the costs of shipping products.

Freight companies understand fully the effect a FAK has on creating additional discounts. They may offer you a FAK at a slightly higher freight class compared to your average freight class. Once again, it becomes critical that you have a thorough understanding of your freight classes because in this example your freight charges would be higher. From a position of knowledge, you can negotiate a better freight program for you and your company.

Another concept that is extremely important is FOB (free on board). FOB helps us to determine who pays the freight, who owns the freight, and when title passes. It also helps determine who is responsible for filing a claim if the shipment is damaged or lost (see **figure 1**).

Consignee: The receiver of the goods.

Tariff: A tariff is simply the contract that a shipper and carrier agree upon before they enter into business. Inside the tariff, the base rates and discounts are defined.

Discount: Freight discounts, sometimes called incentives, are simple percentage reductions off of a freight bill. They are there for the asking, whether it be LTL, truckload, small parcel, air, or intermodal. These basic discounts are often in the range of 35 to 50 percent. Discounts can go much higher based upon the freight class, volume, mix, and other less tangible negotiating points.

Another part of the tariff is the accessorial charges.

Accessorial Charges: Additional charges the carrier may invoice. Examples are

- **Single Shipment Charges**: having only one shipment to pick up at a facility may not allow carrier to spread their pickup fixed costs over several shipments; therefore they want to add additional charges for only one shipment received.
- **Document Fees**: Many times carriers will want to charge to copy the original bill of lading or for making corrections.
- **Proof of Delivery, Redelivery, and Special Equipment Charges**: if your customer requires a lift gate.

Some carriers even have accessorial charges for deliveries to high traffic, congested areas, like the New York City garment district! Many, but not all, of these charges can be negotiated out or minimized as part of your tariff.

Strategies

Developing a strategic freight plan is the fundamental first step to tapping the hidden gold mine the world of transportation management offers. While developing this plan, keep the mindset of creating a win-win strategy for your company, customers, suppliers, and carriers.

First, we create the framework for our desired outcomes, such as a reduction of freight costs as a percentage of cost of goods sold or sales as measured on a monthly profit and loss statement. We determine a transportation plan for both our inbound and outbound freight. We gather hard facts on how much freight we have to bring to the negotiation table. We determine the best course of action for both inbound and outbound transportation requirements and combine them to get us the best discounts or negotiate them separately based on their unique requirements. Transportation strategies should include negotiations between (1) you and your freight carriers, (2) you and your customer, and (3) you and your product supplier (they may have better unique transportation options than anything you may have negotiated). So, having these three options gives you the best possible opportunity to explore finding the lowest landed cost through these sourcing options.

Secondly, determine what type of carrier is best suited to our goals. A regional, short-haul, or long-haul carrier?

Regional carriers can be very niche-oriented and serve a very localized marketplace. In many instances, they can pick up and deliver the same day or next day without expedite charges and do it so effectively that they are profitable and offer a lower cost than a short-haul carrier.

Short-haul carriers have a larger geographical base than most regional carriers and can move your freight in one or two days. Their expertise is in picking up the freight and getting it delivered quickly. Short-haul carriers can be used strategically to minimize your transportation costs.

Long-haul carriers also move freight from point A to point B, but over greater distances, e.g., East Coast to West Coast. They are experts at taking your freight, combining it with other freight, and moving it to your destination quickly. All of the above publish and sell against their transit times to help you determine what mode of transportation is best for your needs.

Lastly, our strategic transportation plan must address our internal ability to rate and route shipments across our multiple portfolio of carriers, suppliers carriers and customers' inbound freight programs. We must assess the use of (1) manual systems, (2) automated information systems, or (3) third-party logistics providers (TPLPs) to accomplish this rating and routing function. This is the function that on a daily basis will save your company a tremendous amount of money. One misrouted shipment could be a difference of $20 to thousands of dollars. Your company cannot afford to neglect this function or let the element of time and convenience override the requirement of finding the most favorable rating and routing.

This takes time, coordination, and effort to rate and route a shipment across your carrier portfolio and can be done fairly quickly and easily if planned and done on a systematic day-to-day basis. The cost savings can have enormous returns on the bottom line.

Companies cannot afford not to manage their freight. Large and medium-size companies often manage their freight themselves. This requires a staff that is capable of managing all freight issues themselves, from rating and routing, to negotiating with carriers, to auditing and paying the bills. This can be done with manual systems and is increasingly being done by robust software systems. They make the rating and routing function much more streamlined and affordable to companies of any size, without adding additional staff in most instances, making the ROI extremely attractive for the dollars invested.

Third-party logistics providers offer a number of services from auditing and paying freight bills, to consulting and negotiations. Some TPLPs will leverage all freight from all clients to obtain the highest discount possible.

Negotiation Expectations

When companies enter negotiations with carriers, they should have a clear understanding of what they expect with respect to service, delivery, reliability, and competitive pricing.

Service: Good customer service and responsiveness are crucial ingredients to a strong relationship with our carriers. Other services, such as load-tracking, may also be of importance. A local, accessible sales representative is important when problems arise.

Delivery: Are the carriers there as promised? Are they flexible with pickup times? What is their delivery performance record compared to their published transit times?

Reliability: Does the carrier invoice you accurately, using the proper freight class and applicable discount? Are you charged only for those shipments for which you are liable? Sometimes, collect shipments are invoiced as prepaid, and vice versa.

Competitive Pricing: If we can achieve a level of comfort with the first three expectations, then competitive pricing will help us make the final decision. Here it is important to not only look at the discount being offered, but also at the base rates each carrier is using. These base rates vary from carrier to carrier.

Transportation Plan

The transportation plan has two elements that must be laid out: (1) expectations you have from the carriers that serve you (what's in it for you) and (2) how you will meet the carrier's expectation (what's in it for them).

Other areas of concern on which to evaluate carriers include their operating ratio, average age of their equipment, and current insurance coverage certificate.

If the carrier's operating ratio is over 100, it means they are operating at a higher cost than revenue received. They are losing money. It is our recommendation that your carrier should be operating below 100 to be a part of your carrier portfolio.

The carrier's average age of equipment gives insight into their commitment to reinvest in their company. If they're buying and maintaining their current equipment, they are committing to the future.

Make sure you are covered under the carrier's current insurance certificate.

How you will meet the carrier's expectations (what's in it for them)?

It is important in negotiating transportation that you give carriers a background on your company and the primary shipping points. Let them know you want to be a partner with them.

You must collect and present to the carrier all your freight characteristics. Define shipping and receiving times. Define your staff's commitments to driver turnaround time. Commit to have loads ready at the times you say they are going to be ready. Have a commitment to the carrier's drivers. Driver retention is one of the bigger problems in the industry at this point and treating a carrier's driver with respect is nothing more than a business expectation.

Financial information is important to a carrier. They want to be paid promptly. Your Dun and Bradstreet ratings tell the story on your commitment to billings. Exploit your good credit ratings. Show also percentage of claims filed to total shipments.

If you have database expectations, you must define them. Do you expect them to give you a database that you can create your bill of ladings and manifest from? If so, do you expect those to be free? Can they be used across multiple carriers? Or do you have your own internally developed database system that you expect them to help you with? Since this might be the strategy of an internal information system driven by rating and routing, the issues must be brought out in the negotiation.

Things you need to bring to the table: We mentioned before freight characteristics. Let's define those a little bit more.

The historical freight data you need to give to your freight carriers to help them determine what kind of program to put forward for you are (1) how much weight, inbound and outbound, (2) the average weight of the shipments, to where outbound, and from where inbound, (3) the freight classifications of your product, and (4) a definition of your service expectations.

When Negotiating, Qualify Negotiator

Let's ask the question, with whom should you negotiate? In most instances, the carrier's sales reps are not empowered to do anything in terms of pricing. Therefore, it is important for you to go as high up the carrier's corporate ladder as possible! It is in the best interest of the shipper and the receiver to actually go out and ask for regional sales managers or even vice presidents to come and visit your company. Let them walk through your company and see firsthand what you have to offer them and why it's worthwhile for them to do business with you. Regional sales managers and vice presidents influence pricing and special requirements. Don't forget to ask for better discounts. They are out there. If the carrier wants your business, they will go after it aggressively. They will have developed a strategy based on the freight characteristics you supplied to move your freight profitably.

One other thing that matters is size. The smaller the company, the less likely you will be able to entice the attention of the powers that influence pricing.

In some instances, using a TPLP as a small company may be worthwhile because you can combine the total weights that the TPLP has to gain the best possible advantage. However, as you're moving from a small to a medium-size company, the amount of weight you are moving may increase and be more enticing to negotiate yourself. The larger you are, the more you may have the ability to have clout with the supplier.

Weight matters as well. Lightweight, heavyweight, and a mixture between light and heavyweight all determine how you might do your negotiations. Again, with whom you negotiate depends on a combination of size and weight. But remember, the higher up the ladder you go, the better off you are.

The Carrier Selection Process

Once you have the new pricing from the carriers, you need to define a review process. Letting the carrier know the process of defining the chosen carriers is important. Define the time frame for choosing the carriers that will be in your carrier mix. Prior to the review process, you must make sure the tariff is in place and effective. If you give a load to a carrier, have you awarded them the contract? Or

Discount results for company A and B		
Results Company A		
	# of LTL Carriers	Average Discount
1996	4	55-62%
1997	7	64-68%
1998	4	64-74%
Results Company B		
	# of LTL Carriers	Average Discount
1996	13	35-40%
1997	4	50-55%
1998	2	62-68%

Figure 2.

are you testing them because you need to evaluate a load to determine their service, delivery, and reliability? However, if they don't have competitive pricing up front, it is not worth tendering a load to make the determination. They must have competitive pricing in order for you to tender a few loads for evaluation. This is your obligation to follow through and evaluate them on service, delivery, and reliability, as defined earlier.

Audit your freight bills, both inbound and outbound. Review incentives in the tariff versus the invoice. It is at this point you may find thousands and thousands of dollars you can save just by taking a few minutes to review the invoice against your tariff. This is the reliability in billing accuracy in the carrier evaluation. Make sure you are not being charged for freight-collect shipments. Errors do happen in billings, and it is your obligation to audit your bills no matter how few or how many there are.

Real-World Examples

Company "A"

OEM, wholesaler, $40 MM sales, and 151 employees.

Strategy: Internal logistics purchasing negotiates and third-party software used internally to rate and route. Freight rated and routed based on rules (clerical). Preferred carrier list based on (1st) service, delivery, reliability and (2nd) cost. We audit and pay freight bills in accounts payable. Own volume generates clout for discounts. Request for LTL published pricing (a one-shot-deal bid).

Modes: Small parcel; ground, hundred wt., air, LTL, TL, international, inbound, freight forwarder.

What's in it for them (carriers): Freight characteristics were collected and presented to carriers for their first look at total freight available. Inbound freight broken down by state weight, total weight of 2.7 MM #'s. Outbound freight broken down by state weight by NMFC class to each state, total orders to each state, average order weight to each state, average freight class to each state and total weight to all states of 7.3 MM #'s.

Results: We saved big bucks! Carriers responded! Refer to **figure 2** for discount incentive changes for both company A and company B. These were received after formal executed transportation plans were developed and negotiated.

Company B

SUPPLIER ROUTING INSTRUCTIONS
(effective January 1, 1996)

All shipments to Company B are to be made FOB Origin, Freight Collect, as indicated below. Reference Company B Purchase Order Number on all Bills of Lading.

Shipment Type	Total Weight	Carrier
Ground Shipments no individual package more than 35 lbs.	1 - 125 lbs	XXX
Air Shipments	1 - 100 lbs	XXX
Air Shipments	101 - 500 lbs	XXX
Air Shipments	more than 500 lbs	Contact Buyer for Routing Prior to Shipment
Truckload	more than 7,000 lbs and/or more than 11 ft. of trailer space	Contact Buyer for Routing Prior to Shipment
L T L (Less Than Truckload)	less than 7,000 lbs	See Below

USE THIS FREIGHT CARRIER	FOR LTL SHIPMENTS TO / FROM:									
Carrier A	CT	DE	MA	MD	ME	NH	NJ	NY	RI	VT
Carrier B	IN	MI	OH							
Carrier C	IL	KY	NC	PA	VA	WV	WI			
Carrier D	AL AR AZ CA CO DC FL GA ID KS LA MN MS MO MT NE NV NM ND OK OR SC SD TN TX UT WA WY									

NOTES:

ALL NEXT-DAY, SECOND-DAY, and AIR SHIPMENTS must be authorized by buyer.

NON-COMPLIANCE WITH THESE ROUTING INSTRUCTIONS WILL RESULT IN A CHARGE-BACK OF EXCESS FREIGHT COSTS, PLUS A $ 25.00 ADMINISTRATIVE FEE FOR EACH CHARGE-BACK.

If you have any problems with any of our designated carriers, please contact Mike McAlpin at (716) 266-3060 extension 139.

File: Knechtges Figure 3

Figure 3.

Company "B"

Company B's strategy focused on using the services of a TPLP. We began using the TPLP simply to audit and pay our freight bills. In doing so, we began to collect historical freight data, which we would eventually use in our freight negotiations.

After one year, we reviewed the data. We were using 13 different carriers for our inbound freight. Our suppliers were using the carriers with whom they had a relationship. Discounts averaged 35 to 40 percent.

With the help of our TPLP, we reduced the number of carriers to four. We then sat down with each of the four and negotiated new discounts (average discounts were now 50 to 55 percent). We also published a supplier routing guide. This guide specifies which carriers all suppliers should use by state and defines a penalty for nonconformance. Large truckload shipments are routed per our TPLP recommendations (see **figure 3**).

In succeeding years, our business (and our freight) increased. We reduced the number of designated LTL carriers to two (one regional and one long-haul carrier), which has enabled us to increase our freight discounts (now average 62 to 68 percent). Negotiations with carriers have shifted back in-house, although bill consolidation and auditing is still through TPLP. Refer to **figure 4** for an analysis of the success both company A and company B have achieved.

The plans were different, but freight as a percentage of COGS has dramatically been reduced in both companies. These results are the new benchmarks for future transportation plans.

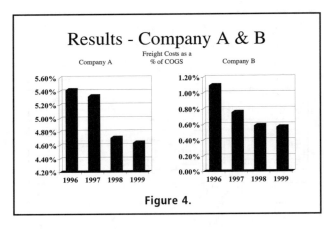

Figure 4.

Summary

The objective to provide small businesses the opportunity to see real-world results from two different companies' successful transportation plans was guided by the desire to help other companies learn from our experiences. We encourage you to develop a strategy for negotiating your freight and formulate a plan that will directly improve your company's profitability through transportation management.

Transportation truly is a hidden gold mine for companies to discover and manage. We ask you to step up to the challenge and unearth the hidden profits available to those that develop, negotiate, implement, and monitor their transportation.

About the Authors

James P. Knechtges is vice president of purchasing for Impact Products, Inc., of Toledo, Ohio, an OEM/wholesaler to the janitorial/sanitary supply industry. He has over 12 years of experience in the areas of purchasing, instructing, production planning, inventory control, distribution, quality control, public warehousing, pricing, software selection, and information systems. Prior to Impact Products, Inc., he held positions as instructor for the Department of Management at Bowling Green State University and lecturer for the Ohio State University. He was a presenter at the 1998 APICS International Conference and has led discussion groups at past APICS International Conference Roundtables for the Small Manufacturing SIG. He has spoken at numerous chapter and student dinner meetings. Mr. Knechtges has served as chairman of the APICS Small Manufacturing SIG, APICS Region III director of chapter management, chairman of the Toledo Chapter of APICS 1998-1999, president 1996-1997. He has earned an M.B.A. and B.S.B.A. from Bowling Green State University.

Michael J. McAlpin, CPIM, is an owner and executive vice president of McAlpin Industries, Inc. He has 13 years of experience in the areas of purchasing, production planning, inventory control, customer service, distribution, and systems administration. He holds a bachelor's degree from Rochester Institute of Technology in chemistry and computer science. He has completed some work toward his M.B.A. He is Certified in Production and Inventory Management (CPIM). He is currently on the Small Manufacturing SIG Committee and is past president of the APICS Rochester, New York, Chapter.

Reprinted from the 1998 APICS Conference Proceedings.

How to Use V-A-T Logical Analysis to Improve Production Performance

Peter W. Langford, CFPIM, CIRM

This paper will show how V-A-T analysis, an element of the logistics portion of Theory of Constraints, will improve production performance by showing alternatives to the "traditional" guidelines of efficiency and activation. The presentation will illustrate how improved product flow is the key to increased market responsiveness and reliability of delivery promises. The presentation objective is to promote an understanding of the complex interactions between current management policies and practices, resources, and the product flows in the plant.

Learning Objective

The attendees will gain an understanding of:
- How problems experienced by a plant result from specific interactions between resources and products that exist in the plant.
- How traditional management strategies typically do not solve, and often aggravate, the problems that characterize different manufacturing environments. These traditional practices often lead good managers to make bad decisions that cause two negative effects: (a) over-activation and/or misallocation of resources, and (b) misallocation of material.
- How to identify and implement management policies that will optimize the performance of the plant.

Definitions

At this point it is generally useful to show the definitions for key terms. The following are taken from the *APICS Dictionary*, 8th Edition:

Theory of Constraints (TOC)—A management philosophy developed by Dr. Eliyahu M. Goldratt that can be viewed as three separate but interrelated areas—logistics, performance measurement, and logical thinking. Logistics include drum-buffer-rope scheduling, buffer management, and V-A-T analysis. Performance measurement includes throughput, inventory and operating expense and the five focusing steps. Thinking process tools are important in identifying the root problem (current reality tree), identifying and expanding win-win solutions (evaporating cloud and future reality tree), and developing implementation plans (prerequisite tree and transition tree). Syn: constraint theory. See: constraint management.

V-A-T analysis—A constraint management procedure for determining the general flow of parts and products from raw materials to finished products (logical product structure). A V logical structure deals with one or a few raw materials, and the product expands into a number of different products as it flows through its routings. The shape of an A logical structure is dominated by converging points.

Many raw materials are fabricated and assembled into a few finished projects. A T logical structure consists of numerous similar finished products assembled from common assemblies and subassemblies. Once the general parts flow is determined, the system control points (gating operations, convergent points, divergent points, constraints, and shipping points) can be identified and managed.

The Product Flow Diagram

The product flow diagram is the basic tool for accurately representing the product flow. It describes the basic flow and the interactions that occur in the manufacturing process. The product flow diagram facilitates understanding production planning and control problems. The product flow diagram provides management with a complete map of the various resource/product interactions that occur. This understanding allows for better identification of critical management problems. The basic building block of the diagram is the operation (or processing) performed on a specific part at a specific resource.

A sample format for presenting the station information is:

Part Identification—Process Identification
Resource Identification

The stations are connected by arrows which designate the direction of the product flow. A station may have zero, one, or more than one incoming arrows. Stations with no incoming arrows represent gateway operations and indicate the entry of material into the process. Multiple incoming arrows indicate an assembly point. Multiple outgoing arrows indicate a divergence point.

Product flow diagrams can be used to identify the dominant resource/product interactions occurring in the plant. These are the keys to understanding the fundamental problems that exist in the plant. Product flow diagrams are a valuable tool to developing a solid basis for application of TOC/CM concepts.

Classifications of Manufacturing Operations

The product flow diagram for most manufacturing operations will contain a variety of resource/product interactions. The dominant resource/product interactions provide the basis for classifying manufacturing into three major categories. The three categories are V-plants, A-plants, and T-plants. Many plants fall into one of these three categories. Some plants exhibits characteristics of more than one of the three categories and are referred to as combination plants.

For each of the three classifications, the bulk of the remainder of the presentation will discuss:

- Dominant Product Flow Characteristics
- General Characteristics
- Consequences of Traditional Management Practices
- Conventional Strategies for Improving Performance
- TOC/CM Concepts Applied.

V-Plants

The dominant product flow characteristic is that products at one stage can be transformed into several distinct products at the next stage (divergent points.) The different products share common resources at most stages.

The general characteristics of V-plants are the existence of the divergence points.

The number of end items are large compared to the number of raw materials.

All end items are produced in essentially the same way.

Equipment is generally capital-intensive and highly specialized.

The consequences of traditional management practices in V-Plants are mostly a function of the presence of the divergence points. Each individual divergence point represents an opportunity for the misallocation of material. Another factor is whether there is the presence or absence of a bottleneck or CCR (Capacity Constrained Resource.) If there is no bottleneck, then the entire plant has excess capacity that results in numerous opportunities for misallocation of material and over-activation that can create excess inventories of the wrong parts.

If there is a bottleneck (or CCR) then the misallocation of material and overproduction before the bottleneck will create large inventory. This inventory is likely not to be material to meet demand. Misallocation after the bottleneck will result in finished goods inventory of the wrong products. It will also have caused misuse of the bottleneck, which now has to make up for the material that has been misallocated.

Managers of V-plants are often puzzled when they have to scramble to satisfy the demand of the market despite the large finished goods inventory. The inability to respond to the market is not in spite of the inventory, but because of the inventory.

Another factor in V-plants is the setup time that occurs. This leads to combining and increasing batch sizes. Managing according to traditional practices results in large and unpredictable lead times. These in turn cause missed due dates.

The conventional strategies for improving performance focus on improving customer service and reducing production costs. This results in a focus on increasing the level of finished goods inventory and improving the forecasting ability of the firm. Unfortunately forecasts tend to come in two flavors, wrong and lucky.

The correct methods (using TOC/CM) to improve performance are:

View improvement in terms of (a) customer service attained by reducing production lead time and (b) reducing product costs by basing each decision and action on the effect it will have on T (Throughput), I (Inventory), and OE (Operating Expense.) The desired direction is to increase T but reduce I and OE. The focus is not on the calculated cost reductions but on the estimated impact of these global measures.

A-Plants

The dominant product flow characteristic is that the resource/product interactions where two or more component parts are assembled together yield only one parent product. Such points in the product flow are commonly known as "assembly points" or as "convergence points."

The number of purchased materials greatly exceeds the number of end items.

The component parts are unique to specific end items.

The production routings for the component parts are highly dissimilar.

General-purpose machines and tools are used in the manufacturing process.

The consequences of traditional management practices in A-Plants are mostly a function of the presence of convergence points. A-plants offer little opportunity for the misallocation of material since the parts being processed are mostly unique to specific end items. More likely, the problems in A-plants result from a misallocation of resources. Products being processed in excessively large batches usually cause this misallocation. These large batches are in response to a perceived need to attempt to cut production costs by reducing the number of setups performed.

Producing products in these excessively large batches causes a wave-like material flow. Like V-plants the misallocation is the result of actions focused on cost and efficiency. Misallocations are the result of managerial actions such as batch sizing (to reduce costs) and early release of material (to maintain labor efficiencies).

Assembly operations normally require that all parts be available before processing can begin. The assembly will constantly be short one or more component(s) to allow assembly to start. The arrival of large batches of parts will not resolve this problem. In many A-plants expediting is the way of life.

Managers of A-plants have trouble understanding inconsistencies that plague their operations. Despite large WIP and components inventories there is a severe shortage of parts. The fact is that the misallocation of resources that creates the excessive inventory also causes shortages and the need to expedite. The unsatisfactory level of resource utilization and the use of overtime seem to be contradictory.

The conventional strategies for improving performance usually focus on two issues: (a) reduction of the unit cost of the product and (b) the improved control of the operation.

In an attempt to reduce the product cost, management will usually stress (a) improve the efficiency of the operation by reducing direct labor, (b) control the use of overtime and (c) focus engineering efforts on reducing the unit cost of production.

The problem of lack of control is usually addressed by selecting and implementing a single integrated production system.

The correct methods (using TOC/CM) to improve performance are:
- To reduce product costs by developing and implementing a strategy that eliminates the root problem. The wave-like material flow, which causes the feast or famine, must be replaced by a more uniform and synchronous flow. This means that transfer batches must be as small as possible.
- The drum-buffer-rope logistical system can help establish the synchronized material flow.
- The constraints that limit the performance of the system must be identified. Next, the time and stock buffers must be determined.

The full review of the solution for A-plants is beyond the scope of this presentation. Suffice it to say that it can be achieved, but not by traditional means.

T-Plants

The dominant product flow characteristics are that a relatively small number of component parts may be combined to form a large number of end items. The number of end items can greatly exceed the number of component parts.

T-plants are mostly found in an assemble-to-order environment where the customer lead time is relatively short, component procurement and processing time is relatively long, and demand for the individual products is difficult to forecast. The components needed to produce the various are master scheduled and stocked prior to final assembly.

The base of the T-plant structure contains no divergence or assembly points.

T-plants are characterized by divergent assembly points. The components parts used in final assembly in T-plants are common to many end items.

The consequences of traditional management practices in T-plants are that dominant interactions occur at divergent assembly points.

Major concerns facing the managers of T-plants are:
- Large finished goods and component part inventories.
- Poor due date performance (30-40% early and 30-40% late).
- Excessive fabrication lead times.
- Unsatisfactory resource utilization in fabrication.
- Fabrication and assembly are treated as separate plants.

The consequences of traditional management in T-plants deal with generally (a) poor levels of customer service and (b) high product cost. The conventional approach to improving performance in a T-plant generally includes the following two strategies:
- Improve deliveries off-the-shelf by developing better product forecasting techniques and improving inventory planning and control functions.
- Reduce the product cost by improving the efficiency of the operation.

The correct methods (using TOC/CM) to improve performance follow:

The primary problem faced by most T-plants is poor delivery performance. Secondary problems include excessive levels of inventory and the inability to respond quickly to a dynamic market. To deal with these conditions the flow of product must be synchronized. Material release, component fabrication, and assembly must be in step with demand. To achieve this synchronized flow it is essential that material misallocation at assembly be eliminated. This will also reduce the amount of inventory required to support the desired service level.

Engineering effort must be focused on improving the operating efficiency of those elements that are most critical to the smooth flow of materials to the assembly operation.

It should be recognized that in many T-plants there are no true bottlenecks.

T-plants can best be managed as two separate plants: an assembly plant that produces the end items, and a fabrication plant that supplies the component parts. The assembly part of the operation is assemble-to-order, with special procedures to guard against stealing from one order to build ahead for future orders. The nonassembly part of the plant should be run as a make-to-stock operation. The MPS must be established to satisfy the needs of both parts of the plant. The schedule release points in a T-plant occur at material release, CCRs, and assembly.

Summary

The product flow diagram is very useful in describing manufacturing operations that have similar characteristics and problems. The dominant interactions represented by the product flow diagram of a firm identify the key business and operating characters of the plant.

It has become evident that the policies employed by too many manufacturing companies are based on the standard cost system. These systems encourage actions that are often counterproductive to the overall productivity and profitability of the firm.

Use the principles given in this presentation and the reading list as an outline for further reading and study to gain further understanding. This understanding becomes a springboard for application of the comprehensive and systematic set of principles, guidelines, and procedures to lead your organizations to increasingly higher level of competitiveness and profitability.

A Short Reading List

Cox, James F. III, and Michael Spencer. *The Constraints Management Handbook.*
Stein, Robert E. *The Next Phase of Total Quality Management.*
Umble, Michael and M. L. Srikanth. *Synchronous Manufacturing.*

All these are available from APICS. Each book lists further references.

About the Author

Peter W. Langford, CFPIM, CIRM, is currently doing business as a principal of the Langford Associates, a firm specializing in manufacturing and materials related consulting and education. He has been president/principal of the Langford Group, Inc., for about ten years.

With over 40 years of experience in industry, he has held positions of manufacturing manager, materials manager, material and inventory control manager, and numerous management positions in production, design engineering, industrial engineering and quality control. He has functioned as a company consultant and troubleshooter in the Far East, United States and Canada. He is recognized by APICS as a Fellow and is Certified in Integrated Resource Management. He has passed all examinations for Certified Purchasing Manager. He has completed the Jonah course given by the Avraham Y. Goldratt Institute.

A member of APICS since the mid 1960s, with service as director on the board of several chapters including two terms as chapter president, he has served seven years as a member of the APICS Repetitive Manufacturing Group SIG Steering Committee, which he chaired from 1984 to 1989. He has served two years as Region I vice president, with one year each on the Membership and Chapter Development Committee and on the Board of the APICS E&R Foundation. He has concluded two terms on the APICS Board of Directors as vice president, education development—SIGs and is currently serving as a member of the Constraints Management SIG Steering Committee.

He has taught and continues to teach a variety of courses, including courses in a degree program in production and materials management. Mr. Langford is a frequent speaker for various organizations including APICS conferences, seminars, workshops and dinner meetings. Auerbach has published him in their series, "Computers in Manufacturing."

He is a graduate of Cambridgeshire Technical College, Cambridge, England.

Reprinted from the 1997 APICS Conference Proceedings.

Forecast Measures to Keep You on Target

Cynthia A. Neuhaus, CPIM, CIRM

Anyone who does forecasting as all or part of their job will tell you that among the most frustrating, confusing, and time-consuming aspects are forecast accuracy measurement and the dreaded month-end exception report. In this practical, real-world presentation, aimed at those who need to build, plan, or buy component stock to a forecast, I will de-mystify some of the typical exception messages standard in several of today's most common forecasting packages, what triggers them, and how to prevent their reoccurrence, cutting down that tree-load of paper. I will offer tips for your own "off the system" tracking that I have successfully used to focus on continuous improvement while minimizing nervous, sometimes counterproductive actions. We will also cover some other traditional methods of measurement, their failings, and how, by looking "outside of the box" we can recognize forecast error as a symptom, not the cause of problems, and use the error to fix root business problems.

Typical System Exception Messages

Let's jump right in and discuss some of the most common standard system messages, what causes them to trip, what the exception message is really telling you, and what to do about them to keep them out of your life for a good long time!

Tracking Signals

If anyone can have a "favorite" exception message (they need a hobby!), the tracking signal is mine. In plain English, the Tracking Signal is a cumulative measure of the demand pattern and the forecast moving farther apart over time. The important thing to remember with a tracking signal is that it is cumulative, and that is why I favor it. It is rare, because it is a measurement over time, for one or two unusual periods of demand to trip the signal, so you can really eliminate many of the "false exceptions" and, in my experience, save a lot of time. When reviewing Tracking Signal exceptions—and most others for that matter—do not ever forget the three basic truisms regarding statistical forecasting packages:

- They do math much faster than you do, but not much else
- No package has as much common sense as you do
- No package has any idea why your customers want the product, or what could cause a trend to change.

That being said and understood, you probably already have an idea what to do with a tracking signal exception—ask yourself if anything unusual is going on with the product.

Maybe catalog coverage has been expanded for it, picking up new applications, or your competitor has undercut your price. Either way, the alpha, or smoothing constant—the method most packages use to modify the base model, trend, and level—likely just can't keep up with the fast pace of the trend change. Or it also can be caused by a slow erosion or decay of growth over time that has begun declining more quickly than expected, which would be a sign that the trend dampening is artificially keeping the forecast higher than it should.

In any event, I find that the best solution to tracking signal errors has simply been to remodel the item. This gives the system a chance to look at the entire demand string with a clean slate. In many systems, this will reset the alpha to a saner value and give a better level and trend as well. If your system is one that requires a lot of work, I would simply adjust the level, or average period forecast. Either way, you've likely cleared up the problem for the foreseeable future.

If your system allows different exception tolerance parameters for A, B, C items, cost, product groups, level of aggregation, not only for Tracking Signals but for any exception message—USE THEM! This is the most often overlooked reason that people drive themselves crazy at month end. Set the parameters tight (I call a tracking signal of 2.5 to 3.5 tight) only on your high-volume items that being out of would be like McDonald's running out of hamburgers, and high-cost items. Set the measure more loosely (4.0 to 8.0) on low-volume, sporadic, or C items so that you aren't bothered because somebody bought two a month instead of one for three months! You may wish to set growth items a little tighter, so you do give them the attention they deserve. If your system allows you to vary the number of times a signal trips before it prints out as an exception, use that in the same way you would use the tighter or looser tracking signal parameters in limiting the number of exception messages that would simply be a waste of your time.

Whenever you review ANY exception item (tracking signal or otherwise), whether you alter the forecast or find that it looks OK and decide to do nothing to it, CHANGE THE EXCEPTION FLAG! Different systems allow you to do this in different ways, but cut the signal, change the exception flag, or do whatever your system allows you to do that tells it not to trip next time. This simple additional step (you're looking at that item anyhow), will make your report smaller next month!

High Sigma

This can be a nasty one. The best way to describe this one in plain English is to say that the system is having a terrible time getting a good fit with the item's trend (or reversal thereof) or seasonal pattern (or total lack thereof). I have noticed this exception occurring most frequently in cases of high-volume items that are sporadic in nature, or that have several disconnected periods of unusual demand, or newer items taking off on a pipeline fill. Unusual promotional activity can also cause this exception to trip. My advice varies with the situation that caused the exception. If it is due to a high-volume sporadic situation, I would likely just remodel, and have the system try to find the best fit, unless that resulted in a forecast that seemed way too high or low. If the new model had a better seasonal fit but did result in an unacceptable high or low forecast, I would accept the new pattern and adjust the forecast quantity. If it was due to several unusual high demand periods, although the traditional advice would be to adjust demand to get a better model, most of the time I found that these seemingly random spikes were due to legitimate repeat orders from good customers, albeit with poor ordering habits. Thus, I recognized this as true demand, not a series of anomalies, and I most likely would adjust the item's level, or base forecast quantity, and realize that I probably would be seeing that item again. If it was a newer item, if your system has such capability (try to fake it manually if it doesn't), a good thing to do is to copy the "pattern" of a past new item with similar attributes (announced the same time of year, was on promotion, etc.) and impose that pattern on the new item.

ABC Change

This is an exception message that is handy for letting you know that an item has increased or decreased to the next classification, above or below. While it may be handy, I've never found a practical use for it as far as the month-end exception report was concerned, and I never remember revising any forecast that tripped out for this reason. In my experience, if the item changed ABC level, it picked up the system parameter for the quantity level I'd already established. Before you turn it on, ask yourself if you really care that it changed levels if the forecast is OK! My advice as far as forecast accuracy goes is why bother?

Check Sporadic

This exception is one that I truly have found useful, though in a more limited sense than the Tracking Signal. This message is alerting you to the fact that an item is now becoming more sporadic in nature than it was before, or vice-versa. On higher volume items, it becomes almost synonymous with the High Sigma in terms of what the system is trying to tell you and what you should do. It also has been very useful to me on those low-volume items that are finally starting to sell, or are on their way to becoming candidates for the obsolete list. In the case of low-volume check sporadic items I found that, with very few exceptions, simply remodeling the item fixes the problem and keeps it gone.

Percentage Errors

Some systems measure error in a very easy to understand way, by measuring the forecast units as a percentage of error compared to the demand units during the same time period. This is great in that aspect but lacks the nice clues that other exception messages may give you as to why the model isn't doing as well as you'd hoped, so you may have to spend a bit more time in your diagnosis before acting. I'd treat this much as a Tracking Signal error in most cases, doing a system remodel to give the system a fresh look at

the item and let it mathematically adapt. If this proves unsatisfactory adjust the item level or item base forecast.

Exception "Bang for the Buck" Advice

I'd now like to offer some of the techniques that I have personally used to get my exception report down to a manageable size (about TWO AND ONE HALF days to work the exceptions resulting from over 83,000 FINISHED GOODS ITEM forecasts—no kidding!) and get better forecasts, too.

Sort Sense

If your system has the capability to group items by product line or group, rather than simply a numeric printout, DO IT! Until you've tried it, you have no idea how much easier your life will become. This helps confirm your observations and find if a pattern exists in the exceptions. Many times if you view the items by logical group, rather than numerically, you will more easily notice if a group, brand, or sales channel has been hit by an unusual demand, such as big pipeline fill orders, that would cause most items in the group to have the same exception. In this case, the right thing to do is usually NOTHING. But if your items aren't grouped to make these patterns easy to see, you may end up putting a lot of time and effort into remodeling and changing forecasts that not only don't need it, but also could give you poorer quality forecasts than you had at the start.

Tracking Exceptions

This is a low-tech favorite of mine. Please try this at work—you will save a lot of time and paper! The next several times you do the exception report, also have a piece of legal paper handy. At the left margin, write down the types of exception messages on your report. At the top, divide the paper into two topic headings, "Action" and "No Action." As you work your report, for each item make a mark on your paper by the exception type under "action" or "no action" depending on whether you changed the forecast or not as a result of the exception message. When you are done, add up the number of marks you have by each exception type, and whether or not it prompted any action on your part. Chances are that, for some exception types you get an awful lot of paper but, after wasting your time reviewing them you do very few actual revisions. Turn 'em off! The side benefit—in addition to the fact that adaptive smoothing manifest in many models makes the system "smarter" the longer it goes—is that the total number of exceptions will fall. As the number falls, tighten the parameter a little so you get the same workable number of exceptions each month, but your forecasts, as a whole, are getting better and better.

An Ounce of Prevention

Although it seems to contradict many of the time savers I've mentioned, revisit the three basic forecasting truisms (especially the one about the system not having a clue as to why your customers would want your products, or what could cause the trend to change). I strongly recommend that you review every item forecast once or twice a year and not wait for the exception report. Although this seems like a lot of work, it generally goes pretty quickly and serves an important purpose—a concerted effort to prevent errors by adding your intelligence to the item forecasts. I also recommend that you time these reviews to coincide with other critical business functions—such as the kickoff of the budget process (BEFORE you impose Sales and Marketing input at the aggregate level); before a new catalog release to make changes to support expanded product coverage, pricing, and the like; or at the beginning of the new fiscal year. The system sees the seasonality and the trend but can't possibly know that your own company has just added a lower-priced competitive item into its own line and anticipate the effect on the existing product. That's where you come in. The system alone is not the answer. I have found this activity to pay dividends in accuracy, problem prevention, and keeping those pesky errors from ever hitting your exception report at all. Recognize that you have the knowledge, not the system—models may be slowly eroding for months before they appear—and that the forecast is the first line of defense in all good execution planning. The benefits far outweigh the time spent, no matter how good your system is.

Other Forecast Measurements

A very common forecast measurement is the Aggregate measurement, that is, taking the sum total of the forecasts for a given group and period and comparing to the actual demand of that group for the same period. This can be a very helpful and easy measurement for certain circumstances, such as dealing with the Sales and Marketing folks as a point of discussion. However, I view forecast error at a group level not as the cause, but as the symptom of a more serious business issue. Let's examine that view in a little more detail.

Generally, group forecasts are developed in conjunction with Sales and/or Marketing during the budget development process and reviewed during the Sales and Operations reviews or stand-alone reviews that take place. Regardless of how it was initially developed or adjusted, it was on the basis of certain assumptions, and it is very important that these assumptions were documented, even if, in the absence of formal sales and operations planning, it's just in your own notes. In many firms, the aggregate is simply used as the forecast measurement, period. But the reality is that if the aggregate is off severely, the issue is generally much more important to the company. For example, a planned promotion (with its planned revenue) not materializing to expectations or unanticipated higher sales that may require costly corrective action such as overtime or outsourcing. If what was expected and why it was expected is documented, it is very easy to use the error as a trigger to discover the root cause of the business issue and take corrective action. Profits are at stake, jobs are at stake, and service levels are at stake—all of which are much more important than the forecast error itself.

A twist on the traditional aggregate forecast measure is the aggregate at lead time. It's the same basic principle; you're just taking a "snapshot" of what the group forecast looked like at full lead time. This is useful in the same respects as the traditional aggregate measure with one additional benefit—it can sometimes explain why, even though the forecast seems OK, the product isn't available as expected. A typical scenario might involve a product line with an average three-month total stacked lead time, for instance. Six weeks into the three-month lead time, Sales may sign up a new account, that will generate a 25 percent increase in sales, but could only secure a one-month product availability lead time. Obviously, upon hearing of the new business, you'd increase the forecast so that the system sees the increased requirements and at least allows the opportunity to expedite or make more material, but you'll likely not have 100 percent coverage in the time allowed. The "snapshot" at lead time allows you to look back and see what the forecast was originally for that period, and this insight could be useful. However, in my experience, I don't recommend the extra work for this additional benefit. If the assumptions and changes are documented, you will know what caused the problem anyhow.

Other than for use as a point of discussion with Sales and Marketing, I personally don't care for aggregate measures or recommend spending a lot of time on them. Why? NOT ONE of my customers, at any firm where I've been employed, has EVER ordered an aggregate! Not a single one has ever sent in a order that read "send three pallets of whatever you've got." And I wish they would—I've got a bunch of obsolete stuff I'd send them, and I'll bet you do, too. No, my customers were always picky. The mechanics wanted parts that fit the car they're working on, dentists wanted attachments that fit the equipment they had, and now, at my current employer, the electricians want wiring ducts that actually fit in the building in which they are to be installed. That is why I recommend that you not get deluded into thinking that everything is OK if the aggregate is OK—it may not be. Don't make the mistake of thinking that the majority of your efforts should be poured into the aggregate level forecasts. Always remember that your customers don't care how accurate your aggregate is—they're interested in delivery on specific items.

Thinking Outside of the Box/ Error as the Trigger

Trying something new and nontraditional can bring unexpected benefits but doesn't always pan out. Before going on to something that has reaped great benefits for me, I do want to mention one that didn't pan out, so that you can think twice before attempting the same. It was a variation of aggregate at lead time—item at lead time. The same concept of taking a snapshot of the aggregate at lead time was applied to the item records, with very little benefit. Not only did it require a lot of data to be saved (remember, I had 83,000 items), but it required a lot of time to review. Just as one of the benefits of a tracking signal being a cumulative error measure dampening the effect of one or two off-periods, the downfall of this method was that it kicked out many items that, upon closer examination, were determined to not require any intervention. One period does not a trend make.

However, something that did work very nicely for me was to do a separate, stand-alone analysis of the items that went on backorder due to forecast error. The reality is that minor errors are typically covered by safety stock, kanban, or traditional expediting, but when the error is enough to cause a backorder, it's a serious problem. This analysis proved extremely useful at uncovering business issues that went beyond traditional exception tracking.

Over time, patterns emerged which pointed to problem clusters. These patterns exposed the need to look at company policies—for instance, keeping a bit more safety stock or looking for another vendor in cases of hideously long (six to nine months) lead times; asking for customer lead times on certain high but sporadic demand items; and asking for advance notice on new account start-up orders, which could consume a three- or four-month supply of product at one time. This additional lead time on new account pipeline fill orders had an additional, but even better benefit, preventing waste for us and the new account.

Since we had much more experience with the product line than the customer generally had, we were able to go back to these new accounts and advise them NOT to stock certain low-volume, limited-application products. In the past, we'd have expedited like crazy, built the product, shipped it out, and had it returned, untouched but much dustier, a couple of years later, to be held by us for a couple more years before we'd throw it in the scrap heap as overstock.

The payoff for your developing a nontraditional forecast measure relative to your business, coupled with other techniques mentioned in this presentation, can be substantial. After personally monitoring items on backorder due to forecast error for about one and one half years and applying the aforementioned continuous improvement techniques, my results were that only about 8.3 percent of backordered items were due to forecast error. And I hope that you'll do even better!

About the Author

Cynthia A. Neuhaus, CPIM, CIRM, is the Material Manager for the E.M. Wiegmann division of Hubbell in Freeburg, Illinois. She has had more than 17 years of Materials and Inventory experience, including more than 10 in forecast Analysis and Management. In addition to speaking at other APICS chapters and technical users groups around the country, she has also presented papers at the 1994, 1995, and 1996 APICS International Conferences. She served on the APICS St. Louis Chapter Board of Directors from 1988 to 1995, and is a Past President of the chapter. She is currently the APICS Region V Director of Membership, a member of Mensa, and an honorary Board Member of the Mid-Missouri Chapter of APICS.

Reprinted from APICS—The Performance Advantage, *February 1992.*

Rough Cut Capacity Planning: The How-To of It

John F. Proud

Imagine that your job is to haul a stack of crates from Los Angeles to San Diego on a flatbed truck. You've decided to take Interstate 5, a highway that you know travels beneath several underpasses. Along the way you discover that your cargo is loaded 15 feet high, but the underpasses only permit 14 feet of clearance. What a time to find out you have a problem. What could you do to continue your journey? As you might guess, there are several alternatives. One might be to unload a portion of your truck and then reload it once it has emerged on the other side. Of course, this option and many others you may think of may not be practical or acceptable. The best solution would be to plan ahead and know the height of the underpasses you'll encounter. You could then plan accordingly, which means stacking the boxes to a compatible height, or picking a route that allows for safe passage of your cargo.

The same holds true in manufacturing. Is it right to take a production plan which has been converted into a master schedule, toss it wildly onto the shop floor and say "good luck"? Chances are that the schedule will likely bump into some low underpasses, i.e., a work center not having enough people to produce the product in a timely manner, if the proper analysis is not done to determine whether the production plan and master schedule are truly realistic. What's needed is to know when and how to successfully use rough cut capacity planning (RCCP) to highlight 80 to 90 percent of the potential manufacturing concerns before these schedules ever get onto the shop floor.

RCCP is a technique that allows you to determine what issues and problems you are going to encounter as you implement the production plan and master schedule. It is one of the most powerful tools available to companies that truly want to run their businesses and manufacturing facilities effectively. However, it does take people who know how to properly use the information provided. People need to know how to develop the necessary resource profiles, identify the demonstrated and planned capacities, determine the required capacity to meet the production plan and master schedule, and how to use the RCCP output to solve potential resource problems before they occur on the manufacturing floor.

Let's start by asking the question, "How many companies do RCCP?" The answer is, everyone does some kind of RCCP. It might be as simple as saying, "I have a plan that calls for shipping $3 million worth of product this month and I've always been able to ship $4 million per month. So we have the proven capacity to meet the plant." Alternatively, you might say, "Management wants us to ship $7 million a month during the summer season. We have no precedent for being able to do that-management's new plan appears to be unrealistic at this time." At the other extreme, you might decide to carry out a formal rough cut capacity plan that evaluates all key resources and determines the feasibility of successfully implementing the sales and operations plans (S&OP). This is where we will focus our attention: the formal approach.

Why Rough Cut?

RCCP basically answers one question: "do we have a chance of meeting the production plan and master schedule (MPS) as currently written?" RCCP shows you where the problem bridges are located before you begin your journey so that you can make the necessary adjustments (i.e., create a production plan and master schedule that does not exceed the factory's capacity). It also gives you some lead time to alter your itinerary before you encounter problem underpasses (i.e., modify the capacity for any problematic resources).

RCCP allows you to:

1. Test the validity of the production plan and master schedule before doing any detailed material or capacity planning.
2. Be able to initiate action for making schedule and capacity adjustments.

Whether or not you formally do RCCP at the production plan and master schedule level, people are going to be out there trying to meet these schedules. Doesn't it make sense to have people working to valid schedules rather than rescheduling everything when a manufacturing center finds a problem?

Some of the advantages of gaining better vision through rough cut are fundamental:

- Rough cut is necessary to establish the validity of the production plan created during the S&OP process.
- Rough cut is necessary if you're going to do a good job of master scheduling.
- Rough cut reduces nervousness in the schedule.
- Rough cut enhances the credibility of the entire MRP II effort-it enables you to begin with a solid plan that drives the rest of the detail scheduling and capacity planning.
- Rough cut is easy and quick to implement.

Defining the Process

To do RCCP in a company with simple products and bills-of-material, you might only need a clipboard, a pencil, and a five-dollar handheld calculator. If your company has products of average complexity and more extensive bills-of-material, you might want to use a personal computer with a spreadsheet program. For very complex planning operations, you will likely need to use a master scheduling system that includes an RCCP module and is run on a

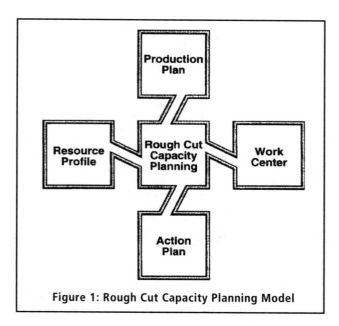

Figure 1: Rough Cut Capacity Planning Model

mainframe or mid-range computer. Whatever the situation, RCCP tools must be interactive with the user.

Let's take a look at the rough cut process itself. RCCP entails three basic steps:

- Calculate the capacity required to meet the production plan and master schedule.
- Compare the required capacity to the planned capacity.
- If necessary, adjust the required or planned capacity so the two are in balance.

Here's what actually happens. As you can see in **Figure 1**, the validation process begins when data from the production plan or MPS are input into the RCCP system. Data from two other sources are then drawn upon: the resource profile database, which contains information about the key resources required to meet the production plan or MPS, and the work center database, which has information about the available, demonstrated, planned and maximum capacity of each key resource that will be used to produce the products in question.

By combining information from the production plan and the resource profiles, the RCCP module determines the gross required capacity necessary to meet the production plan. This required capacity is then compared to the work center's capacity to determine if adequate capacity exists to satisfy the production plan requirements. If the work center's capacity is appropriate, the production plan is deemed realistic and is used to create the master schedule as well as the detailed material and capacity plan. If rough cut determines that the work center's capacity cannot support the plan, that information is fed back to top management, and decisions must be made whether to adjust the production plan requirement or the work center's future capacity.

Essentially, the management team will balance the production plan's required capacity against the work center's planned (demonstrated plus planned changes to the process) capacity by asking, for each key resource in the manufacturing process: What is the required capacity by time period? What is the planned capacity? And what is the difference between the two? This makes it possible to identify potential problem areas and to make adjustments before moving on to any detailed material or capacity planning.

Creating Resource Profiles

The first step in RCCP is to identify the key resources. How is this done? There is a very scientific method to identifying the key resources in a company-ask someone in manufacturing, purchasing or design engineering. People who deal with the production process every day know what the critical resources are. So let's use their knowledge, not ignore it.

Begin the process of key resource identification by asking the people who are close to the action and fill out a resource matrix that not only identifies the resource, but states the reason the resource is critical. Once the matrix is completed, determine if any of the resources identified can be combined because they mirror each other. Remember, we are going to use RCCP to answer the question, "Do we have a chance of meeting this production plan?" In other words, keep the resource profile as simple as possible and with as few entries as absolutely necessary.

Next, we need to determine the set-up and run times associated with each of the identified key resources. Set up and run time both affect the workload on a work center while queue, wait, and move times only affect the time it takes to move work through the work center, not the load at the work center. In validating the production plan and master schedule, we are interested in analyzing the load on the key resources by time period.

The last question is whether we need to take lead times into account in our resource profile. If a resource is needed 35 days before shipment, and production planning is done in months, then the extra five days really won't make much of a difference in determining whether or not you have a realistic plan. If, on the other hand, a resource had a lead time offset of 120 days or more and you do not take that into account, the predictive value of a rough cut will be dramatically diminished. Remember, rough cut is applied on common sense, not hard science. If it's close, it's probably good enough for rough cut purposes.

Determining the Required Capacity

The output of the sales and operation planning process is the production plan, as well as a sales, inventory, backlog and shipment plan. Our goal in RCCP is to validate this production plan. To do this, we take the production plan and explode it through our resource profile. For example, if the production plan calls for 30,000 units of family A in July and the required time for one key resource, lines W and X, is 1.1 hours per 1,000 units, a requirement of 33 hours on the W and X lines would be generated. For family B, our resource profile indicates that 1.8 hours per 1,000 units are required on the W and X lines. If the production plan for family B calls for 10,000 units in July, the required capacity will be 18 hours.

By continuing this simple math for each item in the production plan, we can determine the required capacity to meet the entire production plan. **Table 1** is a stripped-down example of the required capacity necessary to meet a July production plan (only partial capacity requirements are shown).

Critical Resource	Units	Month	Family A	Family B	..... equired Capacity
Lines W & X	Hours	July	33	18	58

Table 1. *Required Capacity Planning...*

Table 1: Required Capacity Planning

Critical Resource	Units	Month	Family A	Family B	...	Required Capacity	Planned Capacity	Maximum Capacity
Lines W & X	Hours	July	33	18	...	58	114	152
		August	27	9		43	60	80
		September	28	9		45	144	192
		Total	88	36		146	318	424
Line W	Hours	July	24	20	...	57	133	171
		August	20	10		43	70	90
		September	20	10		46	168	216
		Total	64	40		146	371	477
Line X	Hours	July	30	0	...	46	95	114
		August	25	0		41	50	60
		September	25	0		45	120	144
		Total	80	0		132	265	318
Finishing	Hours	July	450	280	...	1072	1140	1596
		August	375	140		857	600	840
		September	375	140		929	1140	2016
		Total	1200	560		2858	3180	4452

Table 2. Required Capacity versus Planned Capacity

Once RCCP has calculated the required capacity, the next step is to compare the required capacity to the capacity you actually have at your disposal. Then you can determine whether adjustments need to be made to your resources or the production plan.

Comparing the Required to Planned Capacity

Now that we have identified the required capacity to meet the production plan, it's time to identify the capacity available to satisfy this required capacity. There are several capacity terms which come into play in RCCP. We have already discussed required capacity, which is the capacity necessary to meet the production plan or master schedule. Besides required capacity, we will be discussing three other capacities in our evaluation process.

These three capacities are generally stored on the work center database. The first is the demonstrated capacity-the proven or historical capacity for the key resource. The second is planned capacity, which is defined as the demonstrated capacity plus or minus any planned changes to the manufacturing, engineering, or material flow process. Finally, the maximum capacity, which is the greatest output level that can be achieved for any period of time assuming optimum deployment of all resources.

With this knowledge in hand, we can begin to make a valid comparison of the required capacity to our planned capacity (refer to **Table 2**).

Looking at the figure, there are some periods that are underloaded (less capacity is required than is planned to be available) while in other cases there are overloads (required capacity is greater than the capacity planned to be available). For example, in the finishing operation shown in Table 2, a total of 857 hours is required in August, yet there are only 600 hours planned to be available. Does such a potential overload truly represent the bottom line-we can't do it? Not necessarily. You might, for example, be able to increase or decrease the capacity at selected operations. Additional capacity may be available as noted in the maximum capacity column. But remember, there is no free lunch. If we flex the finishing resource up to maximum capacity, some other key resources' planned capacity could be affected.

Evaluating the Plan

Clearly, "flexing" a capacity up or down or using any other approaches to boost or lower capacity may have a cost impact, and must therefore be carefully evaluated by management. RCCP answers questions about critical capacity and materials requirements in terms of numbers. It points out where potential problems are likely to occur, and reveals what happens when alternatives (i.e., maximum capacity) are applied. But that's as far as the system goes; the rough cut capacity plan provides an opportunity for people to exercise their skills, knowledge, and creativity in balancing demand for product and the supply of resources to produce the product.

By using RCCP, you can really manage by the numbers and evaluate whether your production plan is achievable or just a gleam in someone's unrealistic eyes. You can also determine where to focus your energies. If family A is an "elephant" (refer to Table 2, required capacity data) compared to the other product families-it has by far the largest need for capacity and creates the biggest problem-you can focus your efforts on the family and maximize your effectiveness.

Rough Cut at the MPS Level

What we've done in this article is to develop a rough cut capacity plan by product family, driven by the production plan that is developed during the S&OP process. While all companies need to do RCCP at the production planning level, some manufacturing environments may require a second pass through the rough cut analysis, this time at the master schedule level. Companies with a highly varied mix of product, for example, will have to rough cut at the MPS level.

RCCP at the MPS level uses the same principles as rough cut at the production plan level, but extends the calculations down to the next level. This is done by exploding the master schedule (instead of the production plan) through an item resource profile to generate the required capacity to meet the master schedule. By using rough cut to validate the MPS, it is possible to determine whether the production plan derived during the S&OP process can be met at the product mix level. This validity check brings us full circle in the RCCP process.

How to Implement Rough Cut

Unlike most other manufacturing system techniques, rough cut doesn't require a lengthy cost justification, a large budget, a full project team, or a major educational effort. In fact, for products with simple bills-of-materials and steady mixes, you can get by with a pencil and piece of paper. For more complex procedures, we may need the use of a computer and spreadsheet logic. Whatever the situation, here are the 10 general steps to implement an effective rough cut program:

1. Determine whether RCCP is to be done at the production plan and/or the master schedule level.
2. Identify the company's key resources using a resource matrix that defines the resource as well as the reason it is critical.
3. Develop resource profiles for the identified key resources using the best set-up and run times available.
4. Determine the demonstrated and planned capacity for all resources identified in the resource profile.
5. Determine the total resource requirements for each key resource by exploding the production plan and/or master schedule through the developed resource profiles.
6. Compare the resource requirements to the demonstrated and planned capacity for each identified critical resource.
7. Highlight any potential overloads and underloads by critical resource and time period.
8. Identify alternative plans that balance the requirements and planned capacity.
9. Decide on the best course of action that satisfies management's objectives.
10. Implement your solution by either increasing or decreasing the planned capacity or increasing or decreasing the production plan or master schedule.

As long as people understand how to use rough cut as a capacity planning tool, the payback can be immense in terms of better schedules and a more refined planning process. Rough cut enables management to make good, informed decisions about schedules before they are released to the factory. When that happens, everyone in the company benefits.

(This article is a summary of material written on RCCP by the author.)

About the Author

John F. Proud, CFPIM, is president of Proud Enterprises Corporation, a Los Angeles-based company, and a principal of the Oliver Wight Companies. As a principal of the Oliver Wight Companies, he consults with numerous manufacturing companies helping them achieve Class A MRP II/JIT results. His other responsibilities include teaching the Oliver Wight Middle Management MRP II and Master Scheduling Classes. He currently serves APICS as a member of the 1992 International Conference Committee and National Program Advisory Committee.

Reprinted from the 1996 APICS Conference Proceedings.

Value-Added Forecasting

Joseph Shedlawski, CPIM

To stay ahead of the competition in today's global economy, manufacturing cycle times and customer lead times must continue to shrink, while profit margins grow. Many companies have already taken several steps to improve their chances of success, such as MRP II implementation, JIT, Business Process Reengineering, or Sales and Operations Planning, to name but a few. Those same organizations often continue to be frustrated by the fact that their promised delivery dates are not soon enough for their customers and by the amount of chaos that still exists on the shop floor as a result of attempts to chase the customer demands. Simply holding more inventory, in the hopes that the customer will buy it, is not a feasible solution in the face of carrying costs of over 20%. Long ago, the emphasis shifted away from forecasting as a competitive weapon when it became apparent that forecast error could never be eliminated. Forecasts became a necessary evil, for which no one wanted to claim responsibility! It's time to clear up some of the misconceptions about forecasts and to seize the opportunity inherent in the forecasting process. It is not forecast accuracy, but rather improved understanding and use of forecasting as a tool for reducing both costs and lead times, that will add real value to an enterprise and can improve the results from any and all other initiatives.

Definition and Characteristics

A forecast is an educated guess as to what is going to happen, such as sales demand. It is an attempt to determine who will buy how much of what—and when. As fraught with assumptions as it is, and so often based upon history, the forecast is always going to be wrong. Some forecasts are more wrong than others (the lousy ones versus the lucky ones), so it is important to describe a forecast by two numbers: the prediction and the margin for error, also called the spread. The amount of error resident in a forecast can be calculated and can itself be forecasted. It is useful in analyzing capacity plans and in determining safety stock requirements. Forecasting improvement projects often use error as a benchmark against which to gauge system performance. Just like the weather, product sales are more accurate over the short range than the long range. This truism has many implications with regard to the uses of forecasts, the frequency of their review, and the time buckets used over a forecast horizon. Forecasts will tend to be more accurate for a group, or family, of items that are related by product name, process, etc., than they will be for individual items comprising the family. Forecasting should therefore be done for as small a number of items as possible, by forecasting at the family or group level. Items that have demand planned for them by a production schedule, such as components, don't have to be forecasted, and should not be, because calculated demand is always more reliable than forecasted demand.

Why Forecast?

Given all of the negatives associated with forecasting, a forecast is still required because customers demand delivery of products in less time than the cumulative lead time to order materials, manufacture and deliver them, and because the variety of end items typically offered for sale by make-to-stock manufacturers is too abundant to stock them all by arbitrary inventory rules. Daily decisions of what to procure or produce with limited resources are all based directly or indirectly on the forecast. Long-term decisions on capital procurement, staffing, facilities, and even the nature of a business itself, are all made with input from forecasts. Senior Management, Sales, Manufacturing, Finance, and support functions all require forecasts for distinct purposes. Confusion sometimes sets in because different forecasts are created and maintained to serve each purpose.

In fact, since the uses of the forecast dictate exactly what is measured (units? dollars? SKU? family? competition?) over what time period (months? quarters? years?), then it stands to reason that the numbers, horizons, replanning frequencies, etc., will differ among the various forecasts. Each forecast is valid if there are assumptions and definitions that allow some linkage of the various forecasts.

Methods of Forecasting

That golden age of forecasting, when it was felt that a near-perfect algorithm could be developed for each situation requiring a forecast, is long gone. Abundant forecasting statistical techniques are the legacy of that period of time, many of which, such as Box-Jenkins or X-11, are too complex to be readily understood, and thus are seldom used. Essentially, both qualitative and quantitative methods exist. Qualitative methods are best applied to brand-new products or complex, changing conditions regarding existing products. Judgmental or intuitive in approach, qualitative techniques involve the "gut feel" of experts, or a panel consensus, or an analogy to a previous situation that is deemed relevant, such as what has happened previously in an election year. Quantitative techniques use numerical data either on the product family itself (intrinsic), or related to something outside the company, such as economic factors (extrinsic). History, unfortunately, is not always the best teacher when it comes to forecasting. While data are easy to come by, forecasts constructed solely upon history often yield disappointing results because the circumstances have changed regarding competition, promotional periods, even the market for the product in general. That's why a combination of a quantitative technique, such as exponential smoothing or seasonalizing, with a qualitative, judgmental adjustment is usually better than a quantitative technique alone. Sometimes, extrinsic and intrinsic factors are both used in developing a forecast which is then adjusted based on qualitative assessment. In any case, data should be broken down and analyzed to determine their makeup, which consists of a base number, a trend, a seasonal factor, and randomness. Once these factors have been isolated as components of demand, better forecasts can be constructed.

Another option would be to maintain the forecast to equal the company business plan. By keying in on product strategies and promotions, the strategy in such a case would be to hit the target number. That works well, until the number is achieved and then everyone gets greedy and tries to "beat" the target, which could cause a material or resource dilemma.

If disagreement develops over which technique should be used, or if the forecast package is overwhelming in the number of choices that it offers, then a focus forecasting approach can be applied, to select the best method by comparing what each method would have predicted to the actual results obtained. Again, the danger here is the reliance on history.

Common Pitfalls

There are many reasons why forecasts fail to produce the desired result. A few of the most common pitfalls follow.

1. Forecasting the Wrong Things.

Trying to forecast every singly SKU and every option combination available to the customer, or trying to forecast in too great a specificity of time period, location or customer will quickly lead to disappointment. Besides, it's not necessary.

2. Individual Decisionmaking.

One person does not know enough to come up with the best numbers single-handedly, and could have biases that would skew the forecast. A combination of methods and/or people is best.

3. Second-Guessing.

Once the forecast has been determined, the Sales Plan and Master Production Schedule should follow from it. Switching back and forth or hedging your bets causes the organization to lose its sense of direction. A wish list is certainly not a forecast.

4. Overreaction.

Extrapolating what happened over the first two weeks of a two-month sales promotion over the next six weeks could have disastrous results. Timely monitoring is certainly important, but then so is judiciousness when deciding on when to change the number or the method of forecasting.

5. Conflicting Purposes.

Ask the sales person who's giving you a forecast if that's what he wants you to produce, or if that's what he is promising his boss that he can sell! One number will not usually be enough; each number should be used only for its intended purpose, be it production forecast, yearly goal, or shipping plan. It is better to have two numbers than to try to use one number for two different purposes.

6. Sudden, Unpredictable Change.

Extrinsic factors have to be monitored to recognize the relevance of, for example, a sudden jump in the price of crude oil, or a shutdown of government agencies, to a change in demand for goods or services. A failure to understand forces that affect the market for your products will create a lag time in the forecast system's response to the change.

7. Failure to Recognize All Sources of Demand.

Changes in customers' planned inventory levels, service and repair parts demand, competitors' actions, and incompleteness of internal sales data are all potential contributors to forecast error. The best forecasts are the ones that break down the total demand into its "component parts" so that each piece of the total demand can be managed separately.

8. Lack of Timely Monitoring.

If the forecast is prepared and updated "when we get around to it," then the Master Scheduler might be flying blind, or forced to use the sales numbers from last year or last month to fill out the plan horizon. This is better than nothing, but a dangerous practice. Additionally, a data-entry error or data omission could go unnoticed for a longer period of time. Some systems show a zero in a data field unless or until it is replaced by another number. If the forecasts are not updated regularly, then by default, the plan is told that NOTHING will be sold in that time period!

What to Do?

A forecast policy should be developed to add value to the process and create some harmony among the users and providers of those forecasts. A forecast policy should address all of the following issues.

1. Determine What to Forecast.

Analyze the Bills of Material to find the level at which the fewest number of parts exist, and chances are that is the best place to develop forecasts. For example, if a consumer product is sold in twenty different combinations of size, color, promotional pack, etc., but all contain the same bulk product inside, then forecast at the bulk level and assign probabilities to each of the SKUs. In the case of products from multiple product families that share a common raw material, particularly one that takes a long time to procure, costs a lot, or is in chronic short supply, focus on that raw material. Forecasting and Master Scheduling both work best when performed at some level of aggregation.

2. Modularize Options Bills.

Do not ever try to forecast every combination of buildable end product if you are in an assemble-to-order business! Forecast the assemblies and common components as separate items, and the number of forecasted items will drop from the multiplication product of the number of options to the sum of the options.

3. Assign Responsibility.

While the forecasting effort is a joint one, the accountability for providing and maintaining complete forecast data must reside with a specific individual or group. Preferably, the responsible party is someone who has a vested interest in both Sales and Manufacturing performance.

4. Measure the Forecast.

It is always true that "you get what you measure." Forecast error should be measured, and targets for improvement should be set which measure actual demand compared to the forecast as it existed offset by the manufacturing leadtime. In other words, if the total cycle time from ordering raw materials to finished product is three months, then November's forecast accuracy will compare actual November sales against the November forecast which was entered in August.

5. Monitor the Forecast Method.

Tracking signals are often used to decide when to abandon the current method of forecasting in favor of another which might be more predictive. The most responsive method may not always get the best prediction since it may overreact to subtle changes; every situation is different, but tools exist to allow for this type of monitoring. Focus Forecasting will often suggest a better method.

6. Honor—But Don't Worship—the Time Fence.

A forecast time fence may correspond to the manufacturing leadtime. Within that time, changes in forecast risk changes to the Master Schedule and excessive expediting, so the time fence should be honored by refraining from taking deliberate action, such as scheduling a promotion, which would change the demand. However, whenever an event occurs outside the scope of your control that will affect product demand, such as a strike at your competitor's plant, then it is totally correct to change the forecast starting today! It must be understood that such a change does not guarantee continued supply, but that it will cause a reprioritizing of work outside the time fence, which will speed the recovery from such a change.

7. Don't Just Predict ... Affect!

Good forecasting practices heighten the awareness on the part of Sales and Marketing of the constraints in Operations. Demand "spikes" caused by new product launches, price changes, etc., can be planned to achieve a smoother workload in Manufacturing.

8. Sales and Operations Planning.

Participation in a formal S&OP process is a sure way to increase communication among Sales, Marketing, Finance and Operations, to make major issues more visible, and to bring clarity and consistency to the decision-making processes which affect supply as well as demand. It also suggests that the forecasting effort is performed on a regular basis.

9. Two Numbers, One View.

As previously stated, forecasts should be two numbers, a target and an error. Both can be predicted, measured, and improved. But there must only be *one* set of those numbers, *one* view of what the forecast is throughout the organization at any point in time. And the forecast should not be confused with the master production schedule, which is a lot-sized, inventory-adjusted build plan.

10. Document Assumptions.

The official forecast needs to contain the major assumptions which went into its development so that it can be readily understood, and so that the assumptions can be reconsidered for validity when reviewing the forecast performance, and when replanning. Typically, assumptions involve the market size and the targeted market share, price issues, timing of product launches, competitor's actions and promotion plans. As with any official document, the official forecast, with assumptions attached, should be dated and signed.

Summary

A single view of demand, well thought out and published on a regular basis, gives visibility well beyond the customer-order horizon of financial, personnel, production, material, and capacity needs. Forecasting improvements are opportunities to secure the necessary resources to respond to the customer faster, with less disruption and last-minute heroics. Adding value to such a process is not the job of the computer programmer or the salesman or the Master Scheduler alone, it is a joint effort. Demand is the principal input to all levels of resource management activity. Therefore, the quality of that input affects the quality of all subsequent outputs. Customer service, inventory turnover, and operation efficiency all stand to be enhanced when value is added to the forecast process.

About the Author

Joseph F. Shedlawski, CPIM, is the Manager of Operations Resource Planning for Wyeth-Lederle Vaccines and Pediatrics (WLVP), where he is responsible for inventory, capacity planning, master production scheduling, materials planning, production control, distribution, and demand management for a global enterprise. WLVP is one of the world's leading producers of vaccines, and is located in Pearl River, New York. Joe has sixteen years of experience in Materials Management, including Distribution, Production Control, Material Requirements Planning, Master Scheduling, and Systems. Prior to joining Wyeth-Lederle, he was the Materials Manager for Lederle Consumer Health Products where he was instrumental in the design, implementation, and execution of a successful Sales and Operations Planning process. He also has experience with generic and branded pharmaceutical products, and has worked in multiple plant and subcontract environments. Prior to his experience in Materials Management, Joe held various Quality Management positions.

Joe has a Bachelor of Science degree in Biology from Bucknell University and an MBA in Finance with honors from Iona College. An active APICS member for the past twelve years, Joe was president of the Northern New Jersey Chapter and served on the Board of Directors of Region II for four years, before attaining his current position as Vice President of Region II. Joe has been an instructor for CPIM courses since 1987 and has conducted many seminars and presentations for the APICS community.

Reprinted from the 1996 APICS Conference Proceedings.

Using Distribution Resource Planning to Manage Inventories in Multiple Locations

Bernard T. Smith

This paper covers the following material about DRP:
- Goals
- Performance measurement
- Term definitions
- DRP networks
- Differences between DRP and MRP
- Similarities between DRP and MRP
- Benefits
- Action to take.

Goals

The author has worked in over 400 DRP start ups in different parts of the world. The first thing is to set DRP goals before starting a project. Generally, goals tell why you are going to use DRP in the first place.
- To improve customer service, fill rate, in stock position
- To increase inventory turnover or reduce days of supply
- To improve profit usually lost because of inventory excess write downs
- To reduce cost of operation handling items and setting up orders
- To reduce freight costs by using truck load and car load shipments
- To reduce inventory management expense at remote locations

It's worthwhile to actually start managing a portion of the company inventory with the DRP procedure to measure the impact on these goals. The portion of the inventory should be substantial enough to get the department's attention. It should be from 20 to 30 percent of the business. It should be a problem area now so that even the pilot can get some good results. Don't parallel the test with the old inventory management procedures. It's too easy to fall back into using the old ways of doing things. If you run in parallel, it's hard to tell how much improvement came from DRP and how much just came from focusing attention on the area.

If the DRP procedure will operate in a multilevel distribution network, start at the top level. In other words, there may be regional warehouses shipping to distribution centers who are in turn shipping to customers. Start the DRP inventory management at the regional level. If goods are not available at the regional level, it's a problem to improve performance at the distribution center level.

Performance Measurement

The performance measures should fall in line with the goals of the DRP procedure. The measures should be quite complete so as not to confuse improvement with simple trade offs from one area to another. For example it's possible:

- To improve fill rate but decrease inventory turnover by increasing safety stock.
- To improve turnover but reduce profit by discounting and dumping inventory excesses.
- To improve profit but decrease turnover by ordering large time supplies for discounts.
- To increase turnover but run up the cost of handle and freight by frequent orders.

The performance measure should be summary performance measures of overall progress. It gets confusing when a company shows A item fill rates are up, B items are down, and C items are about the same. The bottom line is what has happened to fill rates overall up or down?

The performance measures should show progress against last time, last month, and the same time last year. Comparing to other companies even in the same industry is difficult because companies have different personalities. Certainly a full line distributor with high profit will have lower turnover and customer service than a distributor who carries only fast movers at a lower profit.

Avoid having more than one measure of the same goal. If you measure dollar service level, don't measure line fill rate as well. Pick one measure of customer service and make it happen.

Term Definitions

DRP, Distribution Resource Planning, uses many of the same terms as MRP, Manufacturing Resource Planning. Both always show information period by period out into the future.
- Gross requirements
  - The forecast whether generated by a computer or by people.
  - Real customer orders by delivery date.
  - Planned orders from a DRP system at a lower level.
  - Exploded requirements from a higher level like an assortment.
- Scheduled receipts
  - Open purchase orders by delivery date.
  - Open production orders by delivery date.
  - Open transfers pending from another location.
- Projected on hand
  - The projected inventory balance adding future inbound and subtracting future outbound.
- Planned orders
  - The quantity DRP would like to order to satisfy the parameters the company is using in the DRP procedure.
- Firm planned orders
  - The overrides the planner or buyer has made to the DRP planned orders.

DRP Networks

The simplest DRP network follows the physical flow of goods from a factory to a distribution center.

More involved networks include:
- Multiple factories shipping to multiple warehouse locations.
- Multiple factories and outside suppliers shipping to multiple warehouses.
- Multiple factory/warehouses shipping selected products to each other.
- Multiple suppliers shipping to a regional warehouse which breaks bulk to other warehouses.
- Dummy consolidation center warehouses that receive and break bulk to other warehouses in the system.
- Retail stores that receive some goods direct and some through the warehouse.
- Factories that use allocation schemes to distribute to multiple warehouses.
- Import order distribution when goods arrive at a domestic port.

The DRP procedure should always follow the physical flow of goods. There should be no make believe. If goods are stocked in five separate warehouse locations, the DRP procedure should treat each location uniquely. Sum up the resultant time-phased planned orders for manufacturing planning. Forecasts should be by individual warehouse location.

The consolidation center should be an expression of the immediate source of the product. The vendor should be an expression of the ultimate source of the product. So an item can be purchased from Whirlpool but flow through the Chicago warehouse to the Seattle warehouse. Seattle would show Chicago as the consolidation center but Whirlpool as the vendor.

Sometimes a consolidation center for a low level distribution point will become a regular warehouse at a higher level. For example, Aleutian Islands warehouse may use Anchorage as their consolidation warehouse source of supply. Anchorage warehouse however may be using Seattle warehouse as its consolidation center source of supply.

All goods should have a primary source of supply. Goods that are consistently rerouted from one source to another have not been planned properly. Goods can come from a secondary source but it should be an exception. If it seems that one source cannot handle the total volume, then the item distribution should be segmented either by sizing, packaging, or location. For example, ship all the 4-foot ladders from Chicago. Ship all the 6 and 8 footers from New York. Or ship the West Coast ladders from Chicago and the East Coast from New York.

Differences Between DRP and MRP

Multiplant Multiwarehouse

MRP generally concerns itself with a total company forecast of an item. It considers things such as capacity and raw material availability. DRP uses forecasts at multiple levels of distribution for an item such as plants, distribution centers, and retail outlets. Rather than using total forecasts of a product's sales in a company, DRP looks at forecasts in individual stocking locations versus the current inventory in those locations. It sums up the planned replenishments of those locations to calculate the total company need.

Allocations

MRP is generally involved in allocating plant and material resources to the production of individual items. DRP concerns itself with the proper distribution of the product to multiple geographic locations as the product is received from the vendor or as the product comes off the manufacturing line.

Joint Replenishment

MRP usually is looking at the right quantity of an item to manufacture. DRP is generally looking at a group of items to purchase or move from one site to another, for example: a mix of products to fill up a container, truck load, car load, or minimum vendor restriction.

Finished Goods

MRP is concerned with the production of finished goods from raw materials and manufacturing resources. DRP is concerned with the inventory management of finished goods and repair parts . . .
- ordering
- expediting
- delaying
- allocating
- measuring performance
- identifying service problems
- identifying inventory excesses
- building economical transportation loads
- tying in with key customers

Schedule to Planned Orders

MRP generally uses company-wide forecasts to determine manufacturing requirements. In many cases these same companies use reorder point procedures to distribute the resultant production. DRP sums the time phased replenishment orders throughout the network to come up with the production needs in the future. DRP determines where the goods should go as they come off the manufacturing line.

Large Number of SKUs

Because DRP operates at the lower levels of distribution there are a great many more stock keeping units to deal with than with MRP. For example a plant that manufacturers 1000 items may distribute to ten distribution centers. DRP would be involved with 10,000 SKUs in this company.

Automated Forecast Input

Because DRP is operating with so many more SKUs than MRP it must have computer generated forecast input. Using ratios of forecast distribution of a company forecast is not an acceptable substitute.

Identifies and Redistributes Excess

DRP can look at the past distribution of production in relation to sales in the form of on-hand balances. Where it sees an imbalance in the distribution of inventory it can redistribute the excess and eliminate the need for additional production.

Links to Nonmanufacturing Customers

MRP for many years has allowed manufacturing companies to link to their raw material suppliers. Now DRP allows nonmanufacturing companies and purchasers-for-resale to link to their suppliers.

Similarities Between DRP and MRP

Bill of Material Explosion

DRP needs time-phased bill of material explosions to handle assortment, pallet load mixes, and kit requirement. MRP uses bill of materials for raw material determination.

Paperless Purchasing

Both MRP and DRP are such busy displays of time-phased requirements that both demand paperless processing.

Action Messages

Both MRP and DRP use the three basic action messages:
1. Order some now.
2. Expedite what was ordered before.
3. Delay or cancel what was ordered before.

Other Similarities

Both are powerful scheduling tools. Both require summary measures of performance. And both use the logic for ordering originally designed for MRP.

Benefits

For over 14 years I used a reorder point system in Servistar Corporation where I was Vice President Inventory Control up until August of 1986. Nobody, including Andre Martin, could talk me into switching over all of my inventory to DRP. Since then, however, my successor, Joan Trach, the new Vice President of Inventory Control, has converted all of the items to DRP with outstanding improvements in inventory turnover and fill rate.

With my own eyes I've witnessed quantum jumps in company performance through the use of this simple concept in hundreds of companies around the world.

Action to Take

For so many years, we consultants have told our clients that computers only present information and that people must make decisions. We've created a class of people who spend their lives making routine decisions the computer can make better. It's time now to move on. It's time we start giving our computer systems guidelines for decision making and then use the decision the computer makes. It's time that either our automatic systems work or we rebel and throw them out.

DRP is an excellent example of a procedure that should work as automatically as the heating system in our home. Whether we grow the system in-house or purchase it from outside it should be an automatic system. Visit a company that is using DRP properly to see the dramatic impact on inventory management.

About the Author

Bernard Smith's clients read like *Who's Who in Business*— Thomas J. Lipton, Northern Telecom, Eveready Battery, Whirlpool Corporation, Pepsi, McDonnell Douglas, Imperial Chemical Industries, Apple Computer, Digital Computing, Servistar Corporation, Stanley Tools, General Electric, Osram Sylvania, Nestle's, and many other fine companies.

Early in his career, Bernie managed a data processing, systems, and programming staff of 75 people and two IBM mainframe computers for Warnaco. Later, Bernie became Vice President Inventory Control and Long Range Planning for Servistar Corporation.

In 1986 he formed his own company, B.T. Smith and Associates, programming and selling computer software for marketing and inventory management. During those years he had the chance to see firsthand the interaction between data processing, systems, and programming departments and users in more than 400 companies worldwide.

Bernie received his B.A. and M.B.A. degrees from the University of Bridgeport in Connecticut. He taught in the graduate studies program—managerial accounting, long range planning, and information systems. In his role as consultant and teacher he has presented to thousands of people—APICS, NPMA, NRMA, Council of Logistics Management, NWHA, NTMA, FIT, ATA, PMI, and many others. He's a past board member of the Red Cross, associate of the Carnegie Mellon management decision games, and past President of the Chamber of Commerce.

Reprinted from the 1999 APICS Conference Proceedings.

Sales and Operations Planning—A Fundamental That Still Works

Robert A. Stahl, CPIM

In today's rapidly shifting global economy, it's very easy to become distracted from ensuring that the fundamentals are performed exceedingly well. In a manufacturing company, one of these fundamentals is keeping the balance between aggregate supply and aggregate demand.

An "out-of-balance" condition is defined as having too much or too little in the way of aggregate resources, that is, people, equipment, inventory, etc. When this imbalance exists, failure to satisfy customers while maintaining the financial objectives of the company is typically the result. As such, the management of the company will have very little time to pay attention to anything else, which, over time, becomes a competitive disadvantage of the highest order.

In other words, in today's highly competitive environment, not being able to do the routine things routinely is a sure sign of troubled waters ahead. Keeping aggregate balance between supply and demand, and making shipments to meet customer's needs, is one of the fundamental things a manufacturing company must learn to do routinely, with a minimum of time, energy, and effort. The good news is that this aggregate planning process does not have to be invented. It already exists, and is known as Sales and Operations Planning (S&OP).

The purpose of this paper is first to refresh the reader's understanding of the basic principles, and second to present a framework that will assist the reader in leading an improvement effort back at their own company. A detailed audit checklist and a detailed implementation plan will also be made available to those who attend the presentation itself.

Background

In a manufacturing company, bringing balance to supply and demand is a fundamental "law of nature"—that is, it happens as a natural course of events. It's only a matter of who will bring about this balance. If the presiding leadership function (management) does not execute this responsibility to the satisfaction of the stakeholders, an outside force will eventually take over bringing about this balance. Among these outside forces that will take over are creditors and competitors, neither of which have the company's best interest in mind.

Over the past 20 to 30 years, many tools and techniques have been developed to assist management in achieving the objective of balancing supply and demand. For aggregate planning, this process has become known as Sales and Operations Planning, and is defined by the *APICS Dictionary* as follows:

- A process that provides management with the ability to strategically direct its businesses to achieve competitive advantage on a continuous basis by integrating customer-focused marketing plans for new and existing products with the management of the supply chain.
- The process brings together all the plans for the business (sales, marketing, development, manufacturing, sourcing, and financial) into one integrated set of plans.
- It is performed at least once a month and is reviewed by management at an aggregate (product family) level. The process must reconcile...and tie to the business plan.
- Executed properly, the S&OP process links the strategic plans for the business with its execution and reviews performance measures for continuous improvement.

While every company in existence is doing S&OP to some degree, a truly competitive company constantly evaluates how well it is performing these cross-functional processes. Additionally, whether or not a company is in a Just-in-Time (JIT) or traditional environment, this process remains an essential function. As a matter of fact, one can make the case that S&OP is more important in a JIT environment than in a traditional one. This is because in a JIT environment, there is less inventory, which in a traditional environment acts as a buffer between supply and demand imbalance.

S&OP Objectives

In concept S&OP can be defined as the "monthly update to the annual business plan." With the increased dynamics that are part of most market places today, this monthly updating of the annual plans is more necessary than ever before.

As such all of the plans that are derived from the annual business plan must be updated and synchronized, if a formal planning process is to function effectively. Graphically, this S&OP process would look like **figure 1** from an input/output standpoint.

Specifically, the monthly S&OP process must provide for proper addressing of the following issues:

1. Variances—Review the past month's actual to plan for sales, production, inventory, or backlog. If the variance is greater than expected, investigate and explain, revising the future plans, as appropriate.
2. Market Conditions—Provide a forum for all disciplines to present and discuss their view of the market, so as to bring about cross-functional understanding of market dynamics.
3. New Products—Present and discuss the status and impact of any pending new product introductions.
4. Alternate Plans—Present, evaluate, discuss, and decide upon alternative plans and actions.
5. Conflict—Raise and constructively resolve any policy conflict that exists within the organization. This often

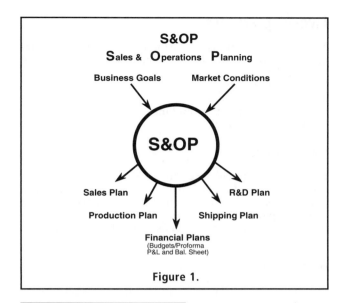

S&OP
Sales & **O**perations **P**lanning

Business Goals   Market Conditions

S&OP

Sales Plan   R&D Plan

Production Plan   Shipping Plan

Financial Plans
(Budgets/Proforma
P&L and Bal. Sheet)

Figure 1.

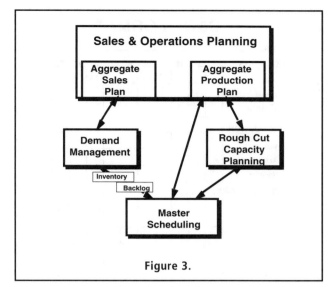

Sales & Operations Planning

Aggregate Sales Plan   Aggregate Production Plan

Demand Management   Rough Cut Capacity Planning

Inventory
Backlog

Master Scheduling

Figure 3.

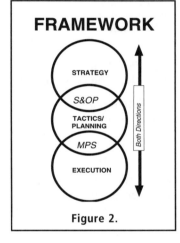

FRAMEWORK

STRATEGY

S&OP

TACTICS/ PLANNING

MPS

EXECUTION

Both Directions

Figure 2.

involves a change in traditional culture from "the person who presents a problem is the problem."

6. Contingency Plans— Develop necessary contingency plans as appropriate to the situation.

7. Accountability— Identify and agree upon necessary actions and changes to plans, creating accountability for results that support the company's goals.

This list implies that S&OP is part strategic and part tactical in nature. In other words, it deals with both policy issues of strategy, as well tactical issues of dealing with the execution of the company's strategy.

In a *Harvard Business Review* article (Nov/Dec 1985) entitled, "Strategic Planning—Forward in Reverse?" Bob Hayes states that a company's strategic planning process must not only be done in one direction—from top to bottom—but it must be done in both directions! This S&OP process provides a means by which this two-directional planning can be take place. This is shown graphically in **figure 2**.

Sales & Operations Planning (S&OP) vs. Master Production Scheduling (MPS)

While S&OP is a very distinct and definable process, it is not a "stand-alone" process. It is, and must be, connected to other business processes. This is graphically shown in **figure 3**.

Additionally, it is important that S&OP and MPS not be viewed as one single process, but rather as two distinct but connected processes. Trying to do both S&OP and MPS in one defined process is often a serious mistake. S&OP fundamentally concerns itself with issues of volume, while MPS concerns itself with issues of product mix, within this volume. There are also many other distinguishing factors, such as the following:

S&OP	MPS
Strategy	Tactics
Volume	Mix
Aggregate	Detail
Months/quarters	Days/weeks
Rate of production	Sequence of prod.
Market perspective	Customer persp.
Business focus	Plant focus
Centralized	Decentralized
Executive resp.	Middle mgmt. resp.

This paper explains the process dealing with the issues listed under S&OP. While the MPS issues are equally important, they are not being dealt with here. From this perspective, it is only important to understand that these two processes are connected, but are not one in the same and are not done as one process.

Product Families

S&OP is done in aggregate by dividing a company's product line into product families. A typical company will have between 5 and 12 product families in which it does S&OP. The *APICS Dictionary* defines product families in the following manner: "A group of end items whose similarity of design, and/or manufacturing facilities, and/or materials are planned in aggregate for sales and production."

The reason for this production-oriented definition of families is because S&OP's main objective is to ensure that proper amounts of resources (capacity, material, etc.) are available to satisfy customers in a cost-effective manner. Therefore, it is important that the final process is designed to accomplish this objective.

If the marketing orientation is significantly different from the production orientation, however, there must be a transparent conversion process that allows marketing to forecast in one group of families, and then convert to a production set of families. This is typically done conceptually through a two-dimensional matrix with marketing groups on one side and production families on the other side. Marketing then forecasts in their set of families, then spreads the mix across the production families.

In any event, the S&OP process must be done with a set of family definitions that allow resources to be planned in

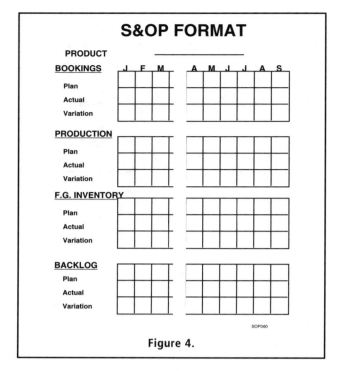

S&OP FORMAT

PRODUCT _____

BOOKINGS   J F M   A M J J A S

Plan

Actual

Variation

PRODUCTION

Plan

Actual

Variation

F.G. INVENTORY

Plan

Actual

Variation

BACKLOG

Plan

Actual

Variation

SOP060

Figure 4.

support of the anticipated demand. By the same token, the family definitions must allow sales and marketing to be able to anticipate the future (alias: forecast) with some degree of certainty. Many times the establishment of these family definitions is quite easy, yet other times it requires a good deal of consideration.

S&OP Data Display

Figure 4 is a very simplified example of a data display. There should be one of these for each product family, and one in total for the business. This is typically developed with the use of spreadsheet software (for example, Lotus or Excel). The arithmetic on this data display is as follows for make-to-stock (MTS) and make-to-order (MTO) environments, respectively:

(MTS) Open Inventory + Production - Sales = Closing Inventory
(MTO) Open Backlog + Sales - Production = Ending Backlog

If a given family is both MTS and MTO, both of these formulas need to be applied in some appropriate fashion, according to the nature of the demand.

Most companies have all of the information for this data display available, but it is typically not all in one place on one page for each family. One of the keys to this process is that the related data is shown in one place on one page. That is sales, production, inventory, and/or backlog are all on one display for each product family. This is a very important issue. There are other issues that also must be addressed, including these:

Issue	Typical
Months of history	3 or 4
Months of future	6 to 18
Size of buckets	Months or quarters
Unit of measure	Each, units, lbs.
Critical time fences	Varies by family
Variance measure	% or numerical

Five-Step Process

The data display shown above then becomes the focal point of the following process, which includes five distinct steps:
1. data closing
2. demand planning
3. production planning
4. partnership (pre-meeting) meeting
5. executive meeting.

Data Closing

In this step, at month-end the actual results for each category (sales, production, inventory, and backlog) for each family is recorded. This information is then distributed to all of the participants. The responsibility of this step can be assigned to anyone who has access to, or can be provided, accurate data.

Demand Planning

This step is the responsibility of the sales/marketing functions. They perform the following actions:
- Review performance; plan to actual.
- Explain any variance out of tolerance.
- Determine future customer needs based on new information.
- Develop a new demand plan (forecast).
- Redefine and inventory or backlog targets as appropriate.
- Run first preliminary set of S&OP reports.
- Pass to production planning and other appropriate people.

Production Planning

While this step may be administered by a function such as material planning, the basic responsibility and accountability is with operations management (plant manager). It includes the following:
- Review performance; plan to actual.
- Explain any variance out of tolerance.
- Determine future impact on capacity: equipment, people, etc.
- Revise production plan based on changes to demand plan and variances.
- Run second preliminary set of S&OP reports.
- Pass to sales/marketing and other appropriate people.

Partnership (Pre-) Meeting

In attendance at the partnership meeting are all the disciplines that have a contribution to make to the planning process. This contribution could be an input to decision-making or will be on the action end of decisions. This would typically include the following: manufacturing (operations), R&D (technical discipline), sales and marketing, and finance. While others could participate, these are typically the primary players.

This step in the process is typically chaired by the materials manager or someone in a similar position. It takes place over the course of one day and may be divided into different segments, determined by product family definitions. This segmentation is so that the detailed discussions of one product family don't unnecessarily waste the time of many uninterested parties.

The objective of this session in general is to sift through the multitude of detail separating the important from the trivial. Proper actions for the trivial issues are settled at this meeting, but the important (or policy issues) are brought forward for executive deliberation. The specific objectives for this meeting should include the following:

- Agree on issues and/or problems that can be solved at this level.
- Recommend changes that involve policy issues.
- Propose alternative solutions and consequences for those issues that can't be decided at this meeting.
- Select alternatives and bring forward to the executive group.
- Prepare an agenda for step 5 (executive meeting).
- Run third preliminary set of S&OP reports.

Executive Meeting

This meeting's purpose is quite simple—make clear decisions about how to run the business from a policy point of view. It is important that clear decisions be made, and that the proper homework be accomplished. Among those present at this meeting to review and finalize decisions should be the following: president, VP sales/marketing, VP operations, VP engineering, and VP finance. The president should chair this meeting. The specific objectives follow:

- Review decisions made by lower levels.
- Resolve disputes (select alternatives).
- Make clear policy decisions.
- Lead management development through this process.
- Publish actions and hold people accountable for performance.
- Run final set of S&OP reports.

Summary

A manufacturing company today can no longer operate without fully integrating its business processes. No longer can the factory be disconnected from the sales/marketing functions. We have entered an age of demand-driven economies, where we must learn how to only run what is needed rather than run as much as we can to optimize output.

This direction of integration begins with the Sales and Operations Planning process. S&OP is the process that connects the marketplace to the factory at the policy or aggregate level of the business. Effective management requires the proper application of the techniques described in this paper. Only those who learn how to use these techniques effectively shall survive the '90s.

About the Author

Robert A. Stahl, CPIM, is the president of the R.A. Stahl Company in Attleboro, Massachusetts, and is a senior partner in the education and consulting firm Partners for Excellence. His 16 years of consulting experience is complemented by his highly successful contributions while in manufacturing line management himself. Mr. Stahl has helped numerous companies in varied environments improve their competitiveness.

Mr. Stahl graduated from Villanova University, is certified (CPIM) by APICS, and is listed in *Who's Who in America*. He is also a member of the Association for Manufacturing Excellence (AME) and the Operations Management Association (OMA). He is a frequent speaker at professional society events, and his articles are published in many trade journals. He was elected the Best Conference Speaker in basic concepts at the 1995 APICS International Conference in Orlando.

Reprinted from the 1998 APICS Conference Proceedings.

Making Consignment- and Vendor-Managed Inventory Work for You

Mark K. Williams, CFPIM

As manager of a manufacturing or distribution operation, you've just been notified by two of your largest customers that they want to purchase goods on consignment. A third very large customer wants to emulate Wal-Mart and begin a Vendor-Managed Inventory (VMI) program—with you as the chosen vendor.

You're beginning to see the pattern: your customers want to increase their profits at your expense. Instead of paying for product within 30 days of delivery, the two who want a consignment program want to delay payment until after using or selling your product. The third wants to go one step further—they want *you* to plan *their* inventory!

It's obvious how these moves will benefit your customers, but is there any benefit for you? We'll examine these issues in a moment, but first, let's define terms.

Consignment and VMI Defined

The *APICS Dictionary*[1] defines consignment as "The process of a supplier placing goods at a customer location *without receiving payment until after the goods are used or sold*" (author's emphasis). This is very different from traditional practice whereby a customer pays for goods within a set time period after receiving them (often 30 days). Under consignment, it makes no difference whether product sits in the customer's warehouse or shelves for two days or two years; the supplier receives nothing until it is used or sold. This could result in a serious cash flow problem for the supplier if goods continue to be produced but money is not collected.

Vendor-Managed Inventory (VMI) is a planning and management system that is not directly tied to inventory ownership. Under VMI, instead of the customer monitoring its sales and inventory for the purpose of triggering replenishment orders, the vendor assumes responsibility for these activities. In the past, many suppliers operated vendor-stocking programs where a representative visited a customer a few times a month and restocked their supplies to an agreed-upon level. Popularized by Wal-Mart, VMI replaces these visits with information gathered from cash registers and transmitted directly to a supplier's computer system via Electronic Data Interchange (EDI). Now, suppliers can monitor sales of their products and decide when to initiate the resupply procedure. This is not an inexpensive proposition for suppliers. Investments must be made in new systems, software, and employee training. Which brings us back to the question: Is there a payoff?

Benefits of VMI

In the article "Integrating Vendor-Managed Inventory into Supply Chain Decision Making," Mary Lou Fox[2] outlines four advantages of VMI:

1. Improved customer service. By receiving timely information directly from cash registers, suppliers can better respond to customers' inventory needs in terms of both quantity and location.
2. Reduced demand uncertainty. By constantly monitoring customers' inventory and demand stream, the number of large, unexpected customer orders will dwindle, or disappear altogether.
3. Reduced inventory requirements. By knowing exactly how much inventory the customer is carrying, a supplier's own inventory requirements are reduced since the need for excess stock to buffer against uncertainty is reduced or eliminated.
4. Reduced costs. To mitigate the up-front costs that VMI demands, Fox suggests that manufacturers reduce costs by reengineering and merging their order fulfillment and distribution center replenishment activities.

While these are all potential benefits of VMI, the most important ones were not cited.

- Improved customer retention. Once a VMI system is developed and installed, it becomes extremely difficult and costly for a customer to change suppliers.
- Reduced reliance on forecasting. With customers for whom a supplier runs VMI programs, the need to forecast their demand is eliminated.

VMI—Binding Customers to Suppliers

Once a VMI system is established, a customer has effectively outsourced its material management function to its supplier. After a period of time, the customer will no longer have the resources to perform this role in-house, making him more dependent upon the supplier. In addition, developing a VMI system entails major costs to the customer. His information services department has to spend time ensuring a smooth transfer of data to the supplier. And his materials management organization has to spend a significant amount of time making sure that the chosen supplier will perform, and beyond that, ironing out a myriad of details ranging from what will trigger a reorder to how returns will be handled. Once all this work is done, nothing short of a major breach in a supplier's performance will prompt the customer to search for a new supplier. With VMI, customer/supplier partnerships are not only encouraged, they are cemented.

Sidestepping the Shortcomings of Forecasting

Traditionally, most manufacturing and distribution operations determine what to sell and how much to sell by way of forecast. Countless hours are spent developing, massaging, and tweaking forecasts—only to have them turn out to be dead wrong. Why? Because a forecast is nothing more than "an estimate of future demand" (*APICS Dictionary*). And, unlike Nostradamus, most of us cannot predict the future! Under VMI, instead of a supplier forecasting what customers will buy—which means guessing at (1) what customers are selling, (2) their inventory positions, and (3) their inventory strategies—a supplier works with real sales and inventory data firsthand. Because the supplier is effectively handling their customers' materials management function, customer inventory strategies are revealed. Soon, the supplier finds that it can provide input on the timing of promotions and safety stock strategies such that it can easily accommodate changes in demand. This reduction in demand uncertainty enables suppliers to operate at higher service levels with lower inventories. Clearly, these are benefits coveted by any and all suppliers.

Benefits of Consignment

Such are the benefits of VMI—what about consignment? Isn't that the same as giving a customer an interest-free loan? Maybe. Before passing judgement, let's take a look at how most companies do business and examine the components of inventory carrying cost.

Most manufacturing and distribution companies, with the exception of make-to-order firms like Boeing, hold inventory for customers in the form of finished goods. This buffers manufacturers against fluctuations in demand. However, this stock of finished goods doesn't come free. As Ross indicates below[3], annual inventory carrying costs for most companies range from 20 to 36 percent.

Cost of Capital	10-15%
Storage & Warehouse Space	2-5%
Obsolescence & Shrinkage	4-6%
Insurance	1-5%
Material Handling	1-2%
Taxes	2-3%
Total Annual Inventory Carrying Costs	20-36%

Let's examine the impact of consignment on two businesses that both have annual carrying costs of 36 percent. Company A holds finished goods inventory and Company B has just decided to provide it on consignment. Company A is responsible for capital, storage, handling, and all other costs listed above. Company B is responsible for providing the capital, and as owner of the goods, is responsible for paying taxes on what isn't sold. However, under consignment, Company B is no longer responsible for storage or material handling. In addition, as with most consignment agreements, Company B's customers now have responsibility for any damage or disappearance of goods on their properties. Thus, Company B has transferred its cost of insurance and "shrinkage." Finally, by closely tracking the use of product and acting swiftly on slow-moving items, Company B can minimize or completely eliminate product obsolescence.

A quick review of cost components demonstrates that by implementing a consignment program, Company B can reduce its annual inventory carrying costs from 36 percent to 18 percent (cost of capital + taxes) in a consignment program, a reduction of 50 percent! However, if too many dollars are put into customers' warehouses on consignment, the negative impact on cash flow could leave a supplier asset-rich and cash-poor, a condition that could lead to bankruptcy. The solution: a well-designed consignment agreement.

Keys Points in Any Consignment Agreement

When negotiating a consignment agreement, it is critical to consider the elements of cost, responsibility, and time. The key elements are as follows:

- Level of consigned inventory. A customer would prefer to hold a large amount of consigned inventory, viewing it as a cheap way of buffering against demand uncertainty. The supplier, however, must determine the level at which it can provide goods profitably. Negotiating a set number of weeks of supply will meet the needs of both parties. If the customer sells/uses $5.2 million dollars a year and the agreement calls for ten weeks of supply, both parties know that $520,000 is the consigned level. The supplier can now budget for the capital required and the potential taxes involved in supporting the inventory. Adjustments can also be made in its cash flow projections. This arrangement also provides the customer with an incentive for increasing sales of the suppliers' products since an increase in sales translates into an increase in consigned inventory.
- Responsibility for slow-moving inventory. Another key element in a successful consignment relationship is to keep the inventory moving. Developing inventory turn goals, by individual product or by product group, can uncover slow-moving items that are inappropriate for consignment. During negotiations, it is important to determine which party will monitor inventory turnover and how slow-moving goods will be handled, whether they will be returned to the supplier or purchased by the customer and removed from the consigned inventory.
- Responsibility for damaged or lost inventory. Another critical factor to address during negotiations is the disposition of stolen or damaged inventory. It is customary for the customer to assume complete responsibility for all consigned inventories—lost, stolen, or damaged—on its premises. A periodic physical inventory needs to be established to account for all consigned inventories.

By following these guidelines, a successful—and profitable—consignment relationship can be established that benefits both parties.

Conclusions

We have examined some of the benefits of VMI and consignment from a supplier's perspective. Indeed, there are benefits to both approaches, as well as costs and risks. By understanding and managing the costs, and controlling the risks through careful negotiations, one can make both consignment and VMI work not only for the customer, but for the supplier as well.

References

1. *APICS Dictionary*, 8th Edition.
2. Fox, Mary Lou, *Integrating Vendor-Managed Inventory into Supply Chain Decision Making*, APICS 39th International Conference Proceedings, 1996.
3. Ross, David Frederick, *Distribution Planning and Control*, Chapman & Hall, 1996.

About the Author

Mark K. Williams, CFPIM, is currently consulting manager with the North Highland Company, a firm based in Atlanta, Georgia, specializing in supply chain management consulting. Prior to this he spent two years at Georgia-Pacific as senior manager of materials and manager of logistics, and over 12 years in manufacturing and materials management in various positions for the Vermont American corporation including operations manager, distribution manager, materials manager, production control manager and corporate internal auditor.

Mr. Williams received a B.A. in political science from the University of Louisville. He is recognized by APICS as a Certified Fellow in Production and Inventory Management (CFPIM). He has taught many APICS certification review courses and spoken to both APICS chapter and region meetings on a variety of topics. He has presented at three APICS International Conferences.

He is past president of the Falls Cities Chapter (Louisville, Kentucky) of APICS. Currently, he is a member of the Inventory Management Committee of the Curricula and Certification Council. In addition, he is also director of education of APICS Region IV, which includes Georgia, Florida, Alabama, Mississippi and Puerto Rico.

Reprinted from the 1998 APICS Conference Proceedings.

Collaborative Planning, Forecasting, and Replenishment

Scott H. Williams

I will talk about Procter & Gamble's current success and future direction of creating consumer value and improving trading partner relationships through electronic data communication.

I will begin with the fit that technology has with efficient consumer response (ECR). I will spend the bulk of my talk providing you with the exciting future vision of P&G's Ultimate Supply System and CPFR—Collaborative Planning, Forecasting and Replenishment.

Look at the ECR definition from the original document published in January of 1993. The question I'm going to ask you, which has been asked earlier here today, is, IS ECR COMPLETED? As I've highlighted it now, does it look like it's complete? Do we have distributors and suppliers working together as business allies? Are we communicating timely and accurate information through paperless systems? Finally, are we questioning every activity and eliminating non-value-added work, or at least reducing it? Is that work complete? When this work is complete, ECR can be labeled as shelf material. As a practitioner in the industry, my answer is that we clearly have a long way to go, and that we have only truly just begun.

The future looks like this: We will let consumer needs drive our business results. We are going to change the way we look at process reliability. Instead of looking at averages and striving for the high 90 percentages, our measurement standard is now zero defects. We're looking to streamline the entire supply system, from the supplier to the customer, and we're going to produce to demand, based on actual consumption. We're going to let the consumers define what's needed and deploy the existing technology to make it happen.

Here's the supply chain: from raw material supplier to the retail point of sale. If you look at what's been going on in today's environment, up to today, you see these individual pieces of the supply system becoming more efficient and working to streamline their own internal organizations and efficiencies. The demand data is created by retail consumption and flows up the supply chain to create the flow of product.

The focus of major industry supply chain activity has been with ECR in the center of the supply chain, between the manufacturer and the distributor—between P&G and our customers' warehouses that distribute product to their retail stores. ECR, through UCS II, CRP, ASN, and FEDI, has focused on distribution efficiencies. The opportunities are now just beginning to be understood around industrial and commercial EDI, which is a recent focus within the Uniform Code Council (UCC), as to how we can build standardization around that connection in the supply chain. My focus today will be at the other end of the supply system, which we refer to as the last 100 yards of the supply system.

Collaborative Planning Forecasting and Replenishment, or CPFR. Four words that, if you don't remember them by the end of today, you will certainly know by the end of this year.

The Ultimate Supply System is all about waste, especially wasted time.

Total Supply Inventory. This is an interesting number. Within our supply systems, with our trading partners, we know there exists around 140 days of inventory. Our retail customer's distribution center and retail stores have 50 of those days with 30 days of actual inventory in the stores and 20 days in their DCs. P&G has 60 days, 30 days of finished product and 30 days of raw materials. Our raw materials suppliers have the remaining 30 days to make up the total 140 days. This inventory ties up cash and it significantly delays product initiatives. New products available right now will not be seen in stores and made available for consumer purchase for four and a half months. When we looked at the value-added time of this on-hand inventory we realized that less than 2% (2 days) of the 140 days was really productive. This is a huge opportunity.

Tied in with all of this extra inventory are retail out-of-stocks. This may seem almost a contradiction. An often-cited Coke study estimates that product out-of-stocks range from 8 to 10%. You go to a store 10 times and one of those 10 times, you can't find the product in the store you want to purchase. If that happened on a regular, consistent basis, over a period of time, you would change your shopping habits. You're either not going to buy that product, or you're not going to shop in that store if it's a product that is critical to your needs.

Batch processing of product and information. Henry Ford established this industry practice, providing consumers with the color of their choice as long as it was black, producing the same thing every day. Keeping the production lines running efficiently meant making a lot of the same thing with as little changeover as possible. Then, when colors became important and production had to changeover from black to another color, the changeover occurred only after ample inventories existed of the current product. Production of the other color continued until sufficient inventory was produced. The key to minimizing changeover was to maximize inventory. We follow this same process today, building huge piles of batched inventories in order to produce efficiently. This process is also the standard for information flow. Data is compiled daily and communicated in "efficient" methods. Product flow and data flow should be based on real-time needs and not forced into artificially created schedules to meet some other measure of efficiency, which ultimately drives total supply system inefficiency. Real-time data communication should drive systems to produce to demand.

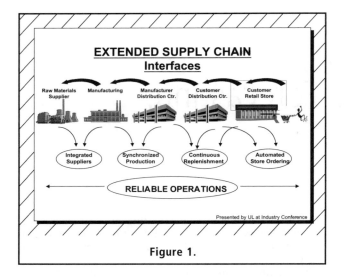

Figure 1.

Another opportunity in streamlining the supply chain deals with improved communications internally and externally. Trust is the key ingredient that will come from improving the business processes and proving that efficiencies can be gained through advanced sharing of information. Examples of this include Product Development personnel collaborating internally with Product Supply and externally with raw materials suppliers to determine production capacities to deploy a new product. Sales managers and customer buyers and merchandising managers and warehousing managers would collaborate on future plans and strategies to generate consumer demand forecasts and effectively receive and distribute product to the stores. Historically, the business practice of promotion and initiative communication was on close-in, need-to-know timing to protect competitive advantages in the market place. This paradigm is giving way to the competitive advance to be gained by providing the exact product quantities exactly when it is needed. Supply system collaboration is the key to making this happen.

All of that has to change if we're going to move forward. The opportunity is to identify the waste of time, convert it to responsiveness, and drive for speed to achieve huge financial gain.

What is the ultimate supply system? P&G is focusing on three concepts to drive this concept: integrate the supply chain, produce to demand and communicate accurate, real-time information. There's a consumer focus to this. It's future-focused and a development project to determine what the possibilities could be. We will test various concepts and develop value propositions based on case study findings because we don't know exactly what the solutions are today. This is a development project to identify methods to compete effectively in the year 2005. We're going to test this and see what we can do with it. The driving force is the consumer's demand for products in the stores, on the shelves and priced at a point that provides a value for the purchase. Supply chain participants—suppliers, manufacturers, and retailers must work together to reduce waste to meet this consumer need. The last piece here is that P&G is not alone. **Figure 1** was presented in a recent industry trade conference by Unilever. It speaks to reliable operations and various pockets of the supply system. Companies are out there at least talking about streamlining supply system.

P&G is actually working supply chain solutions, and here's how. We have four business planks to our Ultimate Supply System. The first is short-cycle production. Produce every SKU that needs to be produced, every day. The supplier connection is a drumbeat integration, so that we're communicating in real time with our suppliers and have built long-term, lasting relationships. The customer connection is designed to get the information at the point closest to the consumer at the point of sale at the retail cash register. And finally, we will let innovation and the technologies drive all the activity.

This brings us to the expected benefits projected for the year 2005: huge dollars for the entire supply system. We have calculated P&G's share of the $4.5 billion supply chain total savings to be in the range of $1.5 to 2.0 billion. This savings largely reflects the inventory in the system that P&G owns.

Likewise, the same relationship exists to calculate our share of the actual system cost reduction. P&G will be testing and measuring the actual opportunities for improving in-stocks, freshness of product, innovation and responsiveness. All of these outcomes will be confirmed as we go forth with our tests and will be contained in our goals for 2005. We are looking for 50% improvement on cycle time, cash, and product availability and speed to market, with 6% on total delivered cost. These are aggressive goals. But they have already been achieved at P&G...

Over a six-year period of time, our Lima, Ohio, plant, which produces heavy-duty laundry liquid, Downy fabric conditioner, and dryer sheets has blown those objectives away. We've increased our volume over that six-year period by 42%. At the same time, diametrically opposed, was a reduction in our finished product inventory by 76%. It can happen. We have done it. We're going to take what we've learned at the Lima Plant and apply it to other supply systems. Here's our approach:

We're going to synchronize inventory data with our suppliers using Lotus Notes and an application known as Simon, which is Shell's application allowing data to be easily communicated online between two trading partners and enabling raw material inventory reduction. On the other side of this supply system, we're going to use the EDI-830, which is the standardized EDI transaction included in the CPFR process between manufacturers and retail distributors. We're going to collaborate with our customers to better project and communicate consumer demand, ultimately to enable our plants to produce to meet this consumer demand information. We will be evaluating product and information flow using a very common currency—time. The process involves documenting the time it takes product and data to flow through the entire supply system. Our current experience with suppliers has confirmed this time mapping process to provide huge learning opportunities. There's a lot of low-hanging fruit that we have already gathered to drive benefits with our supplier connection. We're looking to do the same with customers. This process identifies the longer-term system and process redesign needs as well as the quick wins that will improve the flow of product and time through the supply chain.

How are we testing this? We have six global test supply systems in place today to provide a broad base of understanding and a diverse set of business opportunities on which to experiment. These test systems are located in the following countries: U.S. (2 plants), Mexico, Belgium, Germany, and the Philippines. We are testing six product categories: hair care, heavy duty liquid laundry detergent, tissue/towel, diapers, catamenial (feminine products) and dry powdered laundry detergent. We have engaged over 15 supplier partners providing the raw materials to our plants, and 15 customer partners distributing our products to retail stores. The expectation for participation in these Ultimate Supply System tests is a sincere willingness to compete as a supply system. It's a different concept. We're not going to trade costs back and forth between ourselves and our trading partners and simply push cost in the supply system from one location or company to another. Instead, the objective is to learn how to drive costs out of the total system. This may involve some trade-offs that seek to find the "sweet spot," where some savings incurred by one participant in the supply system make it worthwhile for another participant to incur additional costs. This is where the learning will be most significant in the testing process.

All of this takes considerable cooperation and courage, but, at P&G, we know this is the right thing to work on now to ensure the future growth of our business and that of our supply chain partners. This work involves significant mindset changing and paradigm breaking. But when you review true breakthrough business results that have occurred over time, the common variable has nearly always been the undertaking of something that has changed traditional business activity and, importantly, thinking. P&G believes that the focus on reducing waste and competing as a total supply system are the keys to our future success in the marketplace. This is our vision of creating the Ultimate Supply System.

If you look at this customer connection, which is the side that really deals with CPFR, we're going to let consumer purchases drive the total supply system. We are going to use the point of sale (POS) data to create the initial demand signal in the supply system. This is not just collecting market basket information that gathers information on which products are selling better in what stores, but using the live sales information in the stores to trigger immediate replenishment orders and to be used in long-term promotion and new item demand planning.

Efficient retail replenishment is the single largest opportunity existing in the supply chain today. Shelf out of stocks AND excessive inventories in retail stores are occurring simultaneously. I want to talk about this process as it occurs in most retail grocery, drug and mass merchandisers today.

When you see product being scanned at retail, do you realize all that is happening, and importantly, all that is NOT happening? When product is scanned in stores, package UPC labels are matched to numbers in the retailer's system that associate a selling price to the product. In most cases that is where the process ends—with the price of the product showing on the cash register screen and eventually on the paper receipt you are handed by the clerk who then says "thank you for shopping at (Blank)." The process assigns a price and prints a receipt. In some cases this POS data feeds a market basket database to generate store and customer profiles, but, for the most part, it only performs the two simple functions of assigning a selling price and printing a receipt. Except in the case of a few progressive retailers, this has been the full extent of the use of this scanning functionality in retail stores.

Here's what the store replenishment process looks like: there is daily movement of product from the store to the consumer, from the DC to the stores, and from the manufacturer (P&G) to the customer's distribution center or warehouse. Retail store shelf replenishment orders are created by someone in the stores viewing the product remaining on the shelf at a given point during the day. Usually this process is aided with the use of a hand-held UPC scanner that can read the product number and accept an order

quantity. This order clerk has no real idea how much product has actually been sold or whether there is currently product in the back room.

In this daily replenishment scenario, an order clerk in store number one has overprojected the demand for product in the store, and store number three has underestimated the store demand. This ordering process, therefore, contributes to a worst-case scenario of some stores with too much product and some with too little product and too few stores with exactly the correct amount. This process is the result of not being able to see the actual retail consumption and inventory levels. The customer's warehouse has no idea how much product has actually sold in the stores, and certainly we (the manufacturer) can only see the product movement from the warehouse to the stores, again without knowledge of what has occurred in the stores.

In the promotional replenishment scenario, the same process occurs more dramatically. Because delivery reliability is in question for the manufacturer to ensure product availability to the DC when needed and also for the warehouse to deliver to the store demand, agreement is reached to front-load the customer's warehouse with the promotion product well in advance of the sales event occurring in the stores.

Next, these stores receive standard uniform delivery quantities forced out from the warehouse because the stores are not considered reliable in ordering sufficient merchandising quantities to cover their anticipated demand. Then, guess what, stores sell through the quantities at different rates which are not realized by the store personnel. Last they knew, the back room or aisles were filled with promotional product. Because no active system exists to monitor actual cash register sales, some stores run out and others have too much product remaining after the sales event has ended.

The net result—retail out of stocks of 8 to 12%, customer DC in stores have excess inventory. We're producing the wrong product and not enough of the right product, and stores are either too light or too heavy on inventory.

What happens in the real world now that we have the store POS systems connected? Product flows to where it is needed based on real-time data communication. Perpetual inventory is viewed and communicated for the retail stores, that is, the back room inventory, the shelf inventory, and the sales at the cash register. That information is compiled and transmitted in real time to the distribution center and headquarters to allow instant reaction to the quantities placed on the next truck scheduled for that store.

The last piece of this is that the customer is going to send to us this immediate order forecast and a longer range forecast of promotions and new items planned for weeks into the future. This information is communicated through the EDI-830 to us, and we will feed this information internally to our planning and production systems to enable production to this demand.

Let's take a look at the data. This is an actual East Coast chain customer where we did some analysis with the point-of-sale data they provided us. They are one of the few customers who can utilize this POS information. The base sales rate is very level. Look at that yellow. It's about as predictable as you can make it. You can see the huge sales volume spikes that occurred as the result of a promotion. This could have been a hot-priced sales item for the weeks indicated. The question that becomes really critical is, can these spikes be predicted? If we can, then we can produce to it and we don't have to carry excess inventory to cover these spikes. So, the answer is yes. This customer predicted with 77% accuracy from a base of 35% exactly when and the magnitude of these sales spikes. The improvement in forecast accuracy was directly transferable to reduced safety stock needed to cover this event for both the customer and P&G.

What is the process for predicting these sales spikes? The process is called Collaborative Planning Forecasting Replenishment, or CPFR. This is an industry created process with published models to articulate exactly how the process can be deployed given various business scenarios.

Here's the flow: yellow is data flow, and red is product flow. As customers obtain and use the POS data available from their stores to replenish product as it sells, they need to build the forecast engine in their systems to capture the perpetual inventory and replenish the retail stores. This short-term replenishment information is supplemented with the long-range collaborative planning to include demand projections for promotions and new items. This information represents the joint agreement of the P&G sales manager and the customer buyer/merchandiser using actual historical store sales data captured and held in the POS system. The customer forecasting system then compiles the information and transmits the projected netted demand data (orders) to P&G electronically using the EDI-830 transaction. The data represents weekly totals of orders 1 to 13 weeks out in the future as well as daily totals of orders 1 to 14 days out in the future. This provides P&G with the information to accurately plan production schedules 3 months in advance as well as to provide close-in demand scheduling of production and transportation. At some point, the projections will be determined to be accurate enough to become frozen as actual orders to produce and ship to the customer. The customer will receive the Advance Ship Notice (ASN) and plan their receiving and outbound transportation to the stores prior to receiving the product. It is at this time that the customer's actual store inventories and sales rates will determine how the inbound product will be distributed (cross-docked) to the

trucks for each store without needing to be slotted as inventory.

Here's what partnership looks like within our ultimate supply system. We have top-level managerial support at each of our supplier and customer trading partners to compete as a supply system. And to review the necessary activity involved in the CPFR process, an agreement to share data and collaborate is absolutely critical to allow us to build production responsiveness and meet the customer demand without carrying excessive safety inventory to cover the unknown.

We return to the initial question that asks our internal and external partnerships about the desire to work together as a supply system to eliminate waste. Again, we are seeking to understand the real supply system opportunities and then to test solutions for broad reapplication for year 2005 results. We do not have all the answers, but we have put together a quality process to ensure that we ask the right questions and then develop the right solutions. Once this is complete we will document the findings and share them broadly in the industry. The benefits will be realized for P&G and our trading partners only when a critical mass of partnerships is engaged in the process.

About the Author

Scott H. Williams has been with Procter & Gamble for 19 years in customer business development. He was in sales management for 12 years, was the customer team logistics manager for 3 years, the corporate customer service table maintenance owner for 3 years, and is currently the senior project manager for global customer service and logistics. His responsibilities include CPFR (collaborative planning, forecasting and replenishment) and project manager.

He is the 1998 recipient of the UCC EDI Outstanding Achievement Award for contributions to UCS II Development.

Reprinted from the 1998 APICS Conference Proceedings.

Measuring Up: Performance Measurements for the Twenty-First Century

Ann K. Willis, CFPIM, CIRM

"It is an immutable law in business that words are words, explanations are explanations, promises are promises—but only performance is reality."

—*Harold S. Geneen*

To become and remain competitive in today's global marketplace, companies must develop performance measurements that will reveal current baseline values, highlight opportunities for improvement, and drive operational strategies. This presentation will focus on meeting the objectives of understanding the need for performance measurements, identifying overall performance measurement targets, and utilizing specific measurements to achieve world class goals. Examples and lists are included to enable participants to apply knowledge gained at their own facilities.

Understanding the Need for Performance Measurements

Performance measures are not new. We have been aware for some time that you cannot effectively manage that which you cannot measure. What is new is the recognition that improved performance is necessary for the continued survival of many companies. Today's global competition mandates that manufacturing organizations strive for excellence through continuous improvement in order to remain competitive. Current trends of continuous improvement include viewing inventory as a liability that covers up underlying problems, changing to a more flexible workplace, considering rejects as unacceptable rather than inevitable, learning to respond immediately to customer demand changes, and eliminating all waste.

Why measure? Customer requirements are more stringent than ever, placing tremendous pressure on everyone within the organization. Higher quality, lower prices, rapid product development and reliable service are changing the way we perform. Achieving "best of class" has become the focus for many of us, but how do we answer the question, "Are we there yet?"

Performance measurements are the yardsticks that tell us how we've done, where we are, and where we need to arrive. They help us make decisions on what to change, and on what to change to. They are a checkup on the vital signs of the organization, and serve as communication mechanisms for expectations downward, and results upward.

Performance measurements also motivate us to improve. If a company chooses to measure a process, it is placing priority on that activity, and people will concentrate on improving the process. It is foolish to assume we can continue to repeat the same activity, yet expect to get different results. By measuring performance, feedback is provided to keep us from running into the same walls again and again.

Taking measurements identifies and focuses attention on those areas that need improvement. Changing the mindset that uncovering problems is good, not bad, is the responsibility of management, but once this is achieved, the work force should begin to support the idea of being measured. Everyone reacts to how they are measured, and relating a performance measure to an organizational goal helps people better understand the purpose of the measure and why it is important.

Another reason for establishing measurements is to ensure support of an objective. The first step in the process is to establish that goal or objective, then arrive at a strategy that drives the organization toward achieving the goal. Performance measures ensure continuing progress toward that goal, encouraging actions that are consistent with the company's strategic direction, as well as identifying unnecessary activity which can be eliminated.

Whatever the impetus behind the measurement, the relationship between performance measures and the strategies they are intended to support should be clearly understood by all. How can performance be measured when the company's operational strategies are known only by one or two individuals? A formal system allows everyone to work toward a mutually understood goal.

Steps for Identifying Performance Measurement Targets

How does one build a set of performance measures that are consistent with the strategic goals of the firm and provide feedback on the activities critical to the business?

1. Determine what is needed to manage the business successfully. Focus should be on those activities that contribute to the success of the vision, and measurements of those activities should be consistent with, and support, those policies and practices that will achieve company objectives. Ask "why" five times to make sure the measurement is far enough into the process to facilitate improvement.

2. Decide on the source of information to be used, and the who, what, when, where and why of collecting the data. Selecting measures that are easily attainable assures that they can be started quickly, and continued without difficulty.

3. Clarify and simplify the measures. There should be a clear understanding of what is expected and agreement that the measure is meaningful. The process should be made as mistake-proof as possible, and the process of measuring made simple to ensure results

can be generated easily and consistently. A process that is not well understood by everyone is difficult to measure and improve.

4. Involve or co-develop the measures with the people who participate in the activity being measured. Actual participants usually have the best feel for what activities would be improved by measuring. Managers should be made accountable and delegate resources and authority to those doing the measuring. The workforce must take ownership and responsibility for the measurement

5. Relate local, or functional, measures to global measures, to ensure the activity is consistent with strategic goals of the firm. The measures should be integrated throughout the company so various functional areas are working together for the good of the organization.

6. Establish performance goals that are out of reach, but not out of sight, both short term and long term. People respond to challenges, not impossibilities. Milestones should be set that demonstrate progress made toward the ultimate goal. Achieving milestones validates change and improvement.

7. Collect information for a trial period, and evaluate its effectiveness at both local and global levels. This ensures that data and a collection procedure are available. If the information being collected is not meaningful, change it.

8. Examine every process and activity that is being measured. Ask the following questions: Does measuring contribute significantly to control of the process or improvement of the activity? What would happen if we discontinued this measure?

9. Celebrate achievements of every milestone and goal, resetting the goal to the next level. Successes should be rewarded, and failures coached for success in the future. Seeing progress toward a goal improves morale, garners support, and increases total participation in all improvement activities.

Evaluating Performance Measurement Effectiveness

Once the performance measurement system is in place, it should be audited to ensure its effectiveness. World-class organizations use the following characteristics to evaluate performance measurement systems.

- The cost of the measurement should not exceed the benefit derived.
- Measurements must be simple and easy to use, understand and report.
- Those being measured should clearly understand the relationship between measurements and goals, and should be involved in the selection of the measures.
- Feedback should be provided in a timely manner to both operators and managers, in order for performance to be adjusted toward goals.
- The measurement should convey meaningful detail that can be used and understood at all levels of the organization.
- Measurements must be based on readily and continuously available data, and usable at all levels of the organization.
- Measurements should provide physical as well as financial measures.
- Measurements should be easy to change as needs change.
- Measurements must focus on improvement and corrective action, rather than monitoring or control.

- Measurements should always be expressed as a positive, such as yield of good product rather than reject rate. People are more motivated by upward trends.

World-Class Values

World-class organizations are finding it necessary to change baseline values to determine appropriate, meaningful measurements. Examples of a few of these changes are:

Quality

Quality measurements, coupled with a drive toward a decrease in the cost of quality, focus on a goal of continuous improvement. Monitoring quality improvement costs in conjunction with quality performance data gives a truer picture of the quality progress. Quality measures are also reflecting goals of perfection and customer delight, rather than status quo and just getting by.

Productivity

Today's trends reflect measuring total productivity, rather than drawing traditional lines between direct and indirect, salary and hourly. Measurements focus on getting the most output from current levels of input.

Inventory

Inventory makes up a large part of working capital, many times amounting to one-half to two-thirds of the total investment base. Measurements such as inventory turns are some of the best short-term measurements of utilization, as no credit is given for what is produced, only what is sold.

Time

Reduction of time elements, such as customer response time, manufacturing cycle time, process control feedback time, supplier reorder lead time, and transport time, enable an organization to be better able to respond to dynamic demands.

Innovation

Measures in innovation indicate the ability to achieve and maintain a competitive advantage by introducing more new products, faster, at lower cost and more reliably than competitors. Cheaper, better, faster is becoming the motto for the next century.

Customer Satisfaction

Customer satisfaction has emerged as a strategic goal for many organizations today. Indicators such as customer retention rates, referral rates, repurchase rates, market share trends, complaint rates and satisfaction survey trends are being used to gauge satisfaction levels.

Converting From the Old to the New

Most performance measurements in the past were based on financial and costing information. These types of measurements usually represent outcomes of processes, but do not always provide the best information about what actually occurs behind the scenes. Today's performance measurements must reflect and encourage the new culture of people empowerment, the value of time, emphasis on continuous improvement, a quality mindset, and total people productivity. How we behave is dictated by how we are measured, and we cannot expect people to behave under the new culture if we continue to measure them under old standards.

Eliminating all of the old measurements, such as efficiency and utilization, may be too much change for some organizations and individuals. One alternative would be to change efficiency to labor effectiveness, by dividing standard hours earned by the total hours worked by both direct and indirect employees. Utilization can be changed to machine performance by simply dividing the run hours for scheduled production by the standard hours for scheduled production. This ensures there is no incentive for producing more than the scheduled or needed quantity. The ideal number is one. When the ratio is less than one, it is an indicator of unplanned downtime. When it becomes greater than one, it took more hours than planned to accomplish the schedule.

Specific Measurements to Achieve World-Class Goals

New ways of doing business require new performance measurements. The following are but a few of the measures being used by world-class organizations to foster continuous improvement and achieve strategic goals.

Quality

- Defects per million
- Cost of quality (prevention, appraisal, internal and external failures)
- Supplier certification or certified items
- Reduction of supplier base
- Hours of employee quality training
- Hours of preventive maintenance
- Mean time between failure
- Certification of internal operations
- Unscheduled machine downtime
- Number of customer complaints, warranty claims and recalls
- Unscheduled service call
- Percentage of lots rejected in error.

Cost

- Reduction in data transactions
- Materials shipped to point of use by supplier
- Dollars of product output per employee
- Throughput times from supplier to customer
- Budgeting expense trends
- Projects operating within budget.

Flexibility

- Reduction in cycle time
- Reduction in setup time
- Reduction in lot/batch size
- Increase in standard materials used per product
- Number of parts and levels in bills of material
- Degree of cross training of production personnel.

Reliability

- Increase in overall equipment effectiveness
- Reduction in warranty costs
- Reduction in engineering changes.

People Productivity and Development

- Sales per person
- Value added per person
- Employee turnover ratios
- Number of employees participating in improvement teams
- Competitive compensation packages
- Accident rates
- Absentee rates
- Training hours per employee
- Employee grievances
- Workdays lost due to accidents
- Percentage of appraisals completed on time
- Percentage of positions filled from within the organization.

Inventory

- Inventory turnover
- Inventory days on hand
- Inventory record accuracy.

Lead Times

- Delivery time to customers
- Setup reduction trends
- In-house transit time
- Supplier delivery performance
- Throughput times
- Work in process investment
- Performance to MPS
- Performance to FAS
- Ratio of promised customer delivery lead time to cumulative production lead time
- Administrative process times.

Responsive After-Market Service

- Number of hours of field service training
- Average response time to service calls
- Time to repair
- Availability of spare parts
- Warranty expense
- Overstocked field supplies.

Customer Responsiveness and Satisfaction

- Average customer response time
- Reduction in customer response time
- Number of complete items delivered on time
- Time from customer's recognition of need to delivery
- Quoted lead time
- Customer order processing time
- Time from receipt of order to start of manufacturing
- Number of customer promises met
- Percent of customer orders shipped on customer's request date

- Customer returns, complaints
- Number of customer partnerships established
- Enhanced customer value, via added product features or reduced costs.

Product and Process Design

- Time from idea to market
- Rate of new product introduction
- Percent first firm to market
- Number of engineering changes after design
- Reduction in new product introduction lead time
- New product sales revenue as a percent of total sale revenue
- Project completion cycle times
- Number of errors found during design review and evaluation.

Manufacturing Planning Process

- Master schedule items achieved per week
- Final assembly schedule items achieved per week
- Material requirement plans achieved per week
- Manufacturing orders released on time
- Data accuracy of inventory, bills of materials, routings and forecast
- Material and tooling availability
- MPS on-time performance
- Number and types of changes made to MPS.

Material Procurement Process

- Average procurement cycle time
- On time performance of deliveries
- Reduction in purchasing lead time
- Purchase orders released on time
- Reduction of supplier lead times
- Purchase order errors
- Downtime due to shortages
- Excess inventory.

Manufacturing Process

- Reduction of manufacturing lead time
- Percent queue time in manufacturing lead time
- Percent value-added time in manufacturing lead time
- Shop orders completed on time
- Manufacturing cycle times
- Unscheduled machine downtime
- Number of past due operations
- Yield and scrap rates
- Transactions per person.

Management

- Net income/number of employees
- Total sales/number of employees
- Net income/total direct labor payroll
- Net income/total factory payroll
- Total earned hours direct labor/total factory payroll.

Marketing/Sales and Customer Service

- Total sales/number of employees
- Average lead time in backlog
- Lead time performance
- Premium freight outbound/total freight outbound
- Performance to sales plan

- Accuracy of forecast assumptions
- Number of incorrect order entries.

Delivery Performance

- Timeliness and accuracy of supplier order placement and delivery
- Accuracy of shop floor schedule to customer requirements
- Ability to meet, but not exceed, MPS
- Correct quality and quantity delivery to customer per customer requirements
- Analysis of lost sales due to delivery deficiencies.

Information Services

- Number of errors per line of code
- Percent of reports received on schedule
- Number of rewrites
- Number of test-case runs for successful completion.

Financial/Accounting

- Amount of non-value added activity (scrap, rework, excess queue and move time)
- Total value of usable finished product produced per period per employee
- Total cost and output value ratios
- Time-based overhead usage
- Performance to budget
- Percentage of late payments
- Time to respond to customer requests
- Number of billing errors
- Number of incorrect accounting entries
- Number of payroll errors.

Whatever measures are utilized, one must remember that performance measurements in and of themselves do not add value. Attempts should be made to always focus measures on value-adding activities.

The most useful information derived from performance measurements is the trend of the results as opposed to the actual value of the measurement. We should be more concerned with relative performance over time than with absolute numbers. Small incremental improvements should be encouraged, and celebrated as progress toward the goal. When dramatic changes do occur, these should also be acknowledged. It is often worthwhile to set targets that may at first seem completely unrealistic. But doing so forces us to view the process from a completely fresh perspective, perhaps to find a whole new way to accomplish the objective.

Summary

In order to thrive, or even simply survive, organizations must establish, review and update comprehensive performance measurements. These measurements are the vehicle that drives a company to achievement of its operational goals. Due to the current trends in world-class organizations to develop and sustain customer satisfaction, as well as achieving ongoing improvement, measurements should be designed to drive the improvement process and achieve customer delight.

Often the difficulty is to select measures that satisfy the criteria of meaningfulness, acceptance, reliability, ease of reporting, and consistency. Performance measurements must fit an organization's individual needs, not that of a competitor or another facility. The measurements must be meaningful to the organization using them to achieve strategic objectives.

It is important to remember that performance measurement systems must remain fluid and flexible, in order to change with the constantly changing needs of an organization. How a company measures itself can have significant impact on how well the company performs in the marketplace.

Once measurements are established, success can be measured by marking progress week to week. This progress, no matter how small, must be published internally, rewarded, and used to motivate everyone within the organization to strive for continuous improvement and achieve excellence.

References

Buker, Inc. *World Class Manufacturing Performance Measurements*. Antioch, IL.

Bogan, Christopher E., and Michael J. English. *Benchmarking for Best Practices*. McGraw-Hill, Inc., New York, NY, 1994.

Maskell, Brian H. *Performance Measurement for World Class Manufacturing*. Productivity Press, Portland OR, 1991.

Oliver Wight Publications. *The Oliver Wight ABCD Checklist for Operational Excellence*. Fourth Edition, Essex Junction VT, 1993.

About the Author

Ann K. Willis, CFPIM, CIRM, is operations and education manager for ObTech, an object integration firm dedicated to providing resource management consulting, ERP implementations, and project management to organizations throughout North America. Her seventeen years of supply chain and manufacturing experience encompass all levels from material planning to management. She is responsible for implementation and training of manufacturing systems and has written several customized ERP courses. She has also been responsible for setting up customer-driven partnerships between organizations and has assisted companies in developing and managing strategic methods of customer focus, integration, and people empowerment.

Ms. Willis has been a member of APICS for fourteen years. She currently serves as chair of the CPIM program and is a past member of the MRP/CRP curriculum committee. She has held several chapter and region positions, including three years as chapter president. She was a member of the 1993 International Conference Committee and the 1993 and 1996 TEAM committees. She is a frequent speaker at chapter and regional meetings, and regional and international conferences. She teaches certification review courses, and is a certified Train-the-Trainer and Advanced Train-the-Trainer instructor.